WITHDRAWN

MILLER CENTER SERIES ON THE
AMERICAN PRESIDENCY

JIMMY CARTER AS PRESIDENT

JIMMY CARTER
as President

Leadership and the Politics of
the Public Good

ERWIN C. HARGROVE

Louisiana State University Press
Baton Rouge and London

Copyright © 1988 by Louisiana State University Press
All rights reserved
Manufactured in the United States of America
97 96 95 94 93 92 91 90 89 88   5 4 3 2 1

Designer: Diane B. Didier
Typeface: Sabon
Typesetter: The Composing Room of Michigan, Inc.
Printer: Thomson-Shore, Inc.
Binder: John H. Dekker & Sons, Inc.

Library of Congress Cataloging-in-Publication Data

Hargrove, Erwin C.
    Jimmy Carter as president : leadership and the politics of the
public good / Erwin C. Hargrove.
        p.   cm.—(Miller Center series on the American presidency)
    Bibliography: p.
    Includes index.
    ISBN 0-8071-1499-5 (alk. paper)
    1. Carter, Jimmy, 1924–   2. United States—Politics and
government—1977–1981.   I. Title.   II. Series.
    E873.H36 1989
    973.926'092'4—dc19   88-22051
                                                                      CIP

The transcripts of the White Burkett Miller Center of Public Affairs, University
of Virginia, Project on the Carter Presidency are quoted with permission.

The paper in this book meets the guidelines for permanence and durability of
the Committee on Production Guidelines for Book Longevity of the Council on
Library Resources.∞

CONTENTS

ON THE SERIES

From its creation the Miller Center has devoted a major portion of its efforts to the American presidency and especially the nature of the presidency, particular presidencies, and urgent problems that confront the institutional presidency. In pursuit of such a threefold inquiry, scholars at the Center are engaged in both theoretical and empirical intellectual endeavors. Theoretical inquiry calls for philosophical and intellectual powers of the first order. Empirical research requires a body of facts and information that for any given administration is often obscured for decades from public understanding.

To supply the resource material for understanding the presidency, the Center has turned to oral histories, most notably an extensive history of the Carter White House. However, the Center's commitment to a new kind of oral history begins but does not end with that project. Preceding that effort was an impressive study of the Ford administration in which nine members of the "inner family" came to Charlottesville for two days of debriefing. The group included such leaders as Richard Cheney, Donald Rumsfeld, and James Lynn.

Looking to the future, the Center is committed to continuing attention to presidential studies through oral histories of American presidencies since the Carter administration. The goal is to use whenever possible the same approach to the Reagan and subsequent administrations. However, use of the oral history techniques at the Center is not restricted to studies of the White Houses of certain postwar presidents. Thanks to the example of the Carter Project, oral history is part and parcel of the overall Miller Center approach. Shorter and more concentrated studies are being conducted of each postwar presidency drawing on the participation of some twenty intimates of each president. The full texts of such debriefings are held at the Center, but edited versions are published in single-volume histories. It is fair to say, therefore, that a distinguishing characteristic of the Miller Center is an oral history emphasis responding in part to Elliot Richardson's injunction: "Those of us who have had long tenure in government actually know more than we know we know not only from the standpoint of institutional memory but with respect to principles of governance. However, someone must help us give birth to such insights." The Miller Center has viewed its oral history enterprise as among its foremost responsibilities.

When James Sterling Young joined the staff of the Miller Center in 1978, he was determined to institute what he defined as a new kind of oral history. He had observed some of the efforts in the major oral history projects at Columbia University, where he was a vice-president and professor of government. In the last days of the Carter presidency, Professor Young began extending invitations to members of the Carter White House to visit the Miller Center.

At first, the Carter people were uncertain about devoting the necessary two or three days (including travel time) to the project. A few key people such as Jody Powell made the effort and thereafter engaged in "word-of-mouth advertising." What seemed to attract them was the serious way in which Professor Young organized the agenda, structuring it within a common format for each participant. Young was systematic about preparatory conversations—repeated telephone calls and private meetings with the subjects and dinner and breakfast meetings before the first day of formal discussion.

Another attraction was the quality of the questioners who included not only University of Virginia political scientists but outside scholars of international repute such as Professor Richard Neustadt of Harvard, Professor Richard Fenno of the University of Rochester, former Mount Holyoke president David Truman, and Professor William Leuchtenburg of the University of North Carolina. Some thirty scholars joined in the Carter history:

Henry J. Abraham, University of Virginia
James W. Ceaser, University of Virginia
Inis L. Claude, Jr., University of Virginia
Elmer E. Cornwell, Brown University
Richard F. Fenno, Jr., University of Rochester
Michael B. Grossman, Towson State University
Donald H. Haider, Jr., Northwestern University
Erwin C. Hargrove, Vanderbilt University
Charles O. Jones, University of Virginia

Donald F. Kettl, University of Virginia
Martha J. Kumar, Towson State University
William E. Leuchtenburg, University of North Carolina
Paul C. Light, University of Virginia
David B. Magleby, Brigham Young University
Thomas E. Mann, American Political Science Association
H. Clifton McCleskey, University of Virginia
Richard A. Melanson, Kenyon College
Frederick C. Mosher, University of Virginia
Richard E. Neustadt, Harvard University
David M. O'Brien, University of Virginia
Peter A. Petkas, Miller Center
Don K. Price, Harvard University
Robert J. Pranger, American Enterprise Institute
Emmette S. Redford, University of Texas
Steven E. Rhoads, University of Virginia
Bert A. Rockman, University of Pittsburgh
Francis E. Rourke, Johns Hopkins University
Larry J. Sabato, University of Virginia
David A. Shannon, University of Virginia
Robert A. Strong, Miller Center and Tulane University
David B. Truman, Mount Holyoke (ret.)
Jeffrey Tulis, Princeton University
Stephen J. Wayne, George Washington University

MILLER CENTER STAFF
James S. Young, Chair
Kenneth W. Thompson
W. David Clinton III
Joseph F. Devaney
Lowell S. Gustafson
Daniel C. Lang

Thus, the quality of participants recruited by Professor Young matched the systematic organization of the project.

Full credit for the Carter Oral History Project belongs to James Sterling Young. He conceived of the study, designed and organized it, recruited the participants, and kept major objectives consistently before us all. At each stage, he was ably assisted especially by Professor Robert A. Strong of Tulane University, now associate professor of political science at Tulane, and by Joseph F. Devaney.

It goes without saying that the monographs on the Carter presidency that follow are the result of the Young approach to oral history. The data on which they rest and the insights on the Carter presidency hark back to a concept that Professor Young conceived and formulated before any of the interviews or writings in the project were conducted. Without the intellectual resources and research materials made available through the oral history, none of the projected books in the Carter series could have been written.

Kenneth W. Thompson

FOREWORD

Each presidency nowadays gets studied in two rounds. First, during incumbency, it gets closely studied by Washington observers, especially by journalists whose job it is to keep watch on the White House and keep the world informed of what they learn. Many years after incumbency—usually after the principals have died and their confidential papers have been released—it gets reexamined in the light of history, mainly by scholars who comb through the documents the president and his people have left behind. During the long lull between these two rounds of study, it may be reviewed, defended, or attacked in memoirs, biographies, and other writings. But not much new is learned about it—or in much depth—until the presidential library has been opened and restrictions on the important papers have been lifted.

In the typical pattern, an outgoing presidency loses the attention of journalists and is all but ignored by scholars. It vanishes from the news as the incoming presidency claims press attention and, while scholars wait for access to the documents, disappears into history. The way it looked when last seen, through the eyes of Washington observers, tends to become the accepted portrait. Then, as its documents come to light, things will be discovered that were missed, misconstrued, or not considered newsworthy when it was in office; and sometimes, as in the case of the Eisenhower presidency, the portrait that emerges from the second round differs greatly from the one that emerged from the last.

But what might be learned from the people whose presidency it was, by interviewing them when they leave office? Exit interviews have been done as a matter of policy by government archivists but not by scholars who study the presidency. Oral history interviews have been conducted for presidential libraries and private collections, but only rarely by scholars who study the presidency. Interviews with White House staff members have long been recognized as an important part of presidential scholarship. But interview studies of an outgoing presidency have fallen outside the normal pattern.

Jimmy Carter as President: Leadership and the Politics of the Public

Good and the companion volumes in this series on the Carter presidency are a departure from the pattern. Here a presidency is studied after Washington observers have finished examining it but before the time has come for reexamining it in historical perspective and before the content of the presidential papers has come to light. These studies are based mainly on interviews with the people whose presidency it was, conducted shortly after they left office.

These interviews were undertaken as a new kind of oral history effort by the White Burkett Miller Center of Public Affairs at the University of Virginia. Former president Carter and his principal White House aides were asked to spend a day or two each in private but recorded discussion with a panel of scholars for the purpose of reviewing, reflecting on, and responding to queries about their presidency. With the generous cooperation of Mr. Carter and his staff, twenty-one such sessions were held, most of them in 1981 and 1982. Each session was organized around a single individual or staff group in the Carter White House and consisted of at least five hours of recorded discussion time with a panel of three or more scholars. At least one session was held with each of the principal persons and staff groups. In addition to the former president, the senior-level staff members, most of their deputies, and a number of staff assistants below the deputy level were interviewed. Erwin C. Hargrove participated in many of the sessions as a member of the panel. I directed the project and chaired the sessions.

The Carter Presidency Project was not undertaken with the object of writing books about the thirty-ninth presidency, much less books of revisionist import. Indeed, most of the scholars who participated in the project probably began with the assumption that the essential picture of the Carter White House that had come through to us in news and commentary during incumbency was correct and would be confirmed in the interviews. But as the interviews proceeded, significant disparities emerged. Facets of this presidency came to light under questioning by scholars that had not figured in news and commentary. Contemporary Washingtonian assumptions about power in this White House did not always prove out. Seen from the middle distance of history, in the whole of its four-year term the Carter presidency did not seem quite the same presidency it seemed to observers on the scene day to day during incumbency. New ways of understanding this presidency became possible, and new interpretations of its performance in office suggested themselves.

So the idea jelled, roughly at midcourse in the project, of commissioning a series of monographs in which a few of the participating scholars would report the insights they had gained from the oral history interviews. The respondents gave permission, in most cases on a background basis only, for the transcripts to be used as source material for this purpose. Upon completion of the monograph series, copies of the Miller Center's twenty-one bound volumes of interview transcripts will be furnished to the presidential library in Atlanta, where, as part of the nation's oral history archives, they will be made available to all for reading and research under such terms as the respondents may wish to stipulate. Until that time, in order to assure the anonymity of those respondents who requested it, some of the interview material is cited in this book by the volume number of the transcript rather than by the name of the respondent.

The main data base for the monographs was created by the cooperative effort of some thirty-three scholars and of former president Carter and some fifty persons who were associated with him in a staff capacity. Space does not permit acknowledgment of the particular contribution made by each of these individuals. I single out five without whose cooperation and active support the monograph series could not have come to pass. Jimmy Carter's personal cooperation and support for the idea of the project were essential to its successful completion. He is the first former president to have subjected himself and his staff to the kind of scrutiny and questioning we gave them. He did this generously and conscientiously and asked no favor in return. Jody Powell responded to a number of my requests for specific help, and his counsel and assistance were vital in keeping the interview process going. Kenneth W. Thompson, in addition to contributing as a participant in virtually all the interview sessions, secured the financial and institutional commitments to a project about whose outcome many had reason to be skeptical. His support, through thick and thin, even when we sometimes differed about how to proceed, was key to both the inception and the completion of the project. Robert A. Strong and Joseph F. Devaney made indispensable contributions as chief research assistants on the project.

The subject of study here is a presidency outside the familiar mold. Carter was the first president to be elected from the Deep South since before the Civil War, the first to be elected under the new presidential selection system of the 1970s, and the first true outsider—having no previous experience in Washington—to be elected since Woodrow Wilson. If the ways of Washington were new to Jimmy Carter and most of his Georgia lieutenants when they came to the White House, the ways of their presidency were new to Washingtonians, too. Very little about the thirty-ninth presidency resembled any other one in the memory of Washington observers. And there is little evidence to suggest that Carter and his people meant to cultivate any such resemblance.

There were the Republican presidencies of the recent past. There was the "hidden-hand" presidency of Eisenhower, a former general and diplomat, who brought to the White House his considerable experience in leading politicians while seeming not to. Carter's was no such presidency, and did not mean to be. There was the "imperial" presidency of Nixon, bent upon taking over the government but losing control instead. Carter was at great pains not to resemble that presidency. There was the vetoing presidency of Gerald Ford, confronted with an "imperial" Democratic Congress in the wake of Vietnam and Watergate. Carter's was no such presidency, and did not mean to be.

Neither did the Carter presidency follow in the expected pattern of the Democratic presidencies. After Roosevelt's New Deal, Truman's Fair Deal, Kennedy's New Frontier, and Johnson's Great Society, here was a Democratic president who not only spurned labels but presented a large legislative agenda with a distinctly conservative cast. Carter moved to retrench and reform—not to extend—the welfare state that other Democrats had built; to curb and roll back the regulatory state that other Democrats had built; to reduce intervention in the private sector as a way of solving public problems in the long run; to deregulate and start returning to reliance on market forces in order to achieve desired economic ends. To some, this looked like more than minor deviancy from Democratic doctrine. It looked like an attack on interest-group liberalism itself, and many in the liberal wing of the Democratic party responded accordingly.

Not only programmatically but politically also the Carter presidency fell outside the familiar Democratic mold. While asking a great deal of the government, especially of Congress, in the way of new policy, the administration seemed in the eyes of many Washington observers to be short on political skills and strategies to achieve its policy objectives. The Carter White House seemed not to go by the Roosevelt-Truman-Kennedy-Johnson book on the politics of persuasion. It scored low on the standard Washington political aptitude and achievement tests. If the thirty-ninth presidency was not a hidden-hand, or an imperial, or a veto presidency,

neither was it a "political presidency"—to use Barbara Kellerman's term—
of Democratic vintage. And in all probability Carter did not mean to have a
presidency of that kind, either.

The kind of presidency Carter's was not became a major theme in news
and commentary from Washington, beginning with his inaugural walk
from the Capitol to the White House and continuing throughout his term
in office. In the first round of study, during incumbency, much was learned
from Washington observers about the way the thirty-ninth presidency did
not go about getting things done, what it did *not* do to push its policies
through, what it did *not* do to project its power. Far less was learned about
the kind of presidency it was, the way it did go about getting things done,
what it did do to push its policies through, the way in which it did use a
president's power to persuade—and why so. These aspects are the focus of
this series of retrospectives on the Carter presidency.

Each president has his own way of approaching the opportunities and
problems of office, and each has his own way of pursuing his purposes. His
way is bound to capitalize on what he is good at, to minimize what he is not
good at, and to reflect what he has learned from experience about what
works and what does not work. What was Carter's way? Each presidency
has a *modus operandi* of its own, a methodology of governance. What were
those of the thirty-ninth? Many Washington observers and presidential
scholars have strong ideas about the right way and the wrong way to
organize and conduct a presidency. But presidents and the people who
work with them in the White House have their ideas too—and theirs get
implemented. How was the Carter presidency organized and conducted,
and why so? And, once these questions are answered, what does the election and defeat of this kind of presidency have to teach about the nature and
problems of governance in the American Republic in our time?

These questions will not be fully answered for many years yet, not until
scholars have probed the presidential papers. But the interviews with the
people who constituted and conducted the thirty-ninth presidency brought
the answers much nearer than they were when the first round of study of
this administration came to an end in January, 1981.

In the first volume of this series, Charles O. Jones showed how Carter
approached the task of persuading Congress to adopt his policy proposals.
The nature of Carter's legislative agenda together with the advent of a
resurgent Congress, newly organized and minded to assert policy indepen-
dence from the White House after the Johnson-Nixon era, made this task

formidable. Carter was committed to a program of major policy changes, most of which would have long-term rather than short-term payoffs, many of which had no natural constituency, few of which were popular or could claim a public mandate, and a number of which many legislators had powerful political reasons to oppose. Included, for example, were the Panama Canal treaties, which Carter got the Senate to adopt over the opposition of a majority of Americans, and a comprehensive energy policy, adopted in part over the intense opposition of hordes of lobbyists.

Jones's *The Trusteeship Presidency: Jimmy Carter and the United States Congress* challenges the contemporary portrait of a president who lacked a legislative strategy. It offers the portrait of a president whose legislative strategy seems to have been predicated on the view that congressional "politics as usual" and conventional political incentives could not be counted on to obtain the desired policy results, particularly on the issues on Carter's agenda that divided the congressional Democratic party. Encountering resistance from Congress, Carter pressed Congress to act as public trustee rather than as broker for outside groups. Pressed by legislative leaders to think congressionally, he pressed them to think presidentially. He talked policy rather than politics and lobbied legislators to vote for the best rather than the politically expedient policy. Encountering resistance from the institutional parties of the House and Senate, he set about to build issue parties in support of his legislative agenda. Carter and his people conducted what was probably the most intensive program of policy campaigning and issue-by-issue coalition building that has yet been undertaken in the White House.

This was not the kind of leadership—or the kind of legislative agenda— that a legislative politician in the White House would have been likely to undertake. But it was the kind of leadership that Carter was good at and it was the kind of agenda he had promised to bring to Washington. And Carter's way of working his will on Congress may have been more instrumental to his policy purposes than it seemed at the time. Carter's "trusteeship presidency" helps explain, as conventional Washington wisdom about his congressional relations does not, his formidable legislative successes as well as his failures.

An equally instructive new portrait of Carter in the executive arena is offered by Erwin C. Hargrove. *Jimmy Carter as President: Leadership and the Politics of the Public Good* presents a picture of Carter as a policy maker that differs from those drawn by Washington observers during incumbency, and shows that his way of leading the executive government was of a piece with his way of leading the congressional government.

Soon after Carter's inauguration, word came from Washington commentators of a president who was "all style, no substance." The outsider who had run against Washington would be a symbolic rather than a substantive leader, so the word went, a preacher in the bully pulpit rather than a policy maker. This first reading of Carter as a president who would delegate policy work to others gained credence from his announced intention to give large policy responsibilities to his department heads, and it seemed to be confirmed by Carter's choice of a cabinet with strong policy credentials and Washington connections, in contrast to a low-powered, largely imported, campaign-connected inner circle of White House staff.

Later, however, came word of a president who was "all substance, no style." Observers on the scene now reported a figure in the Oval Office who did little else but policy work, who was no kind of politician, no delegator either—a president who ran policy himself down to the last detail. This second reading gained credence as word of Carter's homework on policy issues got around Washington, as his proposal for a new national energy policy was unveiled, and as it became clear that his commitment to comparable major changes in other policy areas was no mere gesture in the direction of fulfilling his campaign promises. The reading seemed to be confirmed by Carter's dismissal in 1979 of three of his policy chieftains, including one, Califano, who had a strong Washington following.

Erwin C. Hargrove's *Jimmy Carter as President* shows a president who fit neither of these stereotypes. It is the portrait of a new kind of political figure in the Oval Office. This is the figure of what might be called a policy politician: an elected politician who concentrates on policy work and who makes the achievement of good policy his main goal. His métier is issue politics more than party or institutional politics, and his forte is issue leadership rather than the leadership of institutions or organizations. Such figures are becoming increasingly familiar on the American political landscape, especially on Capitol Hill, in this era of congressional activism and assertiveness on policy. Senator Nunn of Georgia is perhaps the most prominent example at the time of this writing. What Hargrove's book reveals—and what the first round of study during Carter's incumbency missed or mistook—is the first true example of the modern policy politician as president.

Jimmy Carter as President shows a chief executive who established his leadership by being on top of policy, by being demanding about policy, and by making the achievement of good policy the discipline of his administration, just as he made it his own discipline and tried to make it so for Congress. Carter set a demanding policy agenda, identifying at the outset the problems in each main issue area that his administration would address and that he would call on Congress to address. To take responsibility for the issues that fell within the provinces of departments he selected a high-powered cabinet whose policy thinking was compatible with his own and gave them broad license to act.

He himself took responsibility for the issues he deemed presidential, including the thorniest of the lot. On "*my* issues," as he called them, he was wont to get educated in depth and detail, and to draw advice and assistance from whatever individuals—staff, cabinet, others—he found most knowledgeable and useful on the particular issue at hand. On the issues he delegated to others, he was wont to be well enough informed to keep the delegates on their toes, to help them out if called on, and to step in if necessary.

Along with a demanding policy agenda, Carter set demanding standards for good policy. What Carter wanted, Hargrove points out, was policy that solved problems, not merely "satisfied," and policy that was strategic rather than expedient in its conception. This meant policy that dealt with the whole of a problem, not just a piece, and that looked to the long run, well beyond one's time in office. It meant policy that could be debated and defended in terms of the goal to be achieved, not just the groups to be served. And it meant policy that was worth what it cost. The point of good policy, as Carter spoke of it, was to show that the American democratic system was in good health, equal to the challenges of the new age; and to restore public confidence in the integrity of the government following the Indochina war and the Watergate scandals by demonstrating the primacy of public serving over self serving in Washington. And the point of presidential leadership, as Carter went about it, was to achieve good policy. In a political system that was tilted in favor of policies that were expedient, constituency-oriented, costly, and good for the short run, it was the president's job to push for policies that were problem-solving, goal-oriented, cost effective, and best in the long run.

This was not the kind of leadership or the kind of policy agenda that a president trained in the ways of bureaucratic politics, any more than a legislative politician, would have been likely to undertake. Certainly it was different from the kind of leadership or the kind of agenda that a president schooled in theater and in ideological politics would be likely to undertake. But it was a kind of leadership that should have surprised no one who was attentive to Carter's pre-presidential career, his public words, his zest for decision making, and his particular personal strengths and skills. It was a kind of leadership that had worked for Carter before, that capitalized on the things he excelled at and avoided what he was not good at, that reflected his political philosophy, and that was true to his character. As Hargrove's insightful portrait of Carter as a political man brings out, the outsider president was at home inside Washington, working his will on the government in the way of a policy politician. In a White House that he saw as preeminently a place of policy leadership, Carter asserted the role of the president as policy premier.

The question about the thirty-ninth presidency, then, is not whether Carter had a strategy of governance or whether he exercised leadership. The question is whether his strategy and his kind of leadership fitted with what the country wanted or needed in his time. Were the late 1970s a time for a policy activist—and a party maverick—in the White House? Was pushing for good policy, as Carter saw it, the way for a president to earn his keep after Vietnam and Watergate? Was the Oval Office a place for a policy politician, after long occupancy by men schooled in the politics of institutions and organizations? In an era when the presidency had lost its license to be the nation's policy boss—when power over the making and managing of national policy had become dispersed among many institutions and groups in Washington—could a president be prime minister of policy instead?

Scholars in the year 2000 will be in a better position to answer such questions than are scholars in the 1980s. But the answers will come the more easily for those who will reexamine and reevaluate the Carter presidency in historical perspective because of Hargrove's illuminating study of presidential policy leadership in the Carter years.

James Sterling Young

PREFACE

Political leadership presents a puzzle difficult to unravel. Highly skillful leaders are most effective when they have an abundance of political support, but which is more crucial, the skill or the support? When less skillful leaders lack political support, is the failure due to limited skill or to political circumstance? Other variations in the quadrant include skillful leaders who achieve limited goals in uncertain situations by virtue of skill, and inept leaders who succeed because they have strong political support. It is not easy to sort through this range of possibilities and evaluate leadership in terms of individual ability versus historical context.

Jimmy Carter is widely thought to have been an ineffective, unsuccessful president for reasons that vary greatly according to the analysis. Some critics charge him with ineptness, a failure to understand the world of power.[1] Others describe a presidency so weakened by the fragmentation of political parties, the democratization of Congress and the public's skepticism toward leadership and authority that skill was irrelevant.[2] If these explanations are combined, ineptness and unfavorable circumstances reinforce each other. But Carter had notable successes. Are these to be attributed to skill or to the actions of others and the circumstances of the moment?

The question to be asked about Carter as president is whether he made the most of his opportunities. Personal skill must be examined against the backdrop of historical context and available political resources. Skill and opportunity may have reinforced each other positively, for example, in Carter's storming of the nomination process and election to the presidency. They may have reinforced each other negatively when seeming ineptitude was matched by overwhelmingly adverse events in Carter's last year in office. Skill may explain such Carter achievements as the Camp David accord, and lack of skill, quite apart from events or context, may help explain clear political mistakes, such as overloading Congress with legislative proposals the first year.

This book is a study of Jimmy Carter as a policy leader. The focus is on his management of policy development within the administration and his style as a decision maker. Processes of policy making are guided, in part, by a president's policy purposes. Clarity of presidential purpose, for example, may produce a different decision-making process from uncertainty, and both purpose and process are shaped by presidential political strategies. Political conceptions of feasibility will influence both goals and decisions. Skillful policy leadership is the ability to fashion a unity among purpose, politics and process, and the source of this unity must be the president himself.

In concentrating on how Jimmy Carter managed policy formation and made decisions, this study does not explore his leadership of public opinion or his relations with Congress, though it does take into account the seamless web joining policy purposes, political strategies and policy-making processes. The idea of congruence among these three elements resists efforts to explain presidential actions in terms of any one of them. A dynamic interaction is always at work. For example, a disjointed process of decision making, with many players and a resulting policy that lacks consistency, may derive both from the president's style of executive management and his policy ideas. The two reinforce each other, and one cannot be reduced to the other. In the final analysis, effective presidential leadership that achieves policy goals depends upon how the president's agenda matches the political "temper" of the times, as well as on presidential skill in making the most of historical opportunities and political resources.

This analysis of Jimmy Carter as a leader builds on the idea of congruence, with particular attention to the artistry a leader uses to fashion a unity among the ingredients of effectiveness. The first two chapters portray Carter's political personality. The chapters on domestic, economic and foreign policy making ask how Carter joined purpose, politics and policy-making processes in these different policy areas. The final chapter assesses Carter's effectiveness as president by matching his skills and strategies of leadership to his historical opportunities. Although the judgments are not definitive and disagreement is possible within the analytic framework provided, the framework itself may have merit.

Oral history interviews provide the raw material for this analysis and interpretation of Jimmy Carter as president. The vantage point, therefore, is from these accounts of Carter and his associates, though the study is more than a simple compilation of what the former president and his lieutenants have said. In painting a portrait of Carter as a leader I have given their words my own interpretation. The gaps in the story, which exist because the oral histories are incomplete, are in places filled by additional interviews and memoirs by members of the Carter administration. Subsequent research on decision making within this administration will surely modify many of the descriptions given here, but I hope that the essential portrait of the president and his way of leading will stand.

My purpose was expressed for me by a colleague who, after reading the manuscript, said he felt that Jimmy Carter had been in the room while he was reading—it was as if they had had an extended conversation. I hope others will feel the same way.

ACKNOWLEDGMENTS

Participation in the oral history interviews of the Project on the Carter Presidency gave me a great opportunity to learn more about the American presidency. The invitation to write a monograph in the series on the Carter presidency was an added benefit and opportunity. I wish to thank Kenneth Thompson, director of the Miller Center, and James Sterling Young, research director, for those opportunities, including my 1982 semester in residence as a research fellow of the White Burkett Miller Center of Public Affairs at the University of Virginia. I am particularly grateful to Jim Young for his careful reading of the evolving manuscript and his incisive advice at key turning points. The manuscript was read by three anonymous scholars for the Miller Center and their criticisms and suggestions were most helpful. I would also like to thank John Egerton, Stuart Eizenstat, Michael Nelson and Bert Rockman for their ideas about the book as it took shape.

Ann Hobbs and Nancy Lawson, of the Miller Center, were helpful in every way during my time there. Sophie Chrysler was a very efficient research assistant at the University of Virginia. Regina Perry and Mildred Tyler, of the Vanderbilt Institute for Public Policy Studies and the Vanderbilt Department of Political Science, respectively, typed and retyped drafts of the manuscript with patience and skill. Kathy Tsaky helped beyond measure in preparing the manuscript for publication.

This book is dedicated to my three grown-up children, John, Amy, and Sarah, with great affection.

JIMMY CARTER AS PRESIDENT

1
FORMING A POLITICAL STYLE

In 1976 the treasurer of the Tennessee Carter for President campaign went to Atlanta to talk with people who knew the candidate in order to find out what kind of man he was supporting. He met Charles Kirbo, a long-time Carter friend, legal and political adviser, who told him, "He is not a politician; as president he will do what he thinks is right, whether it is popular or not, and, if elected, he may be a one-term president."[1] In 1982 one of Carter's closest friends recalled that Carter was always consistent in his basic philosophy and his actions could be predicted if one knew "what he had done previously."[2]

These comments suggest a deeply rooted personal style and a belief system sure to influence Jimmy Carter's style of governing. How did his conceptions of leadership inform the way in which he organized his administration, structured policy development, worked with others and made decisions? These manifestations of style follow from the purposes and operating methods of the man.

The three components of a mature political style are character, cognitive skills and values. Active, creative elements of personality blend these component parts into an operating political style in which the parts reinforce the whole, even though there may be tensions and contradictions among them.[3] A style of leadership is developed through intuitive fumbling and trial and error. Skillful leaders have native abilities but it takes time to discover and develop them as an unfolding variety of situations stimulate the exercise of skill. The strongest skills are most often established in formative times of testing. With success comes the self-confidence that a given approach works and it will be tried and tried again until it becomes natural. Once leaders have developed a range of skills that appear to match the problems they face they will persist in doing what they can do best throughout their careers. They may even construct situations and seek out problems that evoke the skills they most wish to use.[4]

This is not to say that political leaders are entirely prisoners of style. One cannot chart a political career in terms of the politician's responses to inner compulsion, for a mature political leader will have an acute ability to test reality and vary the elements of style in response to particular situations. However, the repertoire of even the most skillful leader is limited. We thus see leaders playing to their strengths as much as possible, and we sometimes see mismatches of skill and situation.

Character is the basis of political style in that it prescribes the fundamental orientations toward the self and others that make up a style of leadership. Needs and drives are fashioned into a loose unity by the conscious, reasoning political personality and are joined to skills and values.

Character is the way a person orients himself or herself toward life, which is a manifestation of how one confronts oneself.[5] High self-esteem permits tolerance of conflict and criticism; low self-esteem may cause defensiveness. The bundle of needs we serve helps shape our character. The need for attention may cause one to create self-dramatizing skills, or the need for achievement may enhance problem-solving skills. Such needs may be stimulated by innate abilities. The core patterns of Carter's character and style were apparent by 1970 when he was elected governor. These patterns had formed through the years, as Carter assimilated qualities he valued in certain character models, added to his store of experiences and acknowledged his personal inclinations.

Jimmy Carter was always ambitious. He told high school friends he would be governor one day, and as a young naval officer he aspired to be chief of naval operations.[6] His models for achievement were his father, Earl Carter, and Admiral Hyman Rickover. In his autobiography the two men are described in much the same terms. He remembers his father as "an extremely competent farmer and businessman" who later developed a wide range of interests in public affairs. He was a natural leader in the community who "always worked harder than did I or anyone else on the farm." His authority was certain.

I never even considered disobeying my father, and he seldom, if ever, ordered me to perform a task; he simply suggested that it needed to be done, and he expected me to do it. . . .
    Admiral Rickover had a profound effect on my life—perhaps more than anyone except my own parents. He was unbelievably hardworking and competent and he demanded total dedication from his subordinates. We feared and respected and strove to please him. I do not, in that period, ever remember his saying a complimentary word to me. The absence of a comment was his compliment. . . . He expected the maximum from us but he always contributed more.[7]

Both men are pictured as very hardworking, competent and tough. They did not easily give out praise, and although they expected the highest performance from subordinates they gave even more of themselves. It is not a great leap to suggest that Jimmy Carter sought to be like these men he admired. He says less about his mother than his father in his autobiography but writes that she was liberal, whereas his father was conservative, and that she "was extremely compassionate" toward all those in need.[8] The mother's liberalism and compassion were perhaps blended in the son with the father's ambition and tough-mindedness.

The first difficult, major task Carter accomplished was to become a nuclear submarine officer in Rickover's program. One can assume that he brought all his energy, drive and ambition to forge the professional identity he had chosen for himself as a young adult. However, just as he was on the verge of attaining success, which was defined as commanding his own ship, he resigned from the navy to return to Georgia to shore up the family enterprises left leaderless by his father's death. The only reason he gives is that someone had to take his father's place. One could speculate that naval advancement in 1953 was unpromising and that the ambition to become governor had not been forgotten. But the more important point is that Carter had to develop a second professional identity at the age of twenty-nine. This could not have been easy because he knew little about farming or business. But one may infer that his eventual success as a farmer and businessman increased his self-confidence and his conviction that he could master any difficult task. He had done twice what most young adults are expected to do only once.[9]

Carter had never been a class leader in high school, college or Annapolis. His greatest skills were not those dramatic qualities that immediately cause a person to stand out in a group, but rather, the careful, painstaking organizational skills needed to develop his own career or a larger collective enterprise. His first independent political success was winning the race for the Georgia state senate against the attempt to deprive him fraudulently of his legal victory. His success in making a legal challenge to the plot to keep him out of office surely contributed to his self-confidence and also gave him a rather jaundiced view of a certain kind of Georgia politics. "But there were other lessons I learned too," he later stated. "The most vital was that people intimidated by corrupt public officials don't necessarily like it; if given some leadership and a chance, they are willing to stand up and be counted on the side of decency and of honest politics and government."[10]

The diverse strands of Carter's political style were woven into a definable and predictable pattern as he served as a state senator. There was strong emphasis on homework; he had pledged to read every bill before he voted on it and did so, perhaps eight hundred to a thousand bills each session. He searched for comprehensive solutions to problems by introducing measures on school finance, education, taxation of utilities, overcrowded state mental hospitals, election laws, budgeting procedures and uniform salaries for state officials.[11] Perhaps most important, he fully developed his disdain for legislative folkways, as he records in his autobiography.

It is difficult for the common good to prevail, especially against the intense concentration of those who have a special interest, especially if the decisions are made behind locked doors. What occurred was not illegal but it was wrong. The 259 members of the legislature were almost all good honest men and women. A tiny portion were not good or honest. In the absence of clear and comprehensive issues, it is simply not possible to marshall the interest of the general public, and under such circumstances legislators often respond to the quiet and professional pressures of lobbyists.[12]

Carter developed a conception of political leadership from this experience in which the virtuous leader articulated the interests of the vast, unorganized public against the demands of groups. "The elected official, then, is the only effective representative and voice for the unorganized citizen, the legal client, the medical patient, the student, the borrower of money or the purchaser of goods."[13]

Carter gave up a virtually certain election to Congress in 1966 to run for governor against Bo Callaway, a Republican graduate of West Point and former congressman with whom he admits he felt competitive.[14] There was no great demand that he run and he was not well known throughout the state, but this was the kind of challenge Carter liked. It evoked tremendous efforts of drive and skill to overcome obstacles. He lost in the Democratic primary and appears to have suffered a deep depression as a result. He told Bill Moyers in a 1976 television interview, "I was going through a stage in my life then that was a very difficult one. I had run for governor and lost. Everything that I did was not gratifying. [Even] when I succeeded in something it was a horrible experience for me."[15] During this period he deepened his personal religious faith through conversations with his sister, Ruth Carter Stapleton, who was an evangelist. He evidently did not have a sudden "born again" experience but rather made a gradual commitment.[16] In 1966 Carter was forty-two years old, the approximate time when men must come to terms with the first half of their lives and decide how to live the second half. If one is a success in worldly terms, that success is often found to be lacking; if one is a failure, some other source of self-esteem must be developed. If this transition is handled maturely the person emerges from a time of uncertainty with a strong sense that self-worth is based on one's own person rather than on worldly achievements.[17] Ambition is not abandoned but is pursued with greater detachment and with the understanding that success or failure is not the foundation of one's integrity as a person. It is plausible that between 1966 and 1970 Carter attained a certain serenity of this kind by deepening his religious faith to cope with the crisis of middle life. He would continue to pursue his ambition, yet could accept failure so long as he was secure in the belief that he had done his best and acted according to his principles. Carter, as governor and president, may thus have been able to detach himself from his successes and failures and justify his actions by his desire to do right. Failure would not then be his fault. This posture gave Carter a certain air of self-righteousness which was used against him when he appeared to depart from his own proclaimed standards.

Carter discovered increased capacities for political leadership in his experience as a missionary in northern cities. As he and fellow Christians visited door to door in Pennsylvania towns Carter came to feel a close rapport with the families he met and, as he later related, he learned to value these people and to feel "then and ever since that when I meet each individual person they are important to me."[18] This belief that each human soul has unique importance may have carried over politically in Carter's ability to strike a strong chord with voters, at factory gates and in political meetings—a talent noticed by a number of observant journalists, one of whom described Carter as a brilliant "one on one" campaigner.[19] In any event, these experiences of political defeat and reaffirmation of faith appear to have strengthened both the man and the politician.

Carter's patterns of character and style showed strong needs for achievement and autonomy. He sought to achieve on his own terms. These needs were complemented by a definition of political leadership that called for independent action by the leader in behalf of the public interest.

For Carter the cognitive aspect of political style was most strongly manifested in his drive for competence. He wished to understand thoroughly the issues for which he assumed primary responsibility, and he characterized his cognitive processes as those of an engineer. In his 1975 auto-biography he describes the style of command he learned from Admiral Hyman Rickover.

He always insisted that we know our jobs in the most minute detail, which is really a necessary characteristic of good submariners. He was often appalled at the incompetence of leaders who knew the theory of management but knew little about what actually occurred within their sphere of responsibility. He has been very critical of our nation's educational system, and particularly of the Naval Academy, because of the graduate's inability to assume technical responsibility for specific naval duties. He believes they should concentrate on engineering, mathematics and other technical courses so that they can understand the ships they are assigned to operate.[20]

In 1982 he told a group of political scientists, "I think I took to the White House the same basic philosophy that I had as governor and the same one that I used in my private affairs even on a submarine when I was younger. I was trained by Rickover, I'm an engineer at heart, and I like to understand details of things that are directly my responsibility. I like to delegate admin-istration to others."[21]

There is ample testimony that this capacity for homework paid off. A long-time colleague from Georgia days described how Carter had pre-sented himself at an informal meeting of the two houses of the Georgia legislature and answered questions on his proposal for the reorganization of state government. A veteran legislator had commented, "I have never seen anybody do as fine a job. . . . He knew more about the state than anybody in the state.[22] Carter regarded knowledge as a recourse for politi-cal persuasion and used his intelligence and capacity for homework to his advantage.

The values advocated by a political leader are usually consistent with his character and cognitive style. Thus Carter's emphasis on achievement through homework was joined to a conception of the public good derived from certain southern political traditions.

As a Georgia politician, Carter developed a style of leadership that joined diverse political traditions into a general formulation of the public good. William Havard has suggested that Carter skillfully combined ele-ments of three southern political traditions. He spoke for the Bourbon tradition in his commitment to agricultural values, his sense of place and extended family and his personal association with the military tradition of the South. He invoked traditional Whig themes in emphasizing modernization of the South through science and industry (he spoke here of his own engineering experience and his life as a businessman), and in the great attention he gave to issues of efficiency and economy in government. Yet he was perhaps most at home in the Populist role of plain farmer, simple Baptist and spokesman for the poor and dispossessed. Havard concludes: "It may be this combination of the three main types of southern politicians in the one man that has caused so many observers to be puzzled over efforts to categorize the President as a liberal, radical, conservative or middle-of-the-roader. His capacity for unification had depended on being all of them in succession, and at times even simultaneously because the old identifications in pure form tend to be more divisive than integrative."[23]

The point here is not necessarily that Carter was some combination of Bourbon, Whig and Populist but that he was experienced in combining diverse strands of southern culture and opinion into a general appeal. When he utilized this synthesizing facility in national politics and policy, others could not always easily categorize him and thus sometimes felt uncomfortable. He fit no one's litmus test.

Dewey W. Grantham's definitive study of southern Progressivism sets forth a collective portrait of southern Progressives in the early twentieth century. Within great variety certain common themes are discernable, and Jimmy Carter reflects those themes. Southern Progressives were middle class, drawn from the professions and commerce (and thus somewhat paternalistic), and they wanted to protect the weak and unfortunate through economic development, community consensus and social reform. They opposed political corruption, machine politics and unethical business practices and preached good government. They eschewed emotion in their politics, advocating that good government be based on expertise rather than popular politics.[24]

One cannot establish a direct link for Carter with the southern Progressive tradition. He was, for one thing, a small-town boy and the Progressives were urban. But as an apostle for southern modernization and an opponent of traditional southern politics and politicians, he clearly had something in common with this older, vanished tradition. He shared a centrist liberalism with the Progressives which may have made it difficult for Democratic party "liberals" to understand him.

Carter also drew on southern religious traditions in his style of leadership. His religious faith was central to his life. Faith shaped his understanding of himself and others, his beliefs about political purposes in government and his style of authority. This faith and the attributes derived from it were clearly grounded in Southern Baptist practices. Carter transcended his church's orthodoxy in that his faith inspired him to throw himself into the world's battles. Southern Baptists typically stress private morality and are inclined to be exclusive; Carter's faith rejected exclusiveness. But Southern Baptists believe that with God all things are possible, that God will triumph, and Carter joined his secular political ideology to this religious optimism. And he saw politics as a moral activity. In a 1976 interview he told Bill Moyers that although he did not look on the presidency as a pastorate, "It gives me a chance to serve, and it also gives me a chance to magnify whatever influence I have, for either good or bad, and I hope it will be for good."[25]

Carter was a New Testament rather than Old Testament Christian. He practiced humility, charity, forgiveness and tolerance as political virtues. He did not see the world as inherently evil and sought peace through understanding rather than confrontation. His style may have carried a trace of the Calvinist themes that permeate southern religion, but the dominant tone was of optimism and hope.

Jimmy Carter's political personality, then, was a unity forged from his character and values, and from his particular way of obtaining and using knowledge. Through his drives for achievement and autonomy he conceived of the leader as a trustee for the public interest. His intelligence and capacity for homework permitted him to use knowledge as a political resource. His commitment to doing good in the world, and his optimism that good could prevail, provided not only direction but reinforced his need to achieve and his intellectual self-confidence.

When he became governor in 1971, Carter's leadership style was fully developed and would not change throughout his governorship or presidency. The governorship of Georgia provided a testing ground for him as a mature politician. All of his skills and values were summoned for an intense drive to be elected and to enact a comprehensive program of reform for the state.

Carter undertook the race for governor in 1970 against great odds, since former Governor Carl Sanders was the strong Democratic front-runner. Most of his friends advised him to run for another office but, he said later, "There was never the slightest hesitancy on my part about what to do. I thought I could run and win, and I never worried at all about who might be in the race against me."[26] Carter displayed in the 1970 campaign the ability to speak to a wider diversity of groups than did his opponents and to appeal to people who were insufficiently represented by government—small farmers, small-town people, the little people. He did this without attacking business or any interests. By appealing as well to the Atlanta business community's desire for modernization of the state's governing structure, he managed to evoke both traditional values of morality and community and modern values of efficiency and progress.[27] Few, if any, politicians in Georgia could cover such a broad scope. The method, however, had its weaknesses for it left a certain fuzziness of image in the minds of specific groups of voters who wondered whether Carter was really with them or whether he had any clear, sharply defined beliefs at all. The fact that his goals were procedural as much as substantive added to this confusion.[28]

In defense of Carter one could argue that the ability to shift among factions was common in a South of weak parties. But two other aspects of his style were also at work. On the positive side he believed that a profound change had taken place in politics in the 1960s and that the time had come to open politics up to the people for greater popular influence in policy making. As a unifier who wished to govern free of factions he needed a strong base of popular support; as a moderate he had no desire to offend important business groups in the state. On the more negative side, Carter was to reveal himself as a gut fighter who in 1970 would hit below the belt to win elections. Carl Sanders' supporters thought he had campaigned unfairly, but after his inaugural speech in which he proclaimed an end to racial segregation in Georgia and the South, all that was forgiven and he entered the governor's office on a positive note.[29]

A discussion of certain features of Carter's governorship will help to identify characteristics of style that were to reappear later.

First, in articulating the public interest, most notably in the reorganization of state government but also in such areas as education, public health, judicial reform, consumer protection and overhaul of tax policy, Carter emphasized equity, plus improved procedures to permit long-range planning and more efficient delivery of services. He avoided strong or divisive themes of social justice and became an institutional modernizer in a "backward" state.

His cognitive mastery was impressive. He was very well informed and continually amazed legislators and others by his great knowledge of problems and proposals.

A disdain for politics as usual was accompanied by a complete willing-ness to use political instruments, such as patronage, against his political opponents. He presented proposals to the legislature in an uncompromis-ing style, vowing that he would not yield, but when necessary he did compromise on details. His strategy was to push as hard as possible at the beginning in order to give away as little as possible at the end.

Carter identified personally with the people against the interests. He and his staff organized elaborate campaigns of public support for his legislative proposals, particularly for reorganization.

Finally, ambiguities in style made Carter politically vulnerable. Moral-ism could be seen as hypocrisy if every action did not conform to the highest principle. The appeal of the nonpolitical stance could lead to disil-lusionment if Carter even once appeared to be playing politics himself. Basing political support upon a diffuse public rather than on a coalition of groups meant that Carter progressively lost public support as his actions alienated segments of the population.

In addition to these characteristic aspects of his style, Carter from the outset rejected conceptions of leadership through compromise that would accommodate the interests of strong legislators. He aimed for a total re-organization of state government, identified opposition with "special in-terest groups" and pleaded that action had to be immediate because "it may be another forty years before we have another chance to reorganize." Recognizing the peril of this approach, Carter after one year as governor commented, "If I have made a mistake it is in undertaking too many things simultaneously."[30]

Carter drove the legislature and made direct appeals to the public on key issues. These appeals were not personal self-dramatizations but carefully orchestrated group efforts in which he played a central part. It would have been difficult, however, repeatedly to mount such organizational cam-paigns and the strategy was confined primarily to reorganization. It was not easy to arouse voters to an intense interest in questions of governmental reform. In his attempt Carter alienated many organized groups, both in and out of government, so that by the end of his term his aides doubted that he could have been reelected. Still, he had come to symbolize Georgia's accommodation with twentieth-century government.[31]

Carter could not succeed himself as governor, but a larger stage was available. He believed that his particular skills, values and approach to politics were precisely what the nation needed. The governorship had provided a vehicle to test the exercise of his operational style and he regarded it as having been a successful testing. From 1974 to 1976 Jimmy Carter was a public man in search of opportunities to display his mastery of difficult problems. He embarked on the quest for the presidency with the drive that he had brought to previous efforts and the self-confident belief that he could resolve the nation's problems.

Carter had been thinking about running for president since 1966 and had regarded the governorship as a stepping-stone.[32] As early as 1972 Carter and his close advisers saw his advantages over other Democratic candidates. McGovern had shown moral leadership, Hamilton Jordan thought, but had not given the image of presidential competence that Carter could present. Jordan later told Jules Witcover:

With the Vietnam war coming to a close, domestic problems and issues were apt to be a more important consideration, the problem-solving ability of the American government was very much in question, and someone outside of Washington, and outside the Senate, a governor who had proved that problems could be dealt with effectively in the state, could win. I thought one of the things that was manifested in the McGovern campaign was the real need for moral leadership in the country, for somebody to stand up and tell the American people to do the things that were unpopular, a feeling that if politicians dealt more openly with the electorate that they would respond well.[33]

The two fundamental questions that were to guide Carter's campaign for the presidency appear on the first page of his 1975 autobiography: "Can our government be honest, decent, open, fair, and compassionate?" and "Can our government be competent?" One of Carter's key advisers saw him as the first southern politician to think through the applicability of a certain southern style of politics to a set of national circumstances. He was a Southern Baptist stylistically in the comfortable manner in which he related the social good to politics. Thus both the moralizing and the technocratic modes of thought were perfectly suited for appeals that the nation must rise above politics as usual and turn to a leader who could provide both honest and competent government on behalf of all the people. The governorship had been a crucial arena for the development of these appeals and a matching style of governance.[34]

The programmatic themes that Carter would stress in the 1976 campaign were listed toward the end of his autobiography. It is important to sample the flavor of his language.

Attempts to reform systems of cash management, taxation, health, welfare, education, transportation or governmental management are doomed unless they are bold and comprehensive. With small and incremental changes there is a focusing of efforts to oppose the change by those who are benefiting from the status quo. There is rarely any public interest in a subject when it is technically or narrowly defined. The special interests almost invariably prevail. But, if political leaders can understand what is right and fair, devise a comprehensive plan for improvement, and describe to the public clearly what should be done, then even the most far-reaching reforms are possible.

To alleviate the understandable concerns about the competence of our government is a tremendous challenge. This is a political issue of utmost importance.

Our nation now has no understandable national purpose, no clearly defined goals, and no organizational mechanism to develop or achieve such purposes or goals. We move from one crisis to the next as if they were fads, even though the previous one hasn't been solved. . . .

As a planner and a businessman and a chief executive, I know from experience that uncertainty is also a devastating affliction in private life and government. Coordination of different programs is impossible. There is no clear vision of what is to be accomplished, everyone struggles for temporary advantage, and there is no way to monitor how effectively services are delivered.

What is our national policy for the production, acquisition, distribution, or consumption of energy in times of shortage or doubtful supply? There is no policy!

What are our long-range goals in health care, transportation, land use, economic development, waste disposal or housing?

The tremendous resources of our people and of our chosen leaders can be harnessed to devise effective, understandable, and practical goals and policies in every realm of public life.

A government that is honest and competent, with clear purpose and strong leadership, can work with the American people to meet the challenges of the present and the future.

We can then face together the tough, long-range solutions to our economic woes. Our people are ready to make personal sacrifices when clear national economic policies are devised and understood.[35]

Carter called for a comprehensive energy conservation program, renewed commitment to protection of the environment, a national transportation policy, tax reform, reform of the judicial system, reorganization of the federal bureaucracy, greater rationalization and efficiency in the system of public welfare for the poor, a practical and comprehensive national health insurance system and greater efficiency in defense programs. He attacked pork barrel public works projects and concluded with a plea for the curbing of nuclear proliferation throughout the world. One sees here a balance of liberal goals and efficient means, a recognition that the institutional capacities of government are crucial to its effectiveness. But even beyond these policy themes, Jimmy Carter had every reason to believe that his style of leadership was not only what the country needed, but what the people wanted.[36]

2
CONCEPTIONS OF LEADERSHIP

In posing a model of the central principles of Carter's style of leadership three important initial considerations are that he had a clear and strong conception of the kind of leader he wished to be as president, that his conception of leadership had been developed and tested to his satisfaction before he became president, and that the central elements in this conception of leadership were deeply rooted in his personality. The keystone of Carter's understanding of himself as a political leader was his belief that the essential responsibility of leadership was to articulate the good of the entire community rather than any part of it. He sought "public goods" that would benefit all citizens. Rather than being antipolitical or nonpolitical leadership, this was, for him, a different kind of leadership that eschewed the normal politician's preoccupation with representing private interests, bargaining and short-term electoral goals. He presented himself to the public as a political leader who represented the public interest.

The public interest, for Carter, was defined through a process of study and discussion. He appears to have implicitly believed in a kind of "right reason" that could be developed to guide action. He wished the policy-making process to combine study and debate, with the goal of reaching agreement on solutions that attacked the nature of a given public problem root and branch and that captured the enduring interest of the community. This in-depth approach could, he believed, overcome the opposition's partial perspectives and interests.

Carter did not believe in fashioning policies according to calculations of political advantage or strategy, but he understood perfectly well that at the end of the day compromise might be necessary. His conception of leadership required a focus on "public goods" when policy was initiated but permitted compromise in due course. This was not nonpolitical leadership tempered by political prudence but rather the principle that compromise was acceptable only after an all-out effort to sell the optimal policy had failed. Anticipated compromises were not built into proposed policy in advance. Thus, although he fiercely held to his preferred strategy of leadership, both because he thought it desirable and because it had worked for him, he kept himself open to political advisers and deliberately sought such diversity in his administration.

His personal values were congruent with this conception of leadership. In economic and social policy he sought to combine liberal goals of equity and justice with fiscal moderation and limited and efficient government. In foreign policy he espoused cooperation among all nations, especially the United States and the Soviet Union, but accepted the reality of competition. In all policy he sought synthesis and balance between seemingly competitive principles and thought it possible to achieve such balance through study and goodwill.

His mode of thought was congruent with these beliefs and with his strategy of leadership. His belief that study could overcome differences and create grounds for agreement matched his personal training and experience as an engineer and his capacity for homework and the assimilation of information. His strategy of leadership thus reflected his intellectual strengths as well as his moral predispositions.

All of these characteristics shaped Carter as a manager of policy formation. He fashioned executive decision-making processes to emphasize homework and free discussion, putting himself at the center of this process, since he was to make the decisions. He was not comfortable with intermediaries who might stand between him and the process of exploration and discussion but preferred to work directly with small groups of advisers who could focus their knowledge and discussion upon specific problems. He neither saw the relationships among such advisers as political in the competitive sense nor felt the need to construct organizational checks and balances. He brought his confidence in reason and goodwill to executive decision making. This approach to decision making will be referred to as Carter's "collegial" style, meaning simply that he liked to work with small groups of trusted advisers in a problem-solving mode with minimal formal structure.

These characteristics formed a unity in Carter's political personality and gave his actions a consistency of purpose—a consistency apparent only if one recognizes the central axioms that guided it. Many of Carter's critics failed to do this and therefore did not understand him or meet him on his own ground. And criticism is incisive only when it captures the essential characteristics of a leader.

FORMING POLICY TO SERVE PUBLIC INTEREST

After his presidency Carter spoke reflectively of his approach to leadership.

I had a different way of governing, I think, than had been the case with my predecessor. . . . I was a southerner, a born-again Christian, a Baptist, a newcomer. Very few of the members of Congress, or members of the major lobbying groups, or the distinguished former Democratic leaders had played much of a role in my election. . . .

As an engineer and as a governor I was more inclined to move rapidly and without equivocation and without the long interminable consultations and so forth that are inherent, I think, in someone who has a more legislative attitude, or psyche, or training, or experience. So for all these reasons I think there was a different tone to our Administration.[1]

One of Carter's closest presidential aides saw the clear relationship between Carter's problem-solving approach and the search for comprehensiveness as a form of political leadership.

One of the things that has always appealed to me was not only Carter's view of the country, his vision for the country, in the sense of confidence in the government and the society at large, but also the idea of how he related the relationships that existed between the host of problems and the short-term solutions that were not going to be significant. He thought you had to move to long-term solutions. That started with an understanding that problems were related, and these issues were related. Everything that he did in his presidency, except for those things that swamped us for the moment, tended to be efforts in the long term, particularly if you look at energy, which was something in which there was not great political outcry in 1977 to do something about. The first discussions as we moved to substance in '77 were how to concentrate attention to gather support in a public that was not all that interested in that issue. . . .

In foreign policy, he thought it was important to consider the relationships the United States had in the Third World, and building those relationships beyond simply the kind of initiatives that you normally take in foreign policy which are dictated by what happened today in El Salvador and yesterday in Iran. He had that sense of long view that we had to go to them.

That's why he so much insisted on leaving politics out of the calculations, as though politics per se would always tend to make these things short-term or incremental, and not deal with long-term solutions.[2]

One domestic policy assistant commented, "Comprehensive in his mind was synonymous with complete solution and in his view a complete solution was the kind of thing the American people wanted because they wanted to change things completely." And another added, "He came to Washington believing, as most Americans probably do believe, that our national problems are some combination of stupidity and venality. He believed that if you demanded intelligence and honesty you would solve these problems."[3]

Some of his associates perceived Carter's hope for comprehensive solutions as strictly a moral stance. "He wasn't going to do the Lord's work on a half-ass basis," one put it. Others saw him strictly as the engineer. "He viewed political problems as cube roots. . . . if you find the right answer and use your powers of logical deduction that was it. You didn't waste a lot of time persuading people about it."[4]

Carter was a planner and a moralist, but he was also a politician whose commitment to long-range plans and comprehensive solutions had grown out of his experience as governor of Georgia. That experience guided his actions in Washington. According to a domestic policy assistant, "He viewed himself as having successfully imposed comprehensive solutions in areas ranging from reform of education . . . from reorganizing the agencies to reorganizing the way they did their state education financing. He viewed himself as having put those characters in the Georgia legislature into shape by having big concepts. It may be that he was right. By coming with those big concepts they couldn't pick them apart."[5]

Carter saw his own approach to leadership as antithetical to the tactics of compromise and bargaining practiced by legislators. Because the legislative norms of addressing only one aspect of a problem at a time opened the door to undue interest group influence, Carter preferred a comprehensive policy proposal that attacked all facets of a problem. Interest groups might be able to defeat an incremental proposal because the public could not be easily mobilized to support it. But the public might rally behind a comprehensive proposal that appealed to public goods. Although this comprehensive approach does not promise solutions, it does institute policy that deals with all facets of a problem. The power of the policy to sustain itself is strengthened by comprehensiveness, which implies a long-term view rather than a quick fix.

Carter thought of himself as a political leader but he could not easily align himself with congressional politicians because, as Charles Jones argues, he saw them as preoccupied with particular interests rather than being trustees for the public interest, as he sought to be. For Carter political leadership was not so much doing what's right instead of what's political as it was doing the political in the right way.[6]

Carter's strategy of policy leadership in the presidency, therefore, was what it had always been for him—to seek to do what was right and hope for political reward in the wake of achievement. He wrote in his diary on January 28, 1977, "Everybody has warned me not to take on too many projects so early in the administration, but it's almost impossible for me to delay something that I see needs to be done." After his presidency he acknowledged the political drawbacks of his strategy of policy leadership but affirmed his initial aims.

We had a very heavy agenda of items that I thought would be beneficial for our country. I can tell you with complete candor that we didn't assess the adverse political consequences of pursuing these goals. . . . I didn't think it was particularly foolhardy. I thought eventually our good efforts would be recognized and our achievements would be adequate to justify my reelection. But I was not under any misapprehension about the adverse consequences of things like China normalization or moving into Africa or getting involved with the Mid East when everybody else had had little success, or moving toward the Panama Canal treaties and so forth. We had a complete agenda and we just tried to fit it all together.[7]

His closest colleagues saw him in these terms. One, who had been with him from the time he became governor, remembered that Carter had developed over a lifetime the idea that he should do what was right and the political rewards would come. His becoming president seemed to validate this strategy. Consequently, this adviser felt, Carter made little initial effort to get along with Congress because he did not think it was necessary.[8] Another assistant remembered,

We used to always joke that the worse way to convince the President to go along with your position was to say that this would help you politically, because . . . he wanted to be a different type of President. He was elected somehow to be a different kind of President. He was running against the sort of system of inside deals and so forth. He saw himself above that system. He did not enjoy politics per se in the same sense that a Humphrey or a Johnson did. . . . It's not something that came naturally to him. He liked to make a decision on the merits and check the decision box that seemed to him the best direction for the nation to go and that was an enormous strength and has an enormous amount of intellectual integrity. It was also however a liability at times because you can't always simply check the right box. . . . He seemed to like sometimes going against the political grain to do what was right. This was viewed as being firm and tough. . . . And of course to some extent it was and one had to admire that.[9]

Carter did not develop policy ideas in order to win popular support but hoped that support would come from bold attacks on unresolved problems. When an assistant told the president that he ought to go for an incremental rather than a comprehensive welfare reform because the latter would be expensive and would create difficult administrative problems, Carter replied, "You know it's people like you that I've been sent to Washington to shape up." Carter did, of course, understand the importance of politics in government. As one associate put it, he "was too smart not to but he often rejected it." During the first two years one aide reported that Carter, in discussing a new policy, would often say, "I will take care of the politics," but then he would fail to do it.[10]

He often rejected advice about prudent political timing of policy initiatives. Clark Clifford was said to have advised him to avoid taking on the Panama Canal treaty, the recognition of China and the effort to mediate between Egypt and Israel, since all appeared to be bad domestic politics. Carter persevered and, in fact, these were three of his achievements. One of his closest advisers had argued that the Panama Canal treaty was a second-term issue, but, he said, Carter wanted to achieve what was on his agenda and was always confident of his ability to deal with the hard issues. Another assistant regarded all of the president's major initiatives as political liabilities—civil service reform, nuclear proliferation, Strategic Arms Limitation Treaty (SALT), the mediation between Egypt and Israel, and the Panama Canal. He felt that Carter, guided by his instinct for the future, was identifying issues that would be much more difficult for the nation to address later. He often overloaded his plate, but "his determination to go beyond marginal improvements led to his big successes."[11]

If Carter was so disdainful of politics as usual why did he choose a vice-presidential running mate with extensive Washington experience and say that it was important to do so? Why did he fill his cabinet with people who had considerable Washington experience, reasoning that this was a way of complementing the inexperience of his personal staff?[12] In fact, he did not disdain political experience, and though his goal was to achieve "public goods" he understood the need to compromise.

Carter did receive and use a great deal of political advice. On domestic issues two separate and steady streams of political analysis existed within the administration. The first, a small group of explicitly "political" friends whom Carter trusted without reservation, consisted of Rosalynn Carter, the Atlanta lawyer Charles Kirbo, Jody Powell and Hamilton Jordan.[13] The second was the Domestic Policy Staff (DPS), directed by Stuart Eizenstat. Eizenstat considered it essential that the DPS, on behalf of the president, test every policy proposal the departments or the DPS itself produced, considering prevailing opinions among Democrats in Congress as well as in the many organized, Washington-based interest groups in the Democratic coalition.[14] The higher echelons of the Office of Management and Budget (OMB) were also able to present their domestic policy views as a counterpoint to the DPS. The OMB view was one of fiscal stringency, less deference to the Democratic constituencies than DPS and an implicit political strategy of appeal to diffuse popular support over the heads of organized groups.[15]

Carter was exposed to these and other streams of advice regularly. Vice-President Mondale, for example, though not a member of the inner group of Georgians, had a personal and privileged relationship with the president. They had lunch together one day each week, but his role as an advocate was most often played in concert with DPS analyses.[16] Hamilton Jordan, assumed to be the chief political adviser, appears to have had little or no formal connection with the other domestic policy advisers. Jordan, primarily interested in the connections between policy and electoral politics, would regularly write Carter long, private memos reminding him of how he had gotten elected and how necessary it was to retain the support of the groups needed for reelection. He thought it unwise, for instance, to antagonize organized labor on the minimum wage issue. One cannot know the extent of Jordan's influence on Carter's policy actions although those close to both thought that Carter paid attention to Jordan and respected his political judgment.[17] Eizenstat and his staff gave little attention to electoral issues but concentrated on the need for the support of Democratic interest groups in forging and passing legislation. The relative influence of the political advice that came, intermingled with policy arguments, from the DPS, OMB and other administration groups can be gauged by examining Carter's actions, particularly in domestic and economic policy decisions. Such descriptions appear in subsequent chapters.

So Carter received these political perspectives regularly, but his domestic policy advisers contend that he did not at first want to hear such advice, even though he listened.[18] He did, however, become increasingly receptive to political learning, and his lieutenants describe his growing political sophistication regarding the kinds of political actions and compromises necessary to win support for programs, particularly in Congress. A domestic policy aide describes the change:

He tended to worry much more in the last couple of years about what the public reaction would be and what the political impact would be. Early on, he was very much, "I only want to know what the best policy is and I'll worry about the politics of it later. You give me the best policy." Later on those kinds of bravado statements tended to disappear and he wanted to know what he could pass, what we could get through, what did this committee chairman want, what did this interest group want. That was a function of worrying more about the reelection as we got closer to it.[19]

This change in Carter was more than just reelection politics, as another aide confirms.

He was not curious about the political aspects of people in the beginning. He took a while to develop respect for other points of view. He began, in effect, to find the right thing and was thus not open to compromise. He eventually got some sense of the deeply conflicting beliefs in Washington. His notion that he was the smartest person made him not want to horse trade. For example, I tried to get him to give in on an issue and he asked if he were right. I said yes and he said, "then why do the wrong thing?" This was not an accurate description by the fourth year. By then he could do as good a political analysis as anyone.[20]

Even with growing sophistication, Carter's fusion of policy and politics was more reactive than creative. He neither assessed his stock of political resources in relation to major policy initiatives nor tied programmatic themes to broad political appeals. However, he did increasingly take political feasibility into account in his own initial decisions, such as the minimum wage level or the kind of Department of Education that would be acceptable to Congress and affected interest groups, and he learned to compromise with members of Congress in terms of their political interests. But no grand political strategy was at work. He hoped the public would reward him in 1980 for having taken on and resolved a number of very hard problems.

Carter consciously played to what he believed to be his personal strengths, and one may infer that he saw his trustee approach to leadership and, indeed, his overall style of leadership as strengths rather than weaknesses. His tenacity in pursuing goals related to this belief in trustee leadership in a mutually reinforcing way. He remembered in 1982,

A lot of my advisers, including Rosalynn, used to argue with me about my decision to move ahead with a project when it was obviously not going to be politically advantageous, or to encourage me to postpone it until a possible second term and so forth. It was just contrary to my nature. . . . I just couldn't do it.

Once I made a decision I was awfully stubborn about it. I think if I could have one political attribute as the cause of my success to begin with, it would be tenacity. Once I get set on something I'm awfully hard to change. And that may also be a cause of some of my political failures.[21]

This suggests that Carter knew himself well and realized that his strengths and weaknesses might be opposite sides of the same coin. But he deliberately and consciously played to these attributes as strengths—as intelligent political leaders typically do.

How can Carter's willingness to fall back on a politics of second best after comprehensive program proposals had failed be reconciled with his expressed disdain for incrementalism, bargaining and compromise and his deeply rooted preference for achieving "public goods"? Contradictory behavior is commonplace among politicians and need not be fully explained. But it may be suggested that the search for the ideal and the later fallback to second best were logically complementary elements of Carter's style. Agreement on the ideal policy was to be achieved by the authority of knowledgeability and the appeal to widely shared values rather than through the building of political coalitions. If this strategy failed one was thrown back on the search for second best if anything was to be achieved at all. Conventional thinking about political feasibility then became useful. An alternative strategy of political leadership is to frame the initial policy in terms of political feasibility. Carter resisted this for fear the second best would overcome the first goal. His assertion of the primary public good in policy making reflected a belief that latent sources of public support could be evoked that would not be available in an incrementalist strategy. But Carter did wish policy achievement and he did wish to be reelected president. He was not so foolish as to refuse a try for second best if that became the only alternative.[22]

Carter's critics take him to task for not exercising "strategic" leadership by joining policy initiatives to strategies of political feasibility.[23] This is fair criticism of his excessive ambition to achieve many goals and his initial reluctance to space the introduction of initiatives. It is perhaps less telling as a criticism of his ambition to achieve public goods. It is easier to calculate in advance the feasibility of incrementalist initiatives than to know whether latent support for a comprehensive policy can be evoked. Carter could live with second best but he refused to compromise at the outset because he hoped to tap potential support for the ideal.

Jimmy Carter was the first modern Democratic president to face the dearth of ideas in the Democratic policy agenda. In any case, economic conditions were not congenial to accepted Democratic remedies, since hyper inflation discourages the introduction of social programs to help people. He could not campaign against government like his Republican successor. So Carter consciously attempted to create new policies for the

Democratic coalition that would combine liberal goals and conservative means. This included a comprehensive redesigning of social programs to create more efficient administration at reduced expense.

Carter sought to balance and reconcile opposites in his approach to foreign policy as well. He thought of himself as "Wilsonian" and wished American foreign policy to be guided by the broad theme of human rights.[24] But he also decided to build up American military defenses after a long period of stasis. He could combine the ideals of international cooperation and national competition in his thinking just as he could be both a liberal in social policy and a fiscal conservative.

Carter gave some clues to his ideology in his 1982 response to the question of whether he had been guided by a long-term strategy to broaden the Democratic coalition.

> Yes. I thought that was the general philosophy that we put together, although I'll use the word loosely because I'm cautious about labels. I [thought] that my conservative approach to fiscal/monetary/budget affairs would increase my base of support beyond what was habitually Democratic. The deregulation of major industries . . . airlines and railroads and trucking . . . I thought that would attract more of, at least, the small business or the business community. And a strong defense . . . [enhanced by a] steady increase after eight years of deep cutting, would be beneficial . . . the public looked upon the Democratic party as more fiscally responsible than the Republican party. It was quite a reversal. . . .
>
> At the same time, I looked on myself as being quite liberal on civil rights . . . human rights on a broad basis, on pursuing peace and nuclear arms control, on social programs, jobs, appointments of minorities and the increased involvement of minorities and women in government. I thought that on environmental quality and those kinds of things that we would retain a basic Democratic constituency. So, I had hopes of building upon the old Democratic coalition and broadening it somewhat.[25]

Not all of Carter's aides, however, saw him as guided by coherent sets of principles. For example, he resisted rhetorical appeals to the public that were not joined to specific issues. He did not want to give a State of the Union speech to Congress in January, 1978, his first opportunity to do so as president, and only reluctantly gave in to staff persuasion. One speech writer felt that Carter could give an "all forest" speech, such as his farewell address, in which he emphasized the themes of human rights, nuclear proliferation and environmental protection, or an "all trees" speech in which he made several unrelated points. But he resisted joining the forest and trees by linking specific issues to larger goals. Ample testimony from associates indicates that when asked to rank his goals or choose among priorities he refused, saying that he hoped to achieve all of his objectives. When he did hint at a larger design with the phrase "New Foundation" to describe his domestic legislative program in the 1979 State of the Union message, he disavowed it soon after in a news conference as being merely a slogan.[26]

The common criticism that Carter as president was an engineer lacking in a political philosophy missed the mark, we have suggested. Why, then, was he so perceived, even by some of his own assistants? His style of leadership perhaps contributed to this perception. His major domestic and foreign policy advisers thought that if a problem existed it was not lack of coherence in goals but rather too many goals which, in his determination to achieve them all, he refused to rank.[27] The attention he gave to homework, his engineer's facility with facts and his disinclination to link specific issues by general rhetorical appeals, when taken together, added to the erroneous impression that he lacked a unified set of guiding principles. And though Carter did not often present himself as a party leader, he did believe it important to bring Democrats back to a center position of liberal goals and fiscal caution, international cooperation and restrained nationalism.

EXECUTIVE ORGANIZATIONAL STYLE

Carter was not unique among presidents in not having given extensive previous thought to the nature of the presidency as an organization. It is a unique institution and presidential candidates do not read political science textbooks as primers. But three major influences seem to have guided his thinking about how to organize his presidency.

The first was his experience as governor of Georgia. Most governorships are organized with a clear division of labor between staff assistants to the governor and comissioners who form the governor's cabinet and head departments. The assistants help a governor with his political work, as legislative aides, public relations and media advisers and legal counselors. The commissioners and the professional staffs in their departments develop programs and administer them; state budget offices assemble budgets and track programs. The chief difference from the institutional presidency is that the lean gubernatorial staffs are not organized for policy analysis or policy development but rather help the governor work with the legislature and the public. This was the way that Carter used his staff in Georgia, keeping a clear distinction in his mind between personal assistants on his staff and department heads. The former were to help him; the latter were to develop and administer programs. He adhered to this model in the White House.

The second influence was Carter's negative reaction to the centralization of government in the Nixon White House. He made this a central theme of the 1976 election campaign, conveniently ignoring President Ford's dismantling of the Nixon White House apparatus. During the campaign Carter promised that no White House staff person would ever be permitted to come between him and the cabinet officers, who were to be his principal advisers. He also publicly charged cabinet officers with the responsibility for policy development in his administration.[28]

The third factor was Carter's own style of problem solving, which was to go after issues himself through intensive study and homework. He resisted the layering of advisory levels between himself and any of his key associates and thus did not initially appoint a White House chief of staff. He liked to receive multiple strands of advice first hand, from staff and departmental advisers, and to integrate such advice himself.[29]

These three influences on Carter's thinking about the organization of the presidency reinforced one another. Between his election and inauguration Carter read Stephen Hess's book on the organization of the presidency and found its prescriptions persuasive. Hess argued that successive presidents, by permitting White House assistants to crowd aside cabinet officers and become principal advisers, cut themselves off from the fullest possible range of policy advice.[30] This provided Carter with a rationale for following his own inclinations.

The result was a White House staff structure sometimes referred to as the "spokes of a wheel," with the president at the center and advisers arrayed around him in a circle.[31] There was no chief of staff and the president directed senior presidential assistants to desist from giving directions to cabinet officers, initially even prohibiting a strong White House coordinating role in policy development. The senior staff were to be advisers to the president and cabinet officers were charged with the responsibility for policy development. The president was not at all interested in the administration of policy and had strong views that this should be handled in the departments.[32]

This way of doing business permitted Carter to play to what he understood to be his strengths as a leader. The president's most important task, he believed, was to make intelligent decisions, and such decisions were most likely to emerge from a process of policy development based on the search for comprehensive policies that attacked problems at the roots. Carter appears to have thought that policy development based on the principle of homework would be a unifying and motivating force in his administration. His role was to lead this process and to set an inspiring example by becoming expert on those issues he considered presidential. He was quite comfortable with ignoring all other questions by delegating them to cabinet officers.

In Carter's mind knowledge developed through such a process of policy development would be a valuable resource in political and administrative persuasion. In 1982 he recalled,

If an issue was mine, I wanted to understand it. And so I spent hour after hour studying the structure of the federal government in preparation of the budgets and really did a lot of detailed work on the budgets because I felt that this was one of the managerial weapons or tools that I had to exert my influence in a definitive way. And my budget came through Congress relatively intact. Even the defense budgets were very seldom modified after I submitted them because I worked them out in detail with Harold Brown [Secretary of Defense] under the Joint Chiefs of Staff and unanimously, I think, the latter supported the final version of the budgets. . . .

If something was of importance to me, like the energy legislation, which was comprised of thousands of meticulous details, I took the time to learn them. When the congressional committees or subcommittees or the House and Senate conferees would be called in the Cabinet room to resolve a particular detail that meant the passage or failure of the entire bill, I wanted to understand what I was talking about as well as the chairman of a Senate subcommittee. And I did. I devoted the time to it. I never did regret it. It was not an onerous chore for me; it was kind of an interesting thing for me to do. At the Camp David discussions with Begin and Sadat I didn't have to turn around to Vance or Quandt or Harold Saunders and say, would you explain to me the history of this particular issue, or will you show me on the map where the lines run or where this is located, because I knew it. And I could negotiate for hours with the subordinates of Begin and Sadat, which I did.[33]

James Fallows, Carter's chief speech writer for two years, recognized Carter's confidence in his persuasiveness. "Carter's performance on first intimate meeting was something special. His intelligence and magnetism soon banished all thoughts of the limits of his background. . . . He was fully aware of this power and used it whenever he could. . . . Lyndon Johnson had the same faith in his famous 'treatment,' but it was based on his intimate knowledge of the other party . . . [whereas] Carter's faith was in himself, and in the impression he would create."[34]

Carter thus played to this strength for knowledgeability in both the policy development and political persuasion processes. He could dominate policy development and set an example for his associates by being on top of issues. And he could persuade members of Congress, newspaper editors and the heads of foreign governments of the correctness of his ideas through the same knowledgeability. Two examples will suffice. An adviser recalled that at a meeting with the deputy secretary of defense and the Joint Chiefs of Staff the president knew the cost of weapons and the military men did not. As Carter's words above suggest, he used his knowledgeability as an example and goad to those who worked for him in policy development. The same adviser had been negotiating with independent energy producers on natural gas rates and they suggested a compromise that seemed reasonable when presented in percentages. Carter's response was that one-tenth of a percentage point was ten billion dollars, and he rejected the proposal.[35] At times this skill could cause Carter to show off when he might have been listening. One aide finally discouraged the president from demonstrating his knowledge to experts who were briefing him with the argument that he was intimidating them and depriving himself of information.[36]

This description of Carter as a decision maker sets him apart from the organizational structure for decision making that he set up. How do we fit him back into it? The short answer is that he wanted a policy development and decision-making process that, in focusing on fact finding and problem solving, would educate him and others. The process was to be collegial rather than competitive, with the president at the center. Carter describes how his favorite meeting, the weekly breakfast with foreign policy advisers Mondale, Vance, Brzezinski and Brown with Jordan and Powell often sitting in, operated on this theme of centralized collegiality.

It was uninterrupted unless it was an extreme emergency and it was an informal group restricted in attendance. We discussed issues that were of [the] utmost importance in a very frank way. It was a compatible group with me, Cy, Zbig, Harold and sometimes others. It was a meeting above all else where I could make a final decision and, ordinarily, the decision would be implemented. We would go through a list of agenda items. We didn't have a prepared agenda ahead of time, but Vance, Brown, Brzezinski and I would have the agenda items. I would ordinarily cover almost all of the issues myself and then I would ask them for additional ones. I would see them crossing off their lists what I had already brought up. At the conclusion of it Brzezinski would read the decisions that we had made or things that were postponed. That was an hour and a half. . . . I think the fact that we could actually make some decisions there was what made it attractive.[37]

Secretary of State Cyrus Vance wrote of the element of centralized collegiality:

In the Carter foreign policy apparatus, the personal dimension would be unusually important. The President's manner of dealing with his senior officials was unpretentious and open minded. He listened carefully and wanted the fullest discussion before making decisions. . . . His policy coordination and review system would therefore have to provide for frequent face to face meetings with his chief advisers. . . .

He emphasized the desire for a "team spirit" among his advisers. He looked for personal compatibility in every candidate for a cabinet level post. . . . "Collegiality" was to be the rule among his principal advisers. He wanted his cabinet to be composed of friends and equals, sure enough of themselves that they would not feel compelled to squabble about who could take the lead on any particular issue.[38]

The principle of centralized collegiality was most clearly embodied in foreign policy decision making because Carter invested the greatest intellectual and emotional effort in foreign policy and the issues could be discussed in one forum of a few key advisers. Here Carter was the central actor, with the secretary of state and the assistant for national security serving as advisers and policy implementers. His role was active and energetic, seeking problems to solve and initiatives to take.

The president was far more detached from the formulation of domestic policy than of foreign policy, in part a reflection of the structural differences in the two realms. Foreign policy can be discussed in one centralized forum among the same officials most of the time, with the president in the chair. But in domestic policy the actors shift from issue to issue and the White House must resolve a much larger number of questions. The president cannot give intensive study to all of them as he can to a relatively few major foreign policy issues. Carter did seek comprehensive policies in domestic policy—energy, welfare reform, tax reform, national health insurance—but he made a major investment of homework only in energy. He relied on Stuart Eizenstat and the Domestic Policy Staff for the coordination of domestic policy development, although Eizenstat was not empowered to overrule or give directions to cabinet officers and departments. Carter met with department heads and read long memoranda about domestic policy, but for the most part he preferred to work off paper, checking yes or no to choices the DPS presented him.[39]

Economic policy-making patterns fell somewhere in between foreign and domestic policy. Presidents must make only a few major macroeconomic policy decisions each year about budgets, taxes and similar broad issues in government management of the economy. Particular microeconomic policy disputes, in labor, agriculture, trade, welfare, etc. may get pushed up to the president if they are thought to have an impact on the health of the economy or if they are politically charged. But Carter was not deeply engaged in economic policy making. It did not provide opportunities for bold, dramatic steps of presidential leadership as did the Camp David treaties, for the constraints on bold economic policy were very strong. The president therefore listened to his economic advisers, who were mostly the same people much of the time since economic policy discussion is well institutionalized. And in making decisions he sought the least damaging course in avoiding inflation or unemployment or balancing the budget.

In all three of these policy areas Carter did homework, read and understood the briefing papers, and made the major decisions. But the amount of effort he put into study, discussion and policy leadership varied according to where he saw his opportunities to make a mark as president; for the most part this was in foreign policy. In all three areas he looked for collegiality and unity among his advisers, not in their ideas but in their commitment to common objectives.

The chapters to follow present little evidence that Carter got bogged down in details and failed to see the forest for the trees, a criticism outsiders sometimes leveled. What critics may have observed superficially was a complex and subtle process well known to Carter's staff. He liked to make decisions, had confidence in his capacity to make good ones and was inclined to make more decisions than he should. This was not getting bogged down in details but rather is an analogue to his tendency to place more issues on the public policy agenda than could be handled easily. In both cases he was ambitious to achieve his goals.

One of his principal assistants reported that Carter, in his desire "to have a sense of conquering the office in its every manifestation," sometimes became overloaded with decisions. This was, however, more common in the earlier part of the administration.

But it still happened too much. Broad decisions would be made and then there would be an inability to make a specific decision. And I think really the answer to that is that first of all people knew that Carter was insisting on making every last decision. And so, if that's the case, you can hold out until the end and go to the President, take everything to him. What should have happened is the President should have said, look here is the PRM [presidential review memorandum]. You've given me the basic issues, here are my decisions, now you go and settle it . . . and don't come back to see me. . . . Even after the first Camp David thing [April, 1978, when Carter delegated coordinating authority to White House staff members for policy development] that never really quite existed, because he just loved to hold on to making those last minute decisions, and as much as he complained about them he kept making them so that people in the agencies knew that there was always another reprieve and another chance.[40]

These comments do not report absorption in detail to the exclusion of the larger picture, but they do describe a president who wished to understand his choices and who at times carried that conviction to a fault.

Policy making through centralized collegiality was designed to serve several purposes for President Carter. It enabled him to set the goal of public goods to be achieved through study, with himself and his way of working as the exemplar for others. It was intended to foster unity among advisers. By exemplifying the search for unity in diversity it would permit Carter to balance and perhaps integrate competing values, such as liberal goals and conservative means, international cooperation and competition, as approximations of public goods. It facilitated the design of policies that articulated public goods—the chief resource of Carter's strategy of presidential leadership, which was to combine knowledge as a political resource with the evocation of shared values in the society.

Alexander George draws on the findings of cognitive psychology to posit a unity of style in political leaders in which beliefs, values and purposes, cognitive style and style of management are congruent.[41] Therefore the mode of policy making a president favors will not only be a manifestation of cognitive style but of presidential purposes. One who wishes to deal primarily with the politics of policy will perhaps favor a loose, disjointed mode of decision making which involves competition among diverse advisers. A president who seeks to find good substantive approaches to problems will favor a decision process of homework and discussion by knowledgeable officials. Purpose shapes process as much as, or more than it is shaped in return.

Carter's style of decision making based on homework and the solving of particular problems gave rise to the impression that issues were decided on an ad hoc basis, according to their merits as the president saw them at the time, without thought for the relation of particular decisions to general policy goals.[42] An alternative explanation, however, is that Jimmy Carter used centralized collegiality in decision making as a way to balance and integrate competing values and goals. His domestic policy advisers were indeed divided, one wishing to play to the politics of the Democratic coalition, particularly the Washington-based interest groups, and a cluster of more conservative advisers wanting the president to emphasize his fiscal conservatism and appeal to the people over the heads of groups in his partisan coalition. Carter found ways to do both by urging the reorganization and rationalization of liberal social programs so that they might work more effectively. He was similarly faced with liberal advisers who continually urged him to increase spending for social programs and economic advisers who warned against the inflationary pressure of spending. He was also anxious to avoid recession and high levels of unemployment. The resulting pattern of decision, for Carter, was to balance between tight and ample annual budgets, depending upon whether the immediate enemy was inflation or recession, with an overall goal of reducing the percentage of increase in federal spending in the interests of economic growth. What may have appeared to be inconsistency was rather, for Carter, the attempt to hold in balance competing demands. He likewise performed a balancing act between Vance and Brzezinski, alternately seeking cooperation with the Soviets and warning them that cooperation was dependent upon good behavior. Observers charged that Carter's only policy was to arbitrate between his key advisers, yet to him the implicit integration of principles of cooperation and competition was clear. Decision making through centralized collegiality was an efficient way for Carter to perform these balancing acts.

People at the top never doubted that Carter was in charge, for he had great confidence in his capacity to make decisions and was not threatened by disagreement among his advisers. His fault was that he permitted the public impression of disarray within the administration to prevail, perhaps because he did not himself feel that things were in disarray. He was also very tolerant of dissidence among his lieutenants, which could be a problem when his associates were not as loyal to him or to the principal of collegiality as he would have liked. According to one aide, Carter was always surprised at these breakdowns, because he wanted his advisers to be a family and did not think of their relationships as political. He assumed that good personal relations would lead to policy agreement.[43]

An aide who had observed Carter for many years and who admired him greatly thought that rather than lacking toughness the president was too tolerant.

Carter is one of the most able and intelligent, most self-disciplined, most self-confident, most determined and most hard working men I have ever known. . . . He's tough and demanding in his personal relationships with the people around him. . . . There was never any doubt in anybody's mind about that. The strongest personalities in our administration—Jim Schlesinger, Harold Brown, Mike Blumenthal, Joe Califano—never doubted for a moment who was in charge. There was never any doubt that the President was well-prepared and able to talk with his expertise on whatever subject was at hand. . . .

You would think by what I have just said that personal loyalty and trepidation within members of the cabinet would have been the natural consequences. It wasn't, for a couple of complicated reasons that I'm not sure I can well articulate. One is that the President was reluctant to sanction anyone. . . . President Carter is a kind man, even though he is as tough intellectually as anyone can be. He is extraordinarily tolerant, perhaps too much so, of other people's shortcomings.[44]

The question of how well Carter managed the occasional breakdown of collegiality among his advisers is an important one that will appear in subsequent chapters. He presumed collegiality to be the fact and achieved it much of the time; it was his nature to expect the best of his lietuenants.

Carter's faith in centralized collegiality as the principle of decision making was not the faith that a well-designed organization would produce good people. He was not an institutional engineer. Rather, he appears to have believed that people of goodwill who had learned to work together would develop the right policies. This was the Baptist rather than the engineer, and was analogous to his trust in the capacity of the American people to respond to leadership in behalf of the public interest. In both policy leadership and public leadership Carter did not want politics to drive policy. A politics of incrementalism, bargaining and the search for feasibility did not evoke the best in people. Carter wanted policy objectives to drive politics. The higher the objective the better the quality of the politics; he hoped to evoke the best in his lieutenants and in the public.

Chapters 1 and 2 have shown Jimmy Carter as a policy leader, politician and manager of policy making. Such a broad portrait is important for understanding how he made policy decisions and managed policy development, for one cannot describe process alone as if the ends and means to policy achievement were not important. But in its focus on how Jimmy Carter managed policy formation this study does not reach out to describe how he led Congress or public opinion. In looking at the beginnings rather than the conclusion of the policy story many interesting themes must be left dangling. For example, Carter's strategy of appealing to public goods was effective when latent constituencies could be marshaled, as in energy policy and the ratification of the Panama Canal treaties, but it failed with welfare reform and tax reform because opposing coalitions could not be transcended. Our story will not reach so far into Carter's style as to describe or assess his strategies of political leadership. We have drawn such a broad portrait in order to place his management of policy formation within a larger context.

The aspiration to frame policies in terms of public goods through decision-making processes that emphasize homework and collegiality does not automatically translate itself into practice. Strategies must be found for organizing and managing centralized collegiality to produce the desired results. Colleagues who can work well together must be appointed. Good collegial working processes must be developed through trial and error. In particular, a constructive division of labor and collaboration among White House staffs, cabinet officers and department officials must be worked out. None of this happens on its own; presidential agencies are given working life by the new players who come into them as the presidency changes hands.

President Carter was more interested in facing issues and solving problems than he was in managing decision-making processes. He had a broad conception of what he loosely called cabinet government, by which he meant policy development in the departments, rather than in the White House. White House staffs were to assist him in making decisions, but beyond that he did not have in mind a well-developed model for the relation of these staffs to the departments should the need for central coordination of policy development appear. And, as such problems emerged, he basically left it up to his chief lieutenants in the White House to work out their relationships with cabinet officers and the departments. They had to find the balances between policy purpose, politics and the organization of policy making.

Chapters 3, 4 and 5 will describe policy-making processes as they developed in domestic, economic and foreign policy. The analysis will link Carter's style of making decisions, the management of conflict, and the search for unity among policy purpose, political calculations and the decision process. Chapter 6 will return to the themes set out in the Preface to ask how Carter's approach to policy and policy making matched the political context of his times and to assess whether he made the most of his opportunities for leadership. This analysis will be set within the context of the canons of presidential skill and effectiveness as revealed in the writings of presidential scholars.

3
DOMESTIC POLICY
FORMATION

The central story of this chapter is the adaptation of Jimmy Carter's style for the management of policy making to the political life of Washington without the sacrifice of comprehensiveness and collegiality. Compromises with both values occurred, of course, but the framework for policy making that developed and became the stable way of doing things preserved collegiality and balanced comprehensiveness against incrementalism. The narrative will illustrate Carter's personal style of managing policy making, the eventual development of greater coordinating authority for the Domestic Policy Staff in the face of cabinet department disagreements, and the increasing role the DPS played in bringing political learning about policy feasibility into the White House and to the president. President Carter responded positively to these developments and learned to use the DPS as a coordinator of policy and for his own political tutelage.

This story was played out against a political background of tension between a centrist Democratic president and a Democratic party and its constituent groups that wished him to be more "liberal" than he wished to be. Carter's search for comprehensive policies that would combine liberal goals with tight financial limits often fell between liberal and conservative poles, too cautious for the first and too radical for the second. The Carter White House was thus feeling its way through the trade offs between the hope for comprehensive initiatives and the need for policy successes that could only be achieved through incremental action.

CONSERVATIVE LIBERALISM

The same confusion Georgia voters had felt about where Carter stood on issues during and after his successful 1970 gubernatorial campaign was present from the beginning of the 1976 presidential campaign. In the New Hampshire primary he had been a puzzle to voters and journalists, not to mention the other candidates, because he was both liberal and conservative and could not be captured by any ideological mold. But he had won the most votes of any candidate in the primary. His achievement in the primaries, which was more difficult to duplicate in the heterogeneous electorate of the general election, was to persuade the voters to trust him, without details. All of this made many traditional Democratic voters very uneasy about him because he did not voice the familiar slogans they wished to hear. A major union leader told David Broder, of the Washington *Post*, "I don't know who he is, where he's going or where he's been."[1]

Clear tensions thus existed between his appeals to groups in the traditional Democratic constituency and groups outside that category, not only issues differences but profound variations in style and approach. The Democratic groups wished to hear what government would do for them; the others were probably responding to Carter's gospel for America. What appeared to be traditionalism in Carter, a yearning for the simplicity of rural life or the social unity of a past era, was not that at all, but a look toward the future and the articulation of the goal of national unity based on planning and organization. Such language was far different from the bread and butter liberalism of traditional Democratic rhetoric.

Carter was a leader in search of "public goods." He clearly believed that the central weakness of American politics and government was the dominance of special interests over social needs, and though he never used the term he was an implacable foe of "interest group liberalism."[2] The chief vehicle for interest group liberalism was the Democratic party and its constituent groups who were practicing a politics of demand generated by the Great Society programs and subsequent environmental, women's and consumer movements. During the general election Carter came under pressures that had not been present in the primary period. The organized constituencies of the Democratic party wanted to know where he stood on their issues. Stuart Eizenstat, head of the campaign issues staff, described the difficulty this presented to the candidate and how he handled it.

He was clearly the most conservative of the Democratic candidates in the '76 campaign. He was the only one talking about balanced budgets and less bureaucracy and less red tape and themes that associate perhaps with Republicans. And then [he] moved to the left [for] the general election in order to accommodate the groups and organizations and institutional interests in the Democratic party. For example the UAW [United Auto Workers] . . . was a key element in any Democratic coalition, organizationally, financially and intellectually. Its big issue was national health insurance. The President had been asked to attend and address the National Medical Association in Washington, which was the predominantly Black medical association, to talk about national health insurance. Well, you know we couldn't go through a national campaign and turn down things like that. . . . And in particular the UAW insisted on knowing what our position was. And we negotiated with them for quite a lengthy period in terms of exact language and there were certain buzz words, "comprehensive," "all inclusive," and so forth that they had to have in order to be enthusiasts in the campaign. Carter, to his credit, held out as much as he could in terms of leaving himself as much flexibility so that he didn't have to implement immediately and it could be done in phases and so forth. And they gave on that and gave up some of the specificity they would have preferred, but he certainly had to give too.

The mayors who are a key part of the Democratic coalition insisted on an urban policy speech. I went to New York and the thing they were most interested in was relieving themselves of the welfare burden, in particular the burden of AFDC [Aid to Families with Dependent Children]. . . . And there were negotiations with the mayors' group . . . and the urban policy paper came out and that was again Carter having to move away from perhaps positions he would have liked to have taken because obviously it cost money to remove the welfare burden and that tended to cut against his balanced budget theme. . . .

[Such tensions were] terribly important in terms of what happened in the presidency, this balancing act between his basic instincts, his basic fiscal conservatism, his basic sort of distrust of Washington and the bureaucracy time and time again during the campaign and during the presidency conflicted with the realities of keeping an election coalition and ultimately a governing coalition together.[3]

Carter attempted to preserve as much latitude and autonomy as possible during the campaign but inevitably he threw up ambiguous images about his intentions, thus generating problems for his presidency. He did not find it easy to integrate his conservative liberalism with that of Democratic interest groups, so the uneasy compromises negotiated during the campaign and the ambiguous rhetoric papered over differences that later were not easily reconciled.[4]

The tension between Carter's ideology and goals and the demands of Democratic constituencies was a continuing theme of his presidency. He had a coherent ideology with which he hoped to transcend competing demands, and these ideas were clearly presented in his first presidential speeches. His inaugural address was a point-counterpoint balancing of opposites—limits to growth and economic stimulus, competence and compassion, national goodness and strength—a good illustration of his wish to embrace both prudence and boldness and perhaps a projection of his own character. His April 18, 1977, speech to the nation on energy emphasized the importance of taking a long-term view, of national unity and fairness.[5]

Stuart Eizenstat, who directed the Domestic Policy staff, captures the administration's dominant ideological theme.

One always knew that he wanted to spend as little money as possible and yet at the same time he wanted welfare reform, he wanted national health insurance, he wanted an urban policy, he wanted job training programs. And I think that that tended to lead to some of the clearest internal conflicts . . . perhaps led to the public perception of an administration without the clearest of courses. You know the question of where are you taking the country. . . . You can't keep a foot in each path without severe cost. . . . What we wanted is to cut spending, but not too much, to be fiscally moderate rather than fiscally austere. . . .

Although Carter was a more conservative Democrat than many of those against whom he ran in 1976 he was a Democrat. He felt deeply about problems of poverty. He'd come from the rural south. . . . He felt deeply about his commitment to try to help people. And he felt that the federal government did have some responsibilities. And yet at the same time I think he recognized that the resources weren't there to do anything he wanted or the groups wanted, that we have to be exercising some fiscal discipline.[6]

Another domestic policy assistant characterized Carter as having been a governor who liked to give reassuring speeches to conservative Chamber of Commerces about his soundness and then to do a few liberal things. The approach had its difficulties as this aide observed.

Carter once said in my hearing that all a Democratic president needed to do was appear to be conservative. For example, he wanted a welfare reform that would serve conservative values. He picked welfare reform as his first big initiative to balance Chamber of Commerce and liberal values. It looked to him like a rational place to start. That overlooks the nature of the problem. If the Chamber of Commerce is cheering the liberal groups will oppose it. . . .

If he had pulled National Health Insurance up first he would have had a better issue than Welfare Reform. National Health Insurance would have had a genuine constituency because of the gaps in coverage. Welfare reform had no constituency. He rejected that because he believed that looked too liberal.[7]

Carter's closest aides understood that he hoped to lead the Democratic coalition in new directions. One remembered that Carter thought the way to change the Democratic party was through new policy and thus was proud of a Spring, 1977, poll showing that a majority of those polled believed the Democrats to be more fiscally responsible than the Republicans. Another stated that Carter was the first president of the party of the disadvantaged to face the fact that, because of the success of past Democratic administrations, the disadvantaged were a smaller group. "I think he had a truer sense of how to move away from the old coalition than I did," this aide added.[8]

DEVELOPMENT OF THE DOMESTIC POLICY STAFF

It is convenient to classify all policies not predominantly in the national security area or clearly economic issues of the standard macroeconomic or microeconomic variety as domestic policy. This includes health, education and social welfare policy. Even though economists may work on such issues in presidential government, they usually do not have ultimate responsibility for them. By the same token economic regulation of business and labor and issues of inflation and employment are regarded as economic issues. Domestic policy is usually understood to include environmental issues and urban policy as well.

Chapters 3 and 4 on domestic and economic policy respectively will follow these conventional distinctions. Thus, although the president's economic stimulus package was an important domestic program early in the administration it will be considered in the chapter on economic policy. Energy policy is clearly a hybrid because all hands worked on it, but the major policy development responsibilities were never given to administration economists and therefore it is treated as domestic policy.

Domestic policy, as defined, flows from the departments that do such business, notably the former Department of Health, Education and Welfare, which became Health and Human Services in 1979 after the Carter administration created the Department of Education. Labor Department employment and training programs were considered domestic policy as were those programs of the Department of Housing and Urban Development that contributed to the legacy of urban programs left over from the Great Society.

These domestic programs flowed into the White House through the Domestic Policy Staff, which is as good a way as any to distinguish them from economic policy issues which the Council of Economic Advisers staffed. But what was the Domestic Policy Staff? Since the Kennedy administration a small body of presidential assistants on the White House staff had gradually become institutionalized to help develop the president's domestic policy program. Bill Moyers and Joe Califano pulled together most of the Great Society programs in the Johnson administration, working with task forces and departmental groups. This group was small, with no more than five members, and their work could not have been accomplished without the institutional knowledge and programmatic expertise of the Bureau of the Budget and the various departments. Lyndon Johnson seldom talked with cabinet officers about new domestic policy but relied upon White House staffs to develop final proposals. In 1970 President Nixon created the formal structure of a Domestic Council, consisting of the cabinet officers of the domestic policy departments, and attached a large staff to the council under the leadership of John Ehrlichman. Policy development was, in fact, preempted by the staff, which worked with the newly created Office of Management and Budget and subcabinet departmental staffs. Cabinet officers and the Domestic Council itself were relegated to secondary roles in policy development. President Ford retained that structure, giving Vice-President Rockefeller authority over the work of the Domestic Council staff. In fact, since Ford had a limited program of domestic policy neither staff nor council had much to do.[9]

Carter abolished the Domestic Council by executive order and created a small Domestic Policy Staff in the White House office under Stuart Eizenstat. He made clear to Eizenstat, the members of the new cabinet and the press that the Nixon system of displacement of cabinet officers by White House staff in policy development was not to be repeated. Some members of the Carter team who had served in the Johnson administration felt that the president should have empowered Eizenstat to take policy initiatives and resolve disputes among departments as Johnson had empowered Califano.[10] But because Carter's intention was to restore cabinet officers to preeminence in policy development, members of the Domestic Policy Staff were to be facilitators and coordinators.

Eizenstat was a young Atlanta attorney who had briefly worked in the Johnson White House and was Hubert Humphrey's research director in the 1968 presidential campaign. He had known Governor Carter but had not served in his administration. He became the director of the Atlanta-based issues staff, at Carter's request, during the extended campaign for the presidency. In mid 1976 Eizenstat recruited the core of the future DPS to work in Atlanta on the issues staff. After the November election he recruited a DPS staff in Washington. He knew exactly what kind of people he wanted because of his belief that the function of a presidential domestic policy staff was to be a coordinating body that would match policy ideas and plans to the political climate. On behalf of the president the DPS would test policy ideas against what the political traffic would bear. He therefore recruited staff members with Washington experience, whether on congressional committee staffs or in public interest law firms. His deputy, for example, was a senior staff member of the Senate Budget Committee and a long-time associate of Vice-President Mondale, and many DPS members were substantive experts in specific policy areas, such as health and energy. For the most part, however, they were not technical experts in what is often called "policy analysis," which has cost-benefit analysis as its core methodology. In Eizenstat's view expertise at policy analysis in this technical sense should reside in the departments and agencies where program proposals would be developed. For example, the complicated calculations of how to combine the income maintenance provisions of welfare reform with the creation of public employment for welfare recipients were best handled by economists in the Department of Health, Education and Welfare and the Department of Labor. For years policy analysts in and out of government had worked on the very complicated estimates of income payment that would increase, rather than reduce, the incentives of welfare recipients to work. Eizenstat did not envision that kind of competence in the DPS staff.

What you want on the Domestic Policy staff at the White House is someone who can synthesize politics and policy. . . . I want someone who, when he sees an issue, has red flags going up. You know, this agency is not going to like it, and I'd better talk to them about it. Or, this guy on the Hill is not going to like it or this interest group is not going to like it. Who understands the issues substantively but who also understands the political implications of it. . . .

We had no capability whatsoever to be able to question when EPA said that their new source performance standards were going to cost X number of dollars. . . . We were able to call CEA [Council of Economic Advisers] in and say, you tell us how much, and we were able to call the industry in and say you tell us how much it's going to cost and of course we knew the industry was going to inflate the figure but it gave you some sense of what the ranges were. And we would call the AFL and say, how important is this cotton dust thing to you . . . [so that] we'd have some idea of what the parameters were and how much we could push EPA. . . . If it were up to the EPA they for damn sure weren't going to call CEA and industry and question the data. But, we felt that we had an obligation to protect the President and give him the conflicting information and . . . synthesize it.[11]

The principal task of the DPS was managing the policy development process with an eye to the president's policy objectives and political needs. As one of Eizenstat's deputies put it,

We put this staff together in order to function within [the parameters of] Carter's very strong commitment to the departments. This meant that we were process managers not program designers. . . . I, having worked in the Senate all my life, obviously was inclined to see this staff as analogous to some operations in the Senate. I think a close model for where we started out from was the Senate Budget Committee which had to have people who understood the issues, understood who the key players were on the Hill, in the academic community . . . and could perform an integration function. You wanted both to have some notion of where the thing ought to come out and some ability to manipulate the process because we could not command it.[12]

In an interview in the early life of the administration Eizenstat described himself as a generalist: "I have a good enough grasp to know the problems in each [policy area], the direction we ought to take, the pitfalls, the positions that interest groups are likely to take, and the probable congressional relations. I try to know enough so I can give the President a reasoned and intelligent judgment on every issue."[13]

Eizenstat's conception of his own role and that of his staff was similar to that of his predecessors in previous administrations. Clark Clifford, Theodore Sorensen, Joseph Califano and John Ehrlichman had been generalists and brokers between the president and program advocates and experts. The differences were in the degree of authority each had to arbitrate among contending parties and decide disputes. On this scale the Eizenstat operation had the least initial authority of any of the White House domestic policy staffs since Johnson.[14]

In contrast to the DPS the Council of Economic Advisers (CEA), both members and staff, and the National Security Council (NSC) staff consist of professional experts. Thus, the three CEA members and fifteen or so professional staff members are economists, the majority drawn from university faculties. National Security Council staff members are usually a combination of academic experts and experienced government professionals but, in both cases, a premium is placed upon substantive expertise. The CEA and NSC staffs are more likely than domestic policy staffs to use expert skills to challenge departmental analysis and plans. The CEA and NSC often assign the agencies detailed tasks of policy analysis, but such work is subjected to expert scrutiny when it is returned to the White House.[15]

This distinction between the domestic policy operation and its counterparts is important because the basis for credibility with the president differs. A domestic policy staff establishes credibility with a president because it helps him politically by assessing policy proposals from a reading of the political context in Congress, interest groups, etc. The credibility of economic and national security staffs with a president is primarily based upon the capacity for formal analysis of difficult policy problems and the clear explication of alternative choices and their consequences. Particularly in national security affairs such analysis may incorporate the experts' political knowledge, for example a political analysis of a particular problem or country.

The CEA and NSC staff functions are based on academic disciplines, especially in the case of economics and the CEA. The ability to analyze domestic policy options derives from no single discipline but from several that are difficult to integrate. Historically formal professional policy analysis for domestic policy developed in the departments rather than in the White House. This was institutionalized in 1965 when President Johnson created the assistant secretaryships for policy analysis in the several domestic policy departments, imitating the model of program-budget analysis Robert McNamara developed at the Pentagon. Microeconomic analysis predominates in such work and it is therefore in the interest of the president to have a domestic policy staff with broader competence. The program-budget analysis carried out by the Office of Management and Budget has become increasingly similar to microeconomic analysis but relies much more heavily on personal knowledge of agencies and programs. But such "neutral competence" is one step removed from the political needs of presidents.[16]

These are important distinctions for understanding domestic policy making in the Carter administration because Stuart Eizenstat and the Domestic Policy staff developed a stronger political role than appears to have been envisioned. For example, a hole that Eizenstat eventually discovered he had to fill was the missing link between political calculation and policy analysis. Hamilton Jordan gave the president advice about electoral politics but did not appear to see himself as the explicit link between political advice and program development. Indeed, one of his former associates argues that the Washington community consistently misunderstood Jordan. He neither considered himself qualified as a policy expert nor believed that he had the administrative ability to be White House chief of staff. So in a sense he refused to accept responsibility, something so unusual as to be misinterpreted in a town that values power and is always asking who is up and who is down.[17] But the consequence was that someone had to be the missing link between politics and domestic policy, particularly since the president did not choose that role for himself. The assignment fell fortuitously to Eizenstat, who kept in touch with interest groups, sounded out congressional opinion as policy was being developed and compensated for Carter's limited interest.[18]

The relation of the DPS political role to presidential decisions was structured by the weakness of the Democratic party as an instrument of government and as a political coalition. The DPS had to fill that gap by necessity because some group in the president's orbit had to assume responsibility for knitting together the various Democratic constituencies in support of administration measures. A division of labor developed in the White House, with the DPS sounding out interest groups and congressional staffs about what the traffic would bear on specific legislative matters and the Office of Public Liaison, established under the leadership of Anne Wexler in early 1978, taking responsibility for creating nationwide support for administration proposals. The model for the latter effort was the successful campaign for ratification of the Panama Canal treaties, led by Hamilton Jordan. In their work with political leaders, mayors, governors, and institutional leaders throughout the country Wexler and her staff created White House forums at which the president and cabinet officers made presentations. The Eizenstat operation worked at an earlier stage to identify interests with stakes in particular proposals, to avoid unnecessary conflicts and develop support in advance through convergence of interests. The Carter administration did not come to Washington with a well established political coalition behind it, for Carter had been elected through a largely independent effort. However, his Domestic Policy Staff did not think it possible for the administration to be effective without support of the groups in the Democratic coalition. Eizenstat was quite explicit about this.

You're going to have to depend on the organized forces in Washington to mobilize their people in terms of legislative process, that's what I was most concerned with. I think that I was also concerned with the President's standing in the Democratic party because although these groups and organizations . . . have certainly had less influence in electing people, it's awfully tough to get elected without them . . . as was shown in the '80 campaign, where a lot of these groups were against him [Carter]. They will make life miserable for you. They will be so publicly critical that they end up tearing down your image among the independent group.[19]

DPS staff members saw themselves in a difficult bind. Domestic policy development had to proceed in concert with the important interest groups within the Democratic coalition such as union labor, farm groups, environmental, consumer and women's groups, yet the support of these groups could not guarantee the passage of legislation proposed by the administration. This was because "liberal" organized groups spoke for a decreasing percentage of the population and members of Congress were consequently more independent and more difficult to lead in terms of a coalition of interests.[20] Carter had become president with the support of both Democratic interest groups and political independents and this increased the paradox of relying on Washington-based interest groups for policy support. Often it was not enough. As a domestic policy aide put it,

You do have a middle class country, a non-aligned country, a non-coalition country which makes it enormously difficult to fashion coalitions for governing, let alone being elected. And I think the President sensed this. I think that they [interest groups] were important to his '76 election. I think that the problem was that these groups and organizations are much more influential in Washington than they are in the nation as a whole. . . . They were pressing Carter for national health insurance . . . for welfare reform and hospital cost containment and . . . a consumer protection agency. And that mass of increasingly well educated independents could care less about all those issues.[21]

Fiscal conservatives within the administration, particularly in the Office of Management and Budget, were critical of the DPS for trying to satisfy the demands of Democratic groups. A former OMB official expressed a view that was strongly supported by his OMB associates.

At the senior policy level at OMB . . . there was a strong concern that the constituency politics that we felt were driving the agencies and some of the White House staff . . . were different from the presidential constituency, which was much wider. The President's constituency transcended and was much broader than all of the various interest groups. The OMB was not only representing that constituency, but when it finally came down to an election issue for the presidency, the OMB issue would serve the President very well. Fiscal responsibility, smaller deficits, controlling program growth, and all of that, were very good political issues to run on. That was not the argument you heard from almost any place else in the government.[22]

Both DPS and OMB officials report that the fundamental issues in the relation of the Carter administration and its domestic policy proposals to popular constituencies were debated over and over in specific cases of policy development. The "liberals" wished to bring the Democratic groups along. As one DPS member said in response to OMB criticisms that DPS was trying too hard to satisfy the groups in the Democratic coalition, "We didn't satisfy them. But we felt that we had to bring the party along in the new direction. The coalition had to be convinced. We had to give them a feeling that they had a stake in it."[23] These remarks reflect the clear understanding that the support of Democratic groups was necessary but not sufficient to carry the president's program.

The OMB strategy was to appeal over the heads of Democratic groups to a diffuse constituency in the population for support for new policy directions. However, OMB did not pursue this strategy consistently. The reports of both sets of advisers reveal that each was aware that its plan for the relation of policy to politics was incomplete. The president did not have a majority coalition in either Washington or the country on which to build his programs. Policy making was characterized by the effort to develop comprehensive programs that would appeal to the general public and then, if this failed, decisions were ad hoc and bent in the direction of appeal to interests, denial of their claims, or attempts to split the difference.

How do we reconcile a political role for Eizenstat and the DPS with Carter's announced determination to be a trustee president who would not focus on politics in policy development? Carter did not initially foresee the political role the DPS would play or the need for it but seems to have changed his mind on the basis of experience. A division of labor gradually developed in which Carter addressed issues as a trustee but considered the political learning of the Domestic Policy Staff as he did so.

The two stories here are the development of the DPS political role and the increasing authority Carter gave Eizenstat and the DPS to arbitrate among agencies and initiate policy proposals on its own behalf, always with presidential support. The first story reveals a modification of Carter's style of leadership though with a continued strong adherence to the trustee model. The second reveals the president's discovery that his original conception of delegating policy development to cabinet officers and the departments had limitations because such officials and agencies often could not agree among themselves. Therefore, the Domestic Policy Staff played an increasingly active role as coordinators. However, at no time did Eizenstat or the DPS displace the responsibility of cabinet officers and the departments for policy development. The modification did not alter Carter's basic conceptions of government.

Eizenstat had not worked intimately with Carter before the campaign, and therefore the two had to get used to each other. It took Carter time to test new people, and in 1982 he described the situation.

As I became more familiar with the overall operation of government, and as we built up a base of generic policy that could be used as a guide for more specific policy evolution, then I trusted Stu and his staff to do much more than we did at first. Stu was one of those who didn't work for me in the state government . . . [but] he was the one who did the issue analysis and worked up domestic policy proposals when I was running for President, so I knew him and I trusted him. But he didn't really have those four years of experience and training within the state government to know exactly how I did things. That didn't take long. I couldn't put a number of months on it, but I would say after the first rash of major proposals that went to the Congress, from then on we had our basic policies understood among each other, and Stu had much more authority from then on than originally in making proposals on his own.[24]

Eventually, Eizenstat became the barometer to others of what Carter thought and would accept, which was possible only because he understood Carter and was trusted by him, again a gradual development. By mid-1977 Carter was telling cabinet officers, "Speak with Stu if you want to know my position."[25]

The members of the Domestic Policy Staff had a sense of what Carter would accept and used such knowledge to develop consensus in the agencies. And the advice the DPS gave Carter was, in the words of an Eizenstat deputy, "colored by what we thought we could get him [Carter] to do."[26]

The most important reason for the increased DPS role, however, was the difficulty of reconciling disagreements among cabinet departments. Eizenstat remembered,

It became clearer and clearer that materials had to flow through my office . . . [because] you simply couldn't run a major study on a major issue out of cabinet departments . . . [and] the welfare [reform] policy . . . is an excellent example of what happens when the White House doesn't coordinate policy but only participates in agency run, interagency activities. And that is that agencies can't agree among themselves. . . . Carter ended up getting a decision memorandum on welfare which was some 60 single-spaced typewritten pages, utterly incomprehensible, in which the Department of Labor and the Department of HEW could not even agree on the language to be used in various sections. . . .

That's what a White House staff is there for. It's a non turf interested, presidentially oriented, neutral arbiter, and when it's not allowed to serve that function, which it was in part not allowed to do because of some of the signals that were sent up by "cabinet government," then you get a policy muddle.[27]

At an April, 1978, Camp David meeting with cabinet officers and senior White House staff members the president gave the Domestic Policy Staff greater authority. Eizenstat recalls the context.

Carter had begun to slip in the polls. There was a sense that there was not enough cohesion, that agencies were going off on their own, that the White House was insufficiently involved in the coordination of policy. That the President was getting too much reading material from too many different sources. And at least one of the decisions made was that there should be a stronger coordinator role for our staff. I frankly think that by that time it was really more a ratification of what was already happening—but at least it did put a clear presidential imprint on what was evolving.[28]

In the early months of the administration, cabinet officers had submitted separate memos to Carter on policy proposals and Eizenstat's role was to add his comments. After April, 1978, the lead role for policy development remained in the agencies but the DPS had a stronger coordinating role. Eizenstat and his staff members worked to eliminate differences among agencies so that one recommendation would go to the president. If this were not possible, DPS would write one memo presenting the several options along with an analysis of the budgetary implications and political risks of each. Carter could then make a decision with one piece of paper in front of him, often simply by checking boxes provided on the memo. "We were coordinators," Eizenstat said, "because we were coordinating the input of material, we were mediating when possible and ultimately we were putting things into a decision making form." Eizenstat was formally called upon to be an arbitrator rather than a mediator on a few issues which involved no fundamental disagreement but rather differences of degree. Often his aim was to protect the president from the need to resolve minor issues. For example, the Energy Department wished to give a 20 percent tax credit for the installation of solar equipment on buildings and the Treasury Department wished to make it 10 percent. Eizenstat split the difference, judging that it was not a presidential issue. Some testimony indicates that Carter was quick to accept compromises the DPS arranged, particularly if the option paper told him that all the parties agreed to the compromise. Of course, as already indicated, many of these compromises took into account what Carter would accept.[29]

The DPS undertook policy initiatives of its own through the Presidential Review Memorandum (PRM), a device Eizenstat borrowed from tne NSC. The DPS would set out a policy question or objective, ask a number of agencies to contribute analysis and papers, and then play the motivating and coordinating role. This was clearly a case of DPS policy entrepreneurship with the president as the ultimate client. The best example, DPS staffers thought, was the youth employment initiative of 1979–1980.[30] The DPS used the PRM process of developing and sifting views throughout the administration as a means to develop support for new policy ideas, both within the administration and throughout the country. For example, during the six- to nine-month period of such activity a number of meetings and public hearings would often be held away from Washington.

Finally, the DPS wrote the president's legislative messages, working with White House speech writers. This was true even if the policy idea had

originated in a cabinet department, so long as the issue was to have promi-
nence in the president's program.[31]

CASES OF POLICY DEVELOPMENT

Three policy stories will illustrate the twin themes of White House coordination and political learning within a commitment to collegiality and
comprehensiveness. The two administration energy policy initiatives, in
1977 and 1979, were handled differently. In 1977 James Schlesinger developed a program secretly, under instructions from the president, that
passed the House of Representatives but ran aground in the Senate and
did not finally pass until late 1978. The 1979 initiative was consciously
coordinated by the Domestic Policy Staff in order to overcome perceived
weaknesses in the first proposal, with good results in Congress. The 1977
welfare reform initiative was a test of the principle of delegating policy development to cabinet officers, in this case Secretary Joseph Califano of the
Department of Health, Education and Welfare. The great difficulty Califano had in bringing the Department of Labor into a common plan
alerted the White House to the need for a greater DPS coordinating role.
Political learning was also deficient in the welfare reform case because the
president and Califano did not understand each other. Unlike energy, welfare reform was a comprehensive policy for which political support was
lacking. Finally, the creation of the Department of Education illustrates
the DPS role as policy coordinator and custodian of political learning for
the president.

ENERGY

The Arab oil embargo of 1974 and the subsequent formation of the Organization of Petroleum Exporting Countries (OPEC), had presented the
United States with increasing dependence on costly foreign oil at a time
when domestic production was declining. Conservation of energy, conver-
sion to other sources such as coal, and increased domestic production of oil
were the obvious remedies. The federal government continued after 1973
to keep the price of oil artificially low through modified price controls and
did little to penalize excessive domestic consumption through taxation.
Neither President Nixon nor President Ford had been able to persuade
Congress to enact an energy program that grappled with these problems.

Carter liked this kind of issue, as it pitted the national interest, and a
public good, against regional and economic interests. It also required

comprehensive treatment, joining conservation and production, oil, gas, coal, nuclear power and taxes. The fact that his precedessors had failed made it even more of a challenge.[32]

Issues of energy policy had not been much discussed in the 1976 campaign and Carter was aware that many Americans questioned whether the energy shortage was genuine or whether the oil-producing countries and companies were gouging the public.[33] One of Carter's advisers reports that the president-elect had been persuaded by his old Navy commander, Admiral Rickover, that the United States was running out of oil. In response Carter felt a moral obligation to exercise stewardship in regard to natural resources. Furthermore, he was critical of the manner in which politicians had failed to face the hard questions. This aide remembers Carter's mood at the time: "With his moral fervor, he had little patience with the normal political tendency toward a policy of drift, opportunism and irresponsibility."[34]

President Carter recalled in his memoirs his perception in 1976 of the need for a "comprehensive" energy program that would encourage conservation, production and the development of alternative forms of domestic energy and reduce dependence on foreign oil. Therefore, he says, "moving with exceeding haste" he decided to develop a national energy plan as quickly as possible. His plan to present to Congress a comprehensive program that it could enact in his first year in office left no time for extensive consultation with Congress. "I felt that the urgency of the issue required such quick action on my part," he recalls. "The plan needed to be completed without detour if Congress was to decide the matter during the first year."[35]

Carter turned to James Schlesinger, a Republican economist and former Nixon and Ford cabinet officer, for help. The two had first met during the campaign when Schlesinger had offered to brief Carter about his recent trip to China. They evidently hit it off very well, both being intelligent and analytic, and Carter resolved to have Schlesinger in his cabinet. Since he had been head of the Atomic Energy Commission under Nixon, he seemed a logical choice for secretary of the Department of Energy whose creation President Carter was to recommend.[36]

The president-elect first mentioned his plan to develop a comprehensive energy policy at a transition briefing on December 9. At that time he said that he hoped to have the proposal ready to send to Congress within ninety days of his inauguration. This decision, however, was kept quiet, with no mention of it being made at a January 31 cabinet meeting. At a February 28 cabinet meeting Schlesinger, now working as an assistant to the president, briefly mentioned that he was at work on a comprehensive energy plan. The decision secretly to develop a plan in ninety days was apparently Carter's. One presidential aide told a journalist who was writing an inside story of the first hundred days that Carter liked deadlines because "he thinks people work better with a gun at their heads." Carter was thought to be worried that if the developing energy plan came to light groups whose interests were threatened would be able to attack pieces of it and dismantle it.

Schlesinger asked the president for a period longer than ninety days in which to develop the plan, fearing that he could not get Congress and interest groups on board in that time, but Carter refused. Carter's style was first to build a bold plan and then try to sell it, and he also wished to get the jump on Congress and introduce his big initiatives early. He thought a president lost popularity over time.[37]

Schlesinger was nominally in the White House but was waiting for the creation of the Department of Energy and his nomination and confirmation as secretary. Because much of his time was taken up with organizing a new department he was not in the flow of the day-to-day business of the Domestic Policy Staff. Thus DPS did not serve as central coordinator of the development of the energy plan, which was between Schlesinger and his staff and Carter. Some of Carter's domestic policy aides thought ninety days to be too hasty, given the need for consultation throughout the government and the Congress and because there had been little discussion of the issue during the campaign. But the president insisted on complete secrecy in order to prevent leaks. In fact, secrecy had not been total because Schlesinger had to draw on the expertise of executive branch officials. His working group consulted with the Treasury Department on tax questions, with the Federal Energy Agency (FEA) and the Energy Research Development Agency (the old Atomic Energy Commission), and with Senator Henry Jackson and Congressman John Dingell, the chairs of the two congressional energy committees. The FEA also held public hearings on energy policy.[38]

One long-time Carter associate saw this approach to policy development as "vintage Carter." The assignment to prepare a plan was given to the man responsible for the policy. It dealt with a national problem requiring a comprehensive solution, so there was no need to compromise or consult.[39]

Another assistant thought the lack of consultation on the energy program was a mistake, but he noted that the administration, having learned a lesson, never repeated this operating style.[40]

Toward the end of March Carter began to hear complaints from White House staff members, cabinet officers and congressional leaders that the plan was being held too close. He was receiving drafts from Schlesinger and checking off pro and con on the options presented, at one point asking Schlesinger to make the plan simpler so that he could fully understand and adequately explain it. At the same time the president asked Eizenstat to have the DPS energy expert look at the plan and then talk with Charles Schultze, the CEA chairman. This was the first time Eizenstat had been asked to concern himself or the DPS with the energy plan.[41]

At about the same time Secretary of the Treasury Michael Blumenthal and CEA chairman Charles Schultze told Hamilton Jordan that they did not know what Schlesinger was doing and feared his plan was being developed with inadequate economic analysis. Jordan told the president and on April 6, two weeks before the program was to be publicly revealed, Carter called together Schlesinger, Blumenthal, Schultze, Lance, Jordan, Jody Powell and Frank Moore to discuss it. Schultze and Blumenthal, according to reports, challenged the plan as retarding growth and contributing to inflation. But Carter reportedly argued that since conservation of energy was so much in the national interest normal economic considerations could be overridden. However, from then on the respective staffs of those principals met regularly to discuss the plan.[42] And they continued to disagree. Blumenthal recommended that the plan be postponed as inflationary, and both he and Vice-President Mondale thought its introduction at that time would weaken the support of organized labor for the tax rebate, which would mean little if the energy measure caused inflation to rise. Some advisers warned that the plan was too close to President Ford's, which Congress had rejected because it promised higher energy costs. The short-term sacrifices asked were not balanced by clearly defined long-term benefits. It was argued, too, that Congress should be consulted more and the time of preparation extended. However, at a cabinet meeting on April 25, the president stressed the necessity of keeping up the pressure or private interest groups would tear the plan apart.[43]

Congressional leaders also began to query the president in April. At a breakfast with the congressional leadership, Senate majority leader Robert Byrd complained that senators had not been sufficiently brought into energy planning. Carter admitted that he had played it too close to the vest in order to protect against premature press leaks. Speaker O'Neill seemed more content, reporting that Schlesinger had talked with key House members.[44]

The energy proposal was announced on April 20, meeting the president's ninety-day deadline. Carter spoke to the nation on television and in a special address gave members of Congress their first view of the program. The key provisions were a tax on gasoline pegged to rise with consumption, a tax on automobiles that burned excessive amounts of fuel, several conservation measures including tax credits for investments in greater fuel efficiency of buildings, taxation of domestic crude oil at the wellhead to raise domestic prices to world levels with a revenue rebate to the public, federal control of intrastate natural gas sales, tax incentives to encourage industries to shift to coal, expansion of uranium production and encouragement of deployment of nuclear reactors, incentives to install solar heating, an end to gasoline price controls.[45]

The president wished Congress to consider the 113 interlocking provisions in one package. No attempt had been made to build a coalition in Congress for the bill as it was being developed, for such an effort would have been inconsistent with the president's considered strategy of achieving comprehensiveness through secrecy and might have diluted the plan at the outset.[46] Speaker O'Neill created an ad hoc committee to consider the entire package as a single measure and, utilizing the discipline upon members that is sometimes possible in the House, was able to obtain passage without serious modification in August, 1977. The Senate, however, lacked such leadership. The Energy and Finance committees and their chairmen strongly disagreed about increased taxes on gasoline—in large part a division between oil-producing and oil-consuming states—and the debate over natural gas deregulation also delayed matters. The president held out for his original bill but eventually compromised by agreeing to a gradual schedule of natural gas and crude oil deregulation and to a greatly reduced tax on energy. Passage finally came at the end of the 1978 congressional session. By that time the administration had experimented with the creation of task forces to oversee legislative battles and had had particular success with that model in the prolonged struggle for ratification of the Panama Canal treaties. The final passage of the energy bill was shepherded by an administration task force consisting of DPS, OMB, the Department of Energy and White House congressional liaison staffs. This was to be the manner in which the second round of administration energy proposals was developed in 1979.[47]

The important insight to be derived from this story for understanding the evolution of the policy development process in the Carter White House is that most of the principal actors decided that a less tightly held, more open consultative process might have increased congressional acceptance and reduced the time required for passage. Whether or not the conclusion was correct, the administration acted upon it by creating task forces to develop new legislation and to aid the lobbying process.

The two flaws legislative analysts for the *National Journal* and the *Congressional Quarterly* identified in the Carter plan were the lack of advance consultation, both within the administration and with Congress, and, more fundamentally, the absence of a constituency for a plan that proposed raising the cost of energy to consumers and also maintained price controls on oil and gas. The package was a hard test of the "public goods" approach to policy. It was too liberal for conservatives in its willingness to continue price regulation and too conservative for liberals in its plan for price increases. James Schlesinger felt that Democratic liberals never forgave Carter for the ultimate decontrol of oil and gas, and environmentalists resented the emphasis on coal and the encouragement of nuclear power development. He reported that Carter's political advisers wondered whether the effort had been worth the cost. Carter himself was unsure of his constituency, noting in his January 19, 1978, diary entry on the energy bill, "In many cases I feel more at home with the conservative Democrats and Republican members of Congress than I do with the others although the others, the liberals, vote with me much more often."[48]

But Carter is reported to have had little doubt of the correctness of his policy. The fall of the Shah of Iran in 1979 precipitated an energy crisis for the United States with subsequent OPEC price increases. A more determined energy program, particularly with higher taxes on oil than Congress had been willing to vote, would have lessened the shock of the OPEC action.[49]

One of Carter's principal domestic policy advisers felt that the president made a mistake in reversing his campaign pledge to deregulate natural gas. The chairmen of the House and Senate energy committees opposed deregulation and Schlesinger, too, thought it unnecessary, since increased prices would stimulate production. Charles Schultze feared the effect on inflation. But this adviser believed the bill would have passed sooner had

Carter realized that the support of senators from the energy-producing states was crucial for passage, as eventually proved to be the case. The failure to perceive this fact was the result of trying to put things together too quickly without sufficient consultation.[50] The White House thus judged that the first energy bill was developed in a faulty manner and moved to correct the flaws.

The first energy program also had rough going because of limited public perception that a problem existed. Despite a strenuous effort President Carter was never able to persuade the American public of that fact. This was not the case with the second program, which responded to a clearly perceived national problem. One result of the 1979 Iranian revolution was the reduction in Iranian oil production and soaring oil prices. Americans became angry because of long gas lines and alternate day gasoline rationing in some states, and governors, truckers and farmers, among many affected groups, pressed the president for action.

Fortunately the administration had a program ready. Early in 1979 Carter had asked Eizenstat to convene an interagency task force to develop a second energy bill. The work of this group was enhanced by the developing oil crisis, and Eizenstat describes the process.

We had every single agency around a table . . . [and the meetings were] attended on the average by fifteen or twenty people every . . . afternoon for weeks and weeks. . . . It was a very open . . . very consultative process and we did a lot of work on the Hill, talked to Jim Wright, talked to Scoop [Jackson], talked to the people who were moving the synthetic [fuels] bill in the House . . . had the agencies involved and we were clearly handling it . . . [and included] extensive discussions with the business community because the business community was key to getting the synthetic fuel corporation passed. . . . I had meeting after meeting of the chief executive officers of the major corporations and we finally got them, including the oil companies to come around, which was very important in ultimately getting it passed. . . .

When we got through with that process we had a really first rate decision memorandum for the President and we had a policy which passed. Every single item passed except for the energy mobilization board. . . . But the synthetic fuel corporation, which was the centerpiece, was passed plus additional conservation initiatives. . . . [It was] a considerable improvement over the '77 process. And there was a lot of talk about energy being now moved to the White House and the Energy department had lost the initiative. . . . That was baloney. We were not initiators, we were coordinators, we were pushing, we were mediating, we were arbitrating, we were getting agencies together. But the substantive work was done by the energy experts in each of the agencies involved.[51]

In other parts of the package the president lifted controls on crude oil prices and persuaded Congress to pass a windfall profits tax on new oil. The total program thus joined incentives for conservation with a plan for developing new sources of energy.

Carter's speech to the nation in July, 1979, about the crisis of national will, with the need for discipline on energy use as the test case, was effective in a way that similar efforts in 1977 were not. There was a visible crisis this time, and Eizenstat admits that this political difference was the critical factor in the passage of the second energy program.[52] But the White House had also organized itself more effectively to develop a legislative proposal, which was a manifestation of the enhanced role of the Domestic Policy Staff, the president's confidence in it and its consequent authority with the agencies.

WELFARE REFORM

This case illustrates the difficulties in delegating the development of presidential policies to cabinet officers when more than one department is involved. The president gave Secretary of HEW Joseph Califano the lead but disagreements between HEW and the Department of Labor finally required a stronger DPS role than had been envisioned.

Carter's experience as governor had convinced him that the national welfare system was inequitable and inefficient.[53] His speech to the National Governor's Conference on July 6, 1976, called for reform that was prowork and profamily and that would provide a uniform standard of payments across the nation.[54] He wanted a more efficient system that provided incentives for people to work. Although in his 1976 urban policy speech he had to give lip service to easing the financial burden of AFDC programs in cities because of the views of Democratic mayors, such relief was not his major goal for welfare reform.[55]

In a December 9 briefing the income security transition team told Carter that they believed a welfare reform bill proposing incremental changes in the existing system would be easier to get through Congress than a comprehensive plan. The president-elect replied that he wanted to deliver the comprehensive bill he had promised, and he also intended to send welfare reform to Congress before national health insurance in order to introduce his administration's social policy with a "conservative" posture. Ben Heineman, an aide to Secretary Califano, reports that the senior liberal advisers in the administration all wanted welfare reform and since none were willing to disagree with the president so early in a new administration the possibility of a more incremental bill was not discussed.[56]

At a meeting of the future cabinet on St. Simon's Island, Georgia, in December, 1976, Carter told Joseph Califano that he wanted a complete overhaul of the welfare system as one of the first proposals to go to Congress. Califano assumed, but did not tell Carter, that welfare reform would cost additional money beyond existing programs so he told reporters that reform would have to await economic recovery. The next day Carter overrode Califano at a press conference by saying that he would send a welfare reform plan to Congress in 1977.[57]

Carter told Califano to develop "a comprehensive plan that was pro-work and pro-family." He did not want to become prematurely engaged and would attend meetings when decisions needed to be made on the basis of a plan.[58] This meant to Califano that the DPS was not to take a lead in welfare reform, and he warned Eizenstat to try and exercise the authority he had had over cabinet officers in Lyndon Johnson's administration. Bert Carp, Eizenstat's deputy, remembered that Carter "viewed Califano and Ray Marshall [secretary of labor] as the key people in putting this together." And indeed Carp, who monitored the issue for Eizenstat, deliberately fended off White House involvement when Califano began to ask about the president's position on key questions.[59]

Califano had difficulty getting the policy analysts in HEW and the Labor Department to agree on a plan. The two sets of economists had different solutions to problems. The HEW analysts affirmed the departmental tradition of favoring income maintenance measures for welfare recipients and the working poor, and the Labor Department people were strongly committed to the principle of providing jobs for the poor who could work, both as a matter of need and from a belief that welfare reform without work requirements and opportunities would not be politically feasible in Congress. The HEW economists were skeptical that a sufficient number of Public Service Employment (PSE) jobs could be created and also believed that work requirements were unrealistic and undesirable for many welfare recipients. After a period of wrangling, Califano found himself unable to convince Secretary of Labor Ray Marshall, who supported his own analysts.[60] So, unable to get any guidance from Carp, Califano asked for a meeting with the president.

Califano was laboring under a deadline of May 1 for the production of a plan that could be made public. He had casually suggested that date to

Carter in a conversation the previous November before his appointment as secretary, and to his surprise Carter in January announced publicly that the welfare reform proposal would be ready by May 1.[61]

Califano wrote a memo to the president before the March 25 meeting, asking which government programs, such as AFDC and food stamps, should be included in welfare reform, what level of income should be set as the national standard, whether intact families should be covered as well as single parent families and if "employable" people on welfare should be guaranteed public service jobs if private jobs were not available. The day before the meeting Eizenstat recommended that Carter ask Califano to develop cost estimates for the different packages and stress the importance of interagency consultation.[62]

At the meeting Califano spoke before a number of White House and departmental officials, including Secretary Marshall, setting out the main elements of the existing system and enumerating the options. Carter was particularly disturbed by the disincentives to work in the existing system and so particularly liked the proposed job programs. But he made no decisions and concluded the meeting by reaffirming his commitment to comprehensive reform and asking Califano to redesign the existing system using existing cost figures. He wanted to simplify the system, put people on welfare in jobs and eliminate fraud, and he would announce the general principles for such a program in May. Califano could later add new program features in one billion dollar increments. Carter added that he, not Califano, would worry about the politics and asked for a report in two weeks. Califano did not see how the government could develop a comprehensive program that met the needs of both those who could not work and the working poor, maintaining national standards and providing new PSE jobs, all at existing cost levels. He did not feel that he had gotten through to Carter that comprehensive reform was incompatible with "zero cost." Benefits would be too low for the plan to win political acceptance.[63]

Frank Raines, a DPS staff member, believed in retrospect that Carter saw the existing welfare program as corrupting people by preventing them from working. Eizenstat suspected, and told Califano, that Carter's "zero cost" injunction with added increments was a management device to get HEW to justify any increases.[64] Since Carter eventually accepted additional costs this would seem an accurate appraisal, a manifestation of Carter's characteristic style of calling for comprehensive reform and then compromising according to political necessities. At the April 11 briefing for the president,

Califano pointed out the inequities and political risks of a zero cost approach and indicated that any of the alternative plans would increase costs. Carter pressed Califano hard as to why benefit levels had to be so high; he wanted welfare recipients to work and asked for a strong employment component as well as reductions in benefit levels. Carter did not choose among Califano's three alternative plans but told him to reconcile differences with Marshall and draft a statement of principles for a May 1 announcement.[65]

At the third White House briefing on April 26 Califano presented two alternative plans, one based on cash assistance and the other on jobs with charts depicting the pros and cons of each. Carter made clear that he wanted both. He said that he would announce principles in May, a program in August and legislation in September. When Secretary of the Treasury Blumenthal asked how the timing would affect tax reform proposals that had to go to the House Ways and Means Committee at the same time, the president replied that his preference was to move on everything at once. He was prepared to push hard for welfare reform because public opinion was favorable, and he was confident that he could sell income assistance as part of a reform that put people to work. But he did not give ground on the zero cost premise. It was still up to Califano to develop a plan that would meet Carter's criteria.[66]

After the April 26 meeting Carter asked Charles Schultze to meet with the Califano and Marshall staffs and mediate the disagreements. Schultze tried, failed, and concluded that the two sides had "two fundamentally opposed ideas, and you could only superficially merge them. They had two fundamentally different views of the way the world ought to work."[67] Schultze told Carter that the two plans could not be easily reconciled and recommended that the May public announcement call for the consolidation of cash assistance programs such as AFDC, Supplemental Security Income and food stamps and say that a program of public jobs would also be included. Carter should then set an internal deadline for the resolution of disagreement. Eizenstat also urged the president not to decide between the two plans in May.[68]

At a meeting on April 30 Carter told Califano, Marshall, Schultze and their staffs that he wanted a large number of public service jobs created, even though new figures indicated that 2.2 million jobs would be required rather than the earlier Labor Department estimate of 1.4 million. When he later met with Califano, Marshall and Eizenstat to establish principles for the public announcement, Carter had written his own statement which read "no higher cost than the original system." All three argued against it but Carter was unyielding. Finally Eizenstat persuaded Carter to add the word "initial" before reference to higher cost. The principles Schultze suggested were then agreed upon and on May 2 Carter, Califano and Marshall met the press and set out general principles for welfare reform. Carter told the press that energy legislation was his first priority and that the same committees which would receive the welfare reform proposal would also get energy, social security revision and tax reform.[69]

Carter gave HEW and the Labor Department two weeks to reconcile their differences. Intense negotiations between the two department staffs ensued but agreement eluded them. So the same Califano who had told Eizenstat to stay out of his business now asked the DPS chief to use the good offices of his staff to resolve the differences. Bert Carp, Eizenstat's deputy, thus met with the two staffs and forcefully worked out a compromise that combined income maintenance and PSE. It was Carp's view that each department got 90 percent of its goals, and the DPS staff liked the compromise because they thought it would appeal to Senator Russell Long and others in Congress who wished above all to increase the incentives of welfare recipients to work.[70] Both department secretaries had gone along because after so much wrangling they were more anxious for agreement than for victory. Carter accepted the compromise. His staff had given him what he had requested, a welfare reform plan with a strong job component. But agreement had been achieved only because the DPS had taken a more forceful role than envisaged in Carter's original concept of delegation of policy development to cabinet officers.

The welfare reform part of the proposed plan, as distinct from the jobs component, reduced income levels for a large number of existing welfare recipients but extended coverage to more people. Just before Califano's May 25 press conference to announce the plan Carter called him to say that the $9,400 which welfare recipients could receive without working was too high by Georgia standards. The American people would not like it. Califano placated Carter by putting his presentation in 1976 rather than 1978 dollar figures.[71]

In August the president announced the Program for Better Jobs and Income, a title he had devised himself. The bill went to Congress but never even reached the floor of the House, since too many other Carter measures, such as energy, social security revision and tax reform, were flooding the two finance committees.[72]

The deep division that had characterized the Nixon attempt to pass comprehensive welfare legislation remained. Conservatives wanted less welfare and more "workfare"; liberals wished to extend benefits with help for the working poor. Carter met with congressional committee and sub-committee chairmen in March, 1978, at Califano's request, but he did not make a strong appeal for the welfare reform bill and said that he would defer to committee calendars. He also said that he would not hold out for the whole package but would take what he could get. On June 6 California passed Proposition 13, a restriction on public spending, and in the judg-ment of congressional leaders welfare reform was dead. Carter later said that he had invested little political capital in welfare reform, and, by im-plication, he did not see the episode as a defeat but as a cutting of losses.[73]

In 1979 the administration developed a second welfare reform plan, with Califano again taking the lead. This time there were two bills, one for cash assistance and the other for PSE jobs, but neither was as ambitious in scope as the initial proposal.[74] The cash assistance bill passed the House but stalled in the Senate. Carter was preoccupied with foreign affairs, inflation and budget balancing.

This story shows Jimmy Carter acting as a politician in his own terms. But he was not the kind of political man Secretary Califano expected him to be. For example, not understanding his style, Califano and the HEW planners did not know how to take Carter's insistence on a welfare pro-gram with zero cost increase. Carter's approach to policy development, however, guaranteed that he would not take congressional opinion into account at the outset but would hold out for an ideal solution. This ap-proach invites easy criticism after the fact, but in any case gathering ad-vance information would have been difficult, since congressional leaders were not anxious to tell the president what they planned to do. Some of his staff thought that a more incremental measure might have passed the first time around, whereas others believed that welfare reform was a no-win issue that should never have been elevated to importance. "Carter's love of comprehensive solutions is rooted in the notion that there is a right and wrong," said one assistant. "He thought that if you hired smart people and carefully reviewed their recommendations, you could develop better solu-tions. It was hard for him to understand that our problems in Washington are the product of high IQ's. I don't think that he understood the problems in welfare reform or how deep the differences are. This was more important than his faith in delegating policy development."[75]

However, Carter was thoroughly political throughout the process. A more conventionally political, incrementalist approach would have required a different kind of policy development process—one giving greater attention to political issues as the prime questions for presidential decision. Carter was political in a different way, on his own terms. He hewed to a conservative image for himself and the program, was very quick to back off when the bill floundered in Congress and would have accepted a lesser bill. His strategy for welfare reform possessed a political logic. He knew that Democratic liberals wanted reform emphasizing equity of benefits yet he also sensed the conservative mood of the country. It was difficult to write a bill that captured both possibilities. The fact that he tried reflected a political strategy.

THE DEPARTMENT OF EDUCATION

In this story one sees Stuart Eizenstat and the DPS playing a much more authoritative policy leadership role than in the previous cases. This may be, in part, because the main story took place in 1978 and 1979 after the DPS hand had been strengthened. But it may also be that the DPS was emboldened by the fact that the primary agent for policy development was the President's Reorganization Project in OMB, over which the DPS might have felt it could assert its White House authority. However, the DPS also acted contrary to the goals of Secretary Califano of HEW, who opposed the creation of a new department. This story also illustrates how the DPS performed a political intelligence gathering and brokering role for the president and how he hoped to stretch the limits of political feasibility to go beyond what the DPS thought possible. But in the end, as the 1980 election year drew near, Carter responded to the need for legislative action according to political feasibility as understood in Washington.

In 1976 candidate Jimmy Carter pledged to support the creation of a Department of Education in responding to a written question from the National Education Association *Reporter:* "I'm in favor of creating a separate Cabinet-level Department of Education. Generally I am opposed to the proliferation of federal agencies. . . . But the Department of Education would consolidate the grant programs, job training, early childhood education, literacy training and many other functions scattered throughout the government. The result would be a stronger voice for education at the federal level."[76]

Carter did not initiate the idea of a new department and it was, in fact, inconsistent with the preference for consolidation of departments that had characterized his governorship. Still, the commitment was apparently not a strategy to win NEA support for his nomination because it was made just before the Democratic convention when the nomination was assured. His chief concern, according to staff assistants, was that education would continue to be neglected so long as the Office of Education was encased in the Department of Health, Education and Welfare. However, he was uncertain on this question and after the election asked for a study of the desirability and feasibility of creating a new department.[77]

Joseph Califano had asked the new president to be cautious about committing himself, with the argument that less rather than more "constituency" departments were needed. In a subsequent meeting with NEA officials Carter hedged and said that he wanted to study the issue. His advisers were also divided. Mondale was committed and Jordan said it was important to keep the campaign pledge but Lance urged a review of the issue.[78]

Senator Abraham Ribicoff, chairman of the Government Operations Committee and a former secretary of HEW, was determined to separate the E from HEW on the basis of his experience as secretary and was waiting to hear from the administration before introducing his bill so that the two plans might not be in conflict. He favored a broad organization that would draw education programs together from a number of departments in order to integrate services. The issue was before his committee because it was seen as a question of government organization rather than a substantive educational matter. The National Education Association favored a new department primarily for the symbolic goal of elevating education to a higher place in the federal hierarchy and at that point was less interested in which programs went into the organizational shell.[79]

An educational study team was assembled in the President's Reorganization Project (PRP) within OMB in April, 1977, and in July was given a charge to develop alternatives. The group was led by Willis Hawley, a Duke political scientist, who reported to Pat Gwaltney, human resources director of the PRP. Hawley and his staff met with Hamilton Jordan who told them that although they should examine political feasibility it should not dominate their analysis. It was his job to worry about politics. If they recommended against a department, it would make things difficult politically but he would worry about that.[80]

The PRP group worked with Califano and his staff, who hoped to scuttle the plan for a separate department in favor of upgrading the Office of

Education in HEW, perhaps by giving it an undersecretary. The PRP study team also worked with the OMB budget staff who, at the program examiner level, were not particularly sympathetic to a new department. They understood the programs in their present structures and did not welcome the idea of having to learn about a new system. In meeting with Ribicoff and his staff, however, the study team discovered a mutuality of interest in a broad department, and the group slowly formulated a plan for a new Department of Education and Human Development that would combine most education and social service programs on the theory that all federal programs that nurtured the capacity of children to learn should be encouraged to cooperate at state and local levels. The PRP staff did not give much weight to either symbolic or political justifications for the creation of a new department but, rather, wished to develop a department that would improve the effectiveness of, and bring about change in, education at the grass roots. Formal education would be linked more effectively to nontraditional sources of learning such as job training, public television, adult education, libraries, child care and diverse social services to families and children.[81]

A narrow department based primarily upon the Office of Education, which was what eventually emerged, was seen by the PRP as less desirable than upgrading in HEW. Califano did not like the plan for a Department of Education and Human Development but, because he believed it to be politically impossible to achieve, supported the idea.[82]

Alternatives were presented to the president at a meeting in the cabinet room on November 28, 1977. Califano and his staff were there, as well as Eizenstat and Bert Carp, his deputy, but the PRP staff made the presentation with budget director James McIntyre presiding as their chief. Jordan and Vice-President Mondale attended, as did two members of the president's executive committee for reorganization, CEA chairman Charles Schultze and Alan Campbell, director of the Civil Service Commission. The three proposed options were a Department of Education and Human Development, an undersecretary for education programs in HEW, or a narrow department comprised mainly of programs in the existing Office of Education. The discussion was on both the merits and the politics. According to reports, Califano supported the first option, perhaps as a straw man, and Campbell concurred. Schultze argued that the president's agenda already carried too many controversial items and did not need education reorganization as another. Eizenstat agreed and argued that the first option was not politically feasible. The vice-president simply called for a separate department, and Jordan argued that the campaign commitment should be honored. McIntyre, though he endorsed the PRP proposal, expressed no strong preference except to follow the president's wishes. Carter listened to the discussion and expressed a preference for as broad a department as possible if there was to be a separate department. He asked the PRP team to go back and figure out which programs should be included in a new department and report back to him. The PRP staff got the impression that he favored a scaled-down version of option one, since he appeared to have gotten the message that a massive reorganization was not politically feasible. Eizenstat and his DPS colleagues made clear, as the meeting concluded, that they wanted a narrow department that would satisfy Carter's commitment to the NEA and not stir up political problems.[83]

The 1978 State of the Union message made only general references to a new Department of Education because although Carter had decided to create a new department he did not yet know which programs would be included. The PRP eventually developed a list of components that might go into a department, making it more or less broad in its jurisdiction, and their recommendation was discussed in March, 1978, in a White House meeting chaired by Eizenstat with the president absent. Eizenstat argued that Carter could not afford to be seen as having a divided staff on the issue of breadth and called for a narrow department. Eventually, a joint DPS-OMB memo went to the president proposing a narrowly based department in place of the previous PRP memo. The DPS-OMB memo went to Carter the day before the administration was to testify at hearings of the Ribicoff committee. Carter read it that night and did not like it. He called Harrison Welford, director of the PRP, and Pat Gwaltney to the White House the next day and asked them to add the original PRP ideas to the DPS-OMB memo as the basis for administration testimony. The president wanted to support as broad a department as possible. The original conception of a Department of Education and Human Development had been scrapped but the PRP memo had included such diverse programs as Indian schools, National Science Foundation education programs, Head Start and school lunch programs from the Agriculture Department, Department of Defense overseas schools for civilian dependents and the HEW Office of Civil Rights. Both Carter and the PRP study team hoped that a broad department would avoid capture by the NEA and other interests that had dominated federal policy making.[84] This was the version that McIntyre and Gwaltney presented to the Ribicoff committee. Carter had overruled his own staff. The Democratic members and staff of the Ribicoff committee were happy with the administration presentation because their bill was also broad. The PRP was itself divided about the merits of a broad department. The study team favored it, but PRP leaders, who worked closely with top DPS and OMB officials, were thinking about the president's political needs and feared that a broad department was not politically feasible.

The interest groups whose programs had been included in the proposals, such as Head Start and civil rights groups, mobilized against inclusion and in 1978 a stripped-down version of the Ribicoff bill passed the Senate. The House version retained a broad department minus Head Start, but group attacks destroyed the chance of passage in 1978. In early 1979 the administration agreed to support a relatively narrow Senate bill, drafted by a White House-led task force in which the DPS was dominant, in close cooperation with Senate and House Government Operations Committee staffs. Secretary Califano was not happy and the White House received reports of his campaigns on the Hill against administration plans. In the judgment of a number of White House assistants this was the primary reason that the president later fired him.[85] He was seen as opposing Carter on an issue that was of increasing political importance to the White House.

The concern with administrative effectiveness in the implementation of education programs in the field, which had been a strong PRP interest at the outset, receded as political and symbolic goals became more important. In 1979 the administration argued that a separate department would increase efficiency by removing education programs from the HEW colossus. In fact, the argument for efficiency was a cover for the importance of passing a bill and creating a department that would meet the president's promise to the education constituency. Therefore he acquiesced realistically in the removal of programs from the broad departmental conception and in other changes that reduced the authority of the secretary of education to reorganize the department, created an assistant secretary for private schools and permitted the director of museums to report directly to the secretary. The new department created by both houses in 1979 was a slightly expanded Office of Education. Domestic Policy Staff members who had been active in this struggle did not believe there had been a defeat or unnecessary compromise, because they had never thought that a comprehensive department had much chance of passing.[86]

It is clear that Carter wanted a comprehensive Department of Education at the outset because he believed in that principle of organization and did not like departments based upon single interests. Therefore he was responsive to the PRP suggestion of a Department of Education and Human Development. But he appears to have understood at the first briefing in November, 1977, that politically this was too ambitious. He then asked PRP to give him options that would permit as broad a department as was politically feasible. But it was also clear that the DPS leadership wanted a narrow department because they thought that a political struggle for a broad department would fail and damage the president. Carter tried to work with Senator Ribicoff in testing the water as to whether a broad department would sell politically. To this end he overruled his own advisers in instructing that administration testimony support the Ribicoff bill for a broad department. But as the unfolding legislative story in 1978 revealed that a broad bill could not pass Congress Carter compromised and supported the passage of a bill for a department of limited scope.

One would require more evidence than is presented here to contend that the 1980 election was on the president's mind. Senator Edward Kennedy was indeed looming in 1979 as a rival for the nomination and Carter's advisers agreed that passage of the bill for a new department would give him a marked legislative success. But whether or not these speculations are valid, we see again Carter's strong effort to achieve a comprehensive program and his willingness to fall back on second best only after experience showed that was all he could expect to achieve. The DPS was ready for this fall-back effort and even anticipated it.

The process of policy development described here met President Carter's criteria that policy making be collegial and that it produce comprehensive program plans. Neither of these goals could have been achieved by the president's original idea of delegating policy development to cabinet officers, a concept that lacked the realistic understanding of the need for a White House coordinating role on issues of presidential policy.

The first energy program and the welfare reform initiative revealed this weakness and the correction was made. However, the increased authority of the DPS to oversee policy development did not bring a lack of commitment to comprehensive programs. The second energy program was certainly far reaching and all encompassing, but it was also informed by the political learning in which the DPS specialized.

However, a single-minded commitment to only comprehensive program initiatives would not have met Carter's political needs as a Democratic president who needed to come to terms with the groups in his coalition and also to achieve legislative successes. The Domestic Policy Staff learned to serve the president's political interests by developing second-best policy strategies, as seen in the Department of Education story. And the president went along after it became clear that his ideal could not be achieved.

The capacity of this adapted policy development process to meet Carter's needs as a problem solver and leader on behalf of "public goods" says nothing about Jimmy Carter's skills as a political strategist in policy development. The possible political blunders of the first energy program, the question of whether welfare reform was politically worth all the energy given to it, the reactive rather than creative presidential politics of the Department of Education structuring all reflect on these skills. The stories do suggest that Carter was not a conventional political strategist who calculated the political feasibility of proposals in advance of their introduction. Instead he hoped to achieve "public goods" and be rewarded politically for such achievement.

Carter's executive style had something of the naval officer in it. He wanted his advisers to bring him recommendations on the basis of their homework, and his task, as he understood it, was to accept or reject the recommendations on the basis of his own homework. One weakness of this approach was that Carter would sometimes overrule his staff when its homework was not in accord with his own. The difficulty in such cases was the absence of a political strategy for presenting the issue to Congress and the public. Carter focused on substantive issues when he should have been giving much of his attention to the politics of the situation so that homework and politics might be combined. This weakness is seen in each of the cases presented in this chapter. Of course, Carter did not believe that conventional incremental and bargaining politics produced good results, so why give time and energy to studying a process that could not produce the results you want? The politics of public goods was based on homework.

Carter was the first modern Democratic president to recognize that new problems were confronting the nation which could not be resolved by the redistributive politics and policy of the New Frontier and the Great Society. The new issues were manifestations of curtailed economic growth. The new policy theme, for Carter, was consolidation and curtailment with equity. This theme united the goal of budget balancing, tax and welfare reform, energy conservation, civil service reform and deregulation of transportation. But the Democratic coalition was still thinking in expansive terms and was not listening to the president.

At the end of the day, Carter was disappointed with his record in domestic policy. He took responsibility for it but also blamed Washington politics.

There is no doubt that I could have done some things better. . . . it would have been advisable to have introduced our legislation in much more careful phases—not in such a rush. We would not have accomplished any more, and perhaps less, but my relations with Congress would have been smoother and the image of undue haste and confusion could have been avoided.

Now I can also see more clearly the problems we created for the legislators. In looking over the list of our proposals that were approved, it was hard to find many goodies for the members to take home. They showed great courage in voting for government reorganization, civil service reform, ethics reforms, our energy bills, deregulation of airlines. . . .

In balance, my feelings toward Congress are mixed. On most issues, the lawmakers treated me well, sometimes under politically difficult circumstances. However, when the interests of powerful lobbyists were at stake, a majority of members often yielded to a combination of political threats and the blandishments of heavy campaign contributions. . . .

Members of Congress, buffeted from all sides, are much more vulnerable to these groups than is the President. One branch of government must stand fast on a particular issue to prevent the triumph of self-interest at the expense of the public.[87]

This was the same Jimmy Carter who had decided when he was a state senator that legislatures could not serve the public interest and that a leader who would articulate the public interest was required. But he was also wiser and sadder.

Domestic issues are the ones that occupy most of his [the president's] time and over which he has least control. Under our Constitution the President has much more authority in foreign affairs—and therefore decisions [in that area] can be made quickly, more incisively, and usually with more immediate results. . . . during most crises in foreign affairs the President can count on the full support of the public. It is almost impossible to arouse such support among a multiplicity of confusing and sometimes conflicting domestic issues. When he can concentrate his attention on one major thrust to the exclusion of other matters, the President can usually prevail, but such an opportunity seldom arises.[88]

Jimmy Carter was chastened but he had not changed his fundamental conception of political leadership.

4
ECONOMIC POLICY MAKING

Throughout his presidency Jimmy Carter sought an economic policy that would permit him to serve both liberal and conservative values. He was a fiscal conservative who believed excessive government spending to be one of the primary causes of inflation. He also believed, from his experience as governor of Georgia, that many federal social programs were wasteful and poorly managed. Fiscal stringency was therefore not antithetical to his liberal values. As a southern reformer who identified with underdogs, especially the poor and minorities, he was responsive to the theme of human development, particularly in regard to children. But he was not particularly friendly to nationally organized establishments and interest groups, whether the AFL-CIO, the American Bar Association or the American Medical Association. The thread of consistency running through his social and economic policies was his support for human service programs combined with attempts to restrain levels of funding, both for better management and as a contribution to the goal of controlling inflation through a balanced budget. He disapproved of "subsidies" to organized groups, whether they were congressionally favored water projects, uncontained hospital costs facilitated by medicare reimbursements or the federally set minimum wage.

These views placed him squarely in the middle of two interrelated dilemmas of economic policy and politics. He campaigned on the need to get the economy moving out of recession and the first policy initiative of the new administration was the economic stimulus program. However, even before that program had passed Congress, Carter perceived that recovery was imminent and decided that inflation was the long-term economic problem. He spent the rest of his term attempting to balance an avoidance of recession and high unemployment (the wish of any Democratic president) with sporadic attacks on rising inflation through budget cutting. This difficult fine tuning of the economy was hazardous politically. Organized Democratic constituencies and congressional Democratic leaders favored economic expansion and resisted restraint. Carter saw microeconomic policies, whether water projects, the minimum wage, or social spending, as bricks in the wall of macroeconomic policy; that is, he believed that spending levels of individual programs had a cumulative effect on the budget and the rate of inflation. Presidential attempts to limit such spending meant proposing policies which offered the various Democratic constituencies only half a loaf.

The story of Carter's economic policy thus parallels that of domestic policy. A centrist president sought synthesis between liberal and conservative principles, and the substantive task of achieving such synthesis was paralleled by the political job of creating constituencies to support it. What appeared to many to be a presidential strategy of zigzag in economic policy, as one annual budget was antirecession and the next was antiinflationary, was not inconsistency but the effort to avoid both extremes.

The two central themes of Carter economic policy were the balancing of the claims of social programs and Democratic interest groups against Carter's desire for fiscal discipline, and the balancing of expansionist budgets directed against recession with tighter budgets directed against inflation. The method of decision making the president and his advisers used was ad hoc, with each decision a correction of previous decisions in light of changed economic conditions and contingent political pressures. The broad policy guidelines were clear to Carter and his advisers, though perhaps not to external observers. The advisory structure was loose and disjointed, reflecting the character of the decisions made.

ORGANIZATION OF THE ECONOMIC POLICY GROUP

President Ford and his advisers had created the Economic Policy Board (EPB) through which important issues of economic policy, domestic and international, macro and micro, passed for discussion. The EPB had a large membership consisting of the secretary of the treasury as chairman, and the heads of the Department of State, Department of Commerce, Department of Labor, Council of Economic Advisers, Office of Management and Budget and Federal Reserve Board. This creation was the culmination of an incremental search in the Nixon and Ford administrations for some body that would increase policy coherence by bringing many loose ends of economic policy together. In the Democratic years, from 1961 through 1968, responsibility for analysis of economic policy choices had been divided. A troika of Treasury Department, CEA and Bureau of the Budget heads reviewed macro policy; the CEA and other Executive Office units managed micro policy recommendations coming from the departments; and international economic policy floated between the CEA and NSC structures.[1]

A second important feature of the EPB under Ford was its link through its secretary and staff to the president. William Seidman, assistant to the president for economic policy, was also secretary of the EPB. His job was to be the honest broker in developing views and preparing options for discussion among the president and his economic advisers. This personal link gave the EPB standing, making it the president's chosen arena for the discussion of economic policy and the group that provided him with coherent choices among alternatives based on free discussion. The system appeared to work because everyone involved trusted Seidman to be an honest broker. He did not try to do anyone else's job.[2]

The actual decision patterns of the EPB may not have been much different from those of the preceding Democratic years. Questions of macro policy were primarily discussed by an informal troika of the heads of the Treasury Department, CEA and OMB. Micro-economic issues were discussed in the EPB but were actually analyzed by Executive Office staffs in an ad hoc manner as in the past.[3]

The precise origins of the Economic Policy Group (EPG) in the Carter administration are unclear. When President Carter announced the appointment of Charles Schultze as chairman of the CEA on December 17, 1976, he stated, "I will not have a separate economic advisor in the White House other than Mr. Schultze."[4] Schultze had not made this exclusivity a condition of his appointment, but he did believe at the time that having another White House economic assistant would not be a good idea. He regarded the chairman of the CEA as the president's personal economic adviser. Why have another?[5] Democratic CEA chairmen have often insisted that there be no staff person between them and the president. Republican chief economists have not made this an issue and, indeed, have functioned well as personal presidential advisers even though others have played a White House role of some kind.[6] The difference may be simply the acceptance by Republicans of more structured presidential staffs in which formal coordination plays a greater role than it does in Democratic presidencies.

In Schultze's view the CEA's job was to do policy analysis, and he had no interest in being a policy coordinator. It was evidently assumed at the beginning of the administration, however, in conversations between

Schultze and Carter, that Schultze would head some kind of economic policy committee in his role as chief economic adviser. When Michael Blumenthal was later appointed secretary of the treasury he told Schultze that it would be impossible for him to be effective, especially in international policy, if Schultze were head of the economic policy group. Blumenthal asked Schultze to serve as executive director under his chairmanship, and the issue was resolved by their agreeing to be cochairmen. Schultze recognized at the time that the treasury secretary would always be the informal head of any advisory group, as had been the case when Schultze was Bureau of the Budget director under Johnson.[7]

This still left unresolved the question of the character of the economic advisory unit. Since it was agreed that the Ford administration terminology would have to be discarded, Economic Policy Group was coined. Schultze's perception of the EPB was that it had functioned well on small issues as a coordinating body but that important questions were handled outside the EPB by smaller groups. He and Blumenthal hoped that the EPG would deal with major issues, with lesser questions being staffed by the CEA, OMB and the Domestic Policy Staff. They were also both determined that the EPG be small enough to permit useful discussion.[8]

It did not begin that way. Schultze and Blumenthal were apparently thinking of an expanded troika that would include the undersecretary of state for economic affairs and the vice-president, should he wish to participate. But Carter permitted a larger membership. Secretary of Commerce Juanita Kreps and Secretary of Labor Ray Marshall were both professional economists and wanted to serve. Secretary of Housing and Urban Development Patricia Harris became a member in ways that were not clear to Schultze and Blumenthal. Stuart Eizenstat was an ex officio member. The vice-president attended. Most of the department heads would bring assistant secretaries who, in turn, would bring staff. The EPG meetings might have forty people in them, and when the president attended a meeting early on, he was clearly bothered by the group's size.[9]

In March, 1977, Schultze resigned as cochairman of the EPG and Blumenthal became chairman. Schultze's reasoning was that he could not simultaneously be a personal presidential adviser and also report collective EPG decisions to Carter. The roles were different and required different relationships with the president. In a memo to EPG members Carter then repeated his commitment to retain Schultze as his only White House assistant for economic policy.[10]

Two issues were, therefore, unresolved in the Spring of 1977—the size of the EPG and its link with the president. The Ford administration had been able to manage an umbrella group in the EPB, in part because William Seidman organized the flow of discussion to the president in a way that connected directly with presidential decisions. Carter had an umbrella group with Blumenthal as chair, but Blumenthal was only one of his several economic advisers. There was no person, position or mechanism for linking the EPG to presidential decisions. In the Nixon administration, John Connally and George Shultz, as secretaries of the treasury, had been explicitly authorized by Nixon to be deputy presidents for economic affairs. In the Kennedy and Johnson administrations, periods of economic policy innovation based on the theoretical insights of economic science, the CEA chairmen had been the prime policy innovators, if not coordinators. Carter did not draw on any of these past models. His advisers did not wish a repeat of the EPB. The CEA chairman was a personal adviser but it became clear over time that he would not be the first among equals. This was perhaps in part because the policy initiatives coming from the Schultze CEA were more uncertain than those from Walter Heller and his immediate successors. And Carter did not designate Blumenthal as first among equals.

The first months of the swollen EPG were rocky and it increasingly came to be regarded by all involved, including the president, as ineffective. The group was too large and the links to Carter were weak. He would receive EPG memos listing too many alternative choices; instead of getting three he might receive six or more because members added their own options at will. Some advisers felt this was Carter's fault because he would not exclude some cabinet officers from membership in the EPG. Another view is that the principal advisers to the president, Blumenthal, Schultze and Lance, all had different ideas and goals and the diversity of options thus reflected the absence of an established administration economic policy. The very dynamics of the situation reinforced the problem because, although none of Carter's advisers wanted an assistant to the president for policy coordination, the absence of such a position meant that the senior advisers had no reliable messenger between the EPG and the president. Fearing their views would be reported inaccurately, they put in their own options.[11]

The puzzle is why Carter, who was unhappy with the overabundance of discordant voices and options in the EPG, initially did nothing to reduce the size or change the structure.[12] The reasons for this are not immediately apparent.

The first effort to improve the EPG came in the Spring of 1977 from recommendations by a President's Reorganization Project team in OMB as a part of a larger study of Executive Office organization. The study concluded that senior White House status for an EPG staff director would be inconsistent with Carter's decision that the CEA chairman be his personal economic adviser. That decision, plus the strength of the other senior economic officials and the general administration emphasis on the primacy of cabinet officers, had led to the original concept of the EPG staff as a coordinating secretariat of limited size (six professionals). EPG meetings had not been effective in developing clear options for debate, the report concluded, because the group size had become unwieldy—eleven principals each with an aide—and frankness was inhibited. The option papers EPG staff had prepared for the president were sometimes outranked by DPS or NSC option papers, because the EPG was separate from the White House. Carter preferred to work off staff papers signed by White House assistants, the report asserted, and participating agencies did not regard EPG as the arena for the central decision-making process because it did not control the presentation of options to the president. Its ability to respond to presidential interests on specific issues was, therefore, less than it could have been. The strongest EPG jurisdictional dispute was with the DPS, whose members saw the EPG staff as supplying economic analysis rather than policy coordination. The PRP report contained several decision-making case studies including an analysis of the administration decision on the new minimum wage; here too many options had been presented without fully analyzing the issues.

The PRP study team recommended cutting EPG membership to a small group of key officials and giving Eizenstat and the DPS additional staff to carry out economic analysis for the EPG. Carter seemed to prefer relying on Eizenstat and therefore the DPS should be given the staff capability to do the work.[13] Instead of implementing this recommendation Carter disbanded the EPG staff. The secretary of the group continued as an assistant to Blumenthal in the Treasury Department. Apparently as a result of discussions between EPG principals and the president, in August, 1977, an EPG steering committee was established consisting of Blumenthal, Schultze, Eizenstat, Undersecretary of State Richard Cooper, the vice-president, and Bert Lance's successor at OMB, James McIntyre. Curtis Hessler, Blumenthal's assistant, prepared the memoranda that went to the president.[14] Even with the new arrangement, for several months EPG members continued to submit uncoordinated options to the president—

until the players became familiar with one another and the lines of division began to cohere in patterns. Eventually, assistants to Blumenthal, Schultze and McIntyre would meet regularly to insure that EPG discussion papers were prepared and to decide who was to take the lead on a given issue. An informal troika, plus two or three, gradually developed. This too changed in the last two years of the administration with the development of wage and price guidelines and an explicit antiinflation program under Alfred Kahn. The president and his key economic advisers then met for breakfast every two weeks. When William Miller succeeded Blumenthal as secretary of the treasury in mid-1979, EPG procedures were tightened and formalized. Miller became Eizenstat's counterpart for economic policy, playing more of a coordinating and less of an advocacy role with his colleagues than had Blumenthal.[15]

Why didn't Carter give the DPS additional staff to do economic analysis for the EPS as recommended by the study team? He did ask Eizenstat to monitor EPG operations and to encourage the other agencies to let the Treasury Department do the paperwork.[16] But Carter never felt well served by the EPG because of the constant friction among its members. He wanted options to come to him in an orderly, harmonious fashion and did not like to play referee. The dilemma, it seems, grew from Carter's promise to have no White House assistant for economic policy and from his commitment to the principle of cabinet collegiality. Since the EPG was a cabinet committee (even though a most unwieldy one) he could or would not give himself the staff link with it that he needed. He resorted to ad hoc devices. Even realizing that he could not easily resolve the undisciplined presentation of options, he still would not authorize staff to do it for him and thus exacerbated his decision problems.

Schultze felt that it took eighteen months to sort out the administration's division of labor for economic analysis and discussion. In the end, the main players regularly discussed the important issues but the formal organization was always messy. Microeconomic issues were staffed on an ad hoc basis by the CEA and other presidential staffs. Hessler staffed macroeconomic issues for the EPG, but the many added options made considerable discussion with the president necessary before decisions were made.[17] The main advisers thought the president should have given someone the authority to limit the options coming to him. The EPG was slow and indecisive, some complained, and made decisions laboriously; its main actors were secretive. No one seemed to be in charge and people were going in different directions. Everyone felt powerless. When Alfred Kahn, head of the Council on Wage and Price Stability, tried to resign in the Summer of 1979 and was dissuaded by the president, he told Schultze that he considered himself a fifth wheel; Schultze responded, "No, I am." And Eizenstat amazed Kahn by saying that he did not feel in on final economic policy decisions either.[18]

Blumenthal spent two and one half years attempting to establish his primacy among economic advisers but never succeeded. By all accounts he was heavy-handed in his relations with colleagues and as EPG chairman, pushing his own strong views and making himself player as well as chairman.[19] One EPG member, in describing executive committee meetings under Blumenthal, said his talk dominated the meetings, and though he pushed through the agenda the group seldom faced hard questions systematically, arrived at decisions or sent anything to Carter. Blumenthal would then lecture the president without knowing when to stop, as he delivered his conservative advice in favor of tight fiscal and monetary policy.[20] In the first year Blumenthal was frustrated by the fact that although he saw himself as leader of the EPG, Bert Lance was closer to Carter. Lance felt that Blumenthal was always trying to weaken that relationship. Disagreements between Blumenthal and Eizenstat were ideological and political, with the latter taking a more liberal line on the need to meet the interests of Democratic coalitions on spending and subsidy issues.[21]

In fairness to Blumenthal, however, he was in a very difficult position. Someone had to lead the EPG in the interests of the president, but Carter refused to give Blumenthal or anyone else that role. Blumenthal's strenuous efforts to be the first among equals could be interpreted as an attempt to establish primacy in the interest of unity. One can infer that Carter wanted the treasury secretary to take such a lead since he deliberately avoided bringing in a White House economic assistant or giving Eizenstat and the DPS the staff to play the coordinating role. Rather, Eizenstat encouraged the treasury secretary to mediate between the EPG and the president. When Miller succeeded Blumenthal, the process was smoother.[22]

The organizational structure for making economic policy decisions at the presidential level thus evolved from an umbrella group that was considered too large and unwieldy to an informal troika of treasury secretary, CEA and OMB heads, assisted by Eizenstat, the vice-president and other senior advisers. This group addressed major issues of macroeconomic policy. Microeconomic questions most often developed at the initiative of the constituency departments and were usually initially analyzed by the CEA and OMB, with Eizenstat and the DPS sometimes playing an advisory role. Such micro issues would often go directly to the president without going through the EPG. In the last two years of the administration the bimonthly inflation breakfasts brought the president and his senior economic advisers together. Since wage and price guidelines were an important aspect of the antiinflation program, both macro and micro policy issues were discussed at those meetings. After William Miller became secretary of the treasury in mid-1979, interactions among senior advisers were more cohesive.[23]

The major advisers for economic policy are easily identified. Charles Schultze, the CEA chairman, was the president's principal economic adviser for four years because the CEA provided expert analysis for presidential choices. They had no other client but Carter. The two secretaries of the treasury were key actors not only because they had the formal lead as EPG chairmen but because the Treasury Department is the chief proposer and advocate of presidential economic policy to Congress. Had Bert Lance remained in government he would have been an important figure in economic policy making because of his interest in the subject and his closeness to the president. His successor, James McIntyre, was not regarded as having similar access or influence on economic issues. Eizenstat, Hamilton Jordan and Vice-President Mondale appear to have considered economic policy issues primarily in political terms, much in the way they approached domestic policy issues. Alfred Kahn, who moved from the Civil Aeronautics Board to the White House in 1978 as chairman of the Council on Wage and Price Stability and as chief inflation fighter, had a specialized role. The inner circle kept their distance from other cabinet officers who contributed to economic policy. This was not unusual, as in any administration the top three economic advisers tend to regard the heads of constituency departments as lacking expertise in macro policy and advocating departmental constituency interests in micro policy. Secretary of Labor Ray Marshall had the clear impression that the troika members did not regard the Labor Department as an equal player and were suspicious of its ties with organized labor. In his view the EPG arrangement prevented the president from fully examining issues because of the policy views key EPG members held. Marshall believed, for example, that administration policy to cut budgets as a means of reducing inflation was mistaken. He did not think the two were related and attributed steep increases in inflation to external energy price rises.[24] However, as we saw in Chapter 3, Carter was personally close to Marshall and valued his views on a number of questions. And it is more likely that Carter himself, rather than the troika, arranged the balance of competing economic views. The central tension was the same as in domestic policy, consolidation and constraint versus responsiveness to Democratic constituencies. The Treasury Department, OMB and the Council on Wage and Price Stability argued for discipline in fiscal policy, and their view was not opposed by a competing economic school of thought. Rather Jordan, Mondale and, to some degree, Eizenstat, presented the claims of Democratic groups in the context of presidential politics. The crucial bridging figure was Schultze, whose approach was very close to the president's: achieve economic growth and avoid recession with minimum inflation. Schultze's Keynesian approach was a theoretical match for Carter's centrism. The difficulties were in achieving such balanced goals, and any failure to do so caused political trouble for the president.

The story of the EPG illustrates Carter's naiveté about administrative arrangements. His economic advisers had to sort themselves out and establish routines for doing their business with one another without any guidance from the president. The same sorting-out process took place in domestic policy, but there the president could rely on the DPS as a coordinating staff. The EPG's ad hoc, disjointed way of considering and making economic policy decisions matched Carter's approach to economic policy in general—competing goals were continually balanced through specific decisions in response to changing conditions. If Carter had laid down a clear and consistent policy line and charged his advisers with implementing it, advisory structures and processes probably would have been more clear-cut. Advisory arrangements take their shape from policy goals as much as they shape those goals.

MICROECONOMIC POLICY AND POLITICS

During the Carter years, public opinion polls revealed a massive contradiction in popular attitudes. People listed inflation as the nation's main economic problem and blamed the government for it. Yet, many of the same people demanded high levels of government social services and economic regulation. The great difficulty was that the economy was not growing at a sufficient rate to outpace inflation and provide money for the expected levels of government activities. At the same time, political parties as representatives of interests were growing weaker and organized interest groups were strong. Economists were unsure of how government might stimulate the economic growth necessary to pay for social programs without feeding inflation. Wage and price levels did not respond to economic slowdown, contrary to received theory, perhaps because business and industry interpreted public policies of commitment to high employment as signs that the government would never permit the economy to falter for long. However, declining economic growth and productivity, combined with inflation, placed the government in the dilemma of having to satisfy group demands for services and regulation with fewer resources than in the past.[25]

Jimmy Carter was the first modern Democratic president to face these dilemmas. His fiscal conservatism and dislike of interest groups disposed him to resist inflationary demands. But his leadership of the Democratic coalition required him to balance his apprehensions about the new economic conditions against the claims of Democratic groups. Carter dealt with such demands by trying to scale them down to acceptable levels. It was not his political strategy to give each group what it wanted, but he did not wish to turn away from them either. The very structure of the political situation, however, put the president on the defensive. From the perspective of the affected groups, half a loaf was not as good as a full loaf.

Eizenstat and his Domestic Policy Staff generally considered it important to keep labor, farmers, environmentalists, women's advocates and other Democratic groups on Carter's side while, at the same time, moderating their demands. Congress was not prepared to turn all requests of such groups into law, and it was important that Carter not be blamed for this. One difficulty was that Carter did not feel close to most of these groups. One aide remembers that at a luncheon meeting Carter had with AFL-CIO President George Meany and the presidents of the international unions, the labor leaders showed Carter very little respect and criticized his half-hearted support of social programs. One union head told an off-color story that offended Carter, who afterward told his assistants that he never wanted to have a meeting like that again.[26]

Carter was not interested in providing rhetorical leadership for these traditional Democratic groups. The 1977 economic stimulus package was, in fact, a boon to the Democratic constituencies but, as one of Carter's assistants said, "Because of the way it was done, because nobody ever had to come and ask him for it, because it was so easy to get out, there was a sense on the part of the mayors and governors and different civil rights groups and different constituencies that it never happened."[27]

At the end of each budget cycle the president, vice-president, Eizenstat and McIntyre would meet to divide two or three billion dollars for "liberal" causes, such as compensatory education and employment and training programs. The purpose was to do something for friends of the administration. But rather than taking rhetorical advantage of such actions, Carter did just the opposite by talking a conservative game. Because he wished his symbolic language to be conservative rather than liberal, he set himself apart from groups in his coalition at the same time that he was attempting to work out agreements with them.[28]

Carter's economists, particularly Charles Schultze, were acutely aware that difficult microeconomic decisions were even more difficult as political choices. It was not easy to calculate with accuracy the effect of a proposed increase in the minimum wage on other economic forces. And it was hard for a Democratic president to give the unions less than they wanted. Carter attempted to combine difficult analyses about policy trade offs of specific choices with the thorny politics of group claims. One Carter economic adviser remarked that Reagan's conservative constituency would support any liberal actions he took because they knew him to be sound, and liberals like Hubert Humphrey could act conservatively without offending their supporters. But Carter had neither a liberal nor a conservative constituency, which often made it difficult to know what he would do in advance of a decision. His preferences were clear—a moderate fiscal conservatism as a policy against inflation. But on specific issues this position would often get whittled down by departments, congressional Democrats and some of his own aides. The direction he favored differed from the one his horses wanted to take. Although his aides found Carter willing to take big risks, such as the canal treaties and mediation of Middle East disputes, "On the smaller issues," one of them said, "there was an awful lot of trying over and over again to cut the cloth just to fit."[29] Carter is described as feeling his way between two alignments of advisers, those such as the DPS and the vice-president who wished to keep constituent groups happy, and those like Blumenthal and the OMB who wished to throw down the gauntlet. Schultze and the CEA staff appear to have been in the balance with Carter, seeking a middle way but leaning toward fiscal restraint, particularly after the stimulus package was in place. Keynesian economists differ little from neoclassical economists on issues of microeconomic policy, since both usually favor market competition over regulation and subsidies. The major ideological divisions among economists are over macroeconomic policy questions. Schultze felt that Carter was cross pressured in making hard microeconomic decisions. Economic analysis pushed in one direction and politics in the opposite. Over and over again the president and his advisers would split the difference, often making no one happy.[30]

McIntyre and his principal aides at OMB thought Democratic politics dominated White House decisions and criticized the administration for not drawing the line much more decisively against group claims. OMB regarded the farm bill of 1977 as inflationary, for example, and felt it should have been vetoed. Bert Lance had wanted the president to veto the 1977 Labor-HEW appropriations bill because it was higher than Carter wanted. But Carter had pledged not to veto in the first year. Many decisions made in the first two years in response to constituency needs had to be rescinded in the last two years of Carter's term. Too many public housing units and CETA public service employment jobs were pledged and had to be taken back; food stamp extensions, black lung benefits and trade adjustment assistance became entitlement programs of increasing cost each subsequent year. The OMB therefore saw Carter as a fiscal conservative who also, like other Democratic presidents, wished to be remembered for expanding the assistance that government gave to people.[31]

Carter's handling of the conflicting advice he received is characterized by OMB observers and other presidential staff members as a balancing of opposites. For example, in the heated discussion in late 1978 about the wisdom of reducing CETA job levels, the vice-president and the DPS opposed the reductions whereas the president regarded them as one of many necessary steps to reduce the size of the budget. McIntyre and OMB also favored the reductions. So Carter split the difference, a rational decision strategy in the absence of a more explicit criterion, but not a style calculated to make Democratic interest groups happy.[32]

SETTING THE MINIMUM WAGE

Two documents describing the development of a Carter administration position on the new minimum wage level provide a case study—and illustrate a broader pattern—of microeconomic policy and politics. The President's Reorganization Project did a case study of the decision, and it appears as well in one Carter assistant's running memorandum on early economic policy decisions.

In 1977 the federal minimum wage was $2.30 an hour. On March 10, 1977, the AFL-CIO staff informed the White House that they would push for a $3.00 minimum wage with subsequent upward adjustments in January using the formula of 60 percent of average hourly wages for manufacturing. They saw no inflationary impact in such an increase.[33] On March 17, both the CEA and the Department of Labor submitted analyses to the EPG. The Labor Department memo, from Secretary Ray Marshall, supported a bill, then in Congress, that would raise the minimum wage to $2.85 in the summer and to $3.31 by January, 1978. The CEA memo described the bill (introduced by Congressman John Dent, a Pennsylvania Democrat) as inflationary and raised the question of whether the minimum wage should be indexed. An OMB memo also argued against indexing and suggested that a new $2.65 level was reasonable. The EPG met on March 21 and Secretary Blumenthal subsequently presented the president with two options. The first was to support a variation of the Dent bill, supported in the EPG by the Labor Department and Housing and Urban Development (HUD). The second option, proposed by the CEA and supported by the Commerce and Treasury departments and OMB, called for an immediate increase in the minimum wage from $2.30 to $2.40 with indexing at a rate of about 45 percent of average manufacturing earnings. The EPG memo was routed through Eizenstat, who added two new compromise options and sent it on to the president. The next day Schultze, Marshall and Eizenstat each submitted an additional memorandum, further elaborating their positions.[34]

When the president met with his economic advisers on March 23 it was clear that he wished to find a middle ground, as did Eizenstat. After conferring with Congressman Dent, Carter met again with his advisers and decided to support an increase to $2.50 with the technical details on automatic increases to be worked out by the others. The next day Secretary Marshall testified before the Dent committee in favor of the $2.50 rate. The president later told his advisers that he had been afraid to go to $2.60 (as Congressman Dent had evidently recommended) so early in the congressional process.[35]

On April 7 at a stormy meeting in the White House between the president and vice-president and top labor leaders, George Meany strongly criticized the administration for its minimum wage decision. On April 9, Lane Kirkland of the AFL-CIO told Blumenthal that they had not appreciated finding out about Carter's decision on the $2.50 level through the news ticker rather than directly. He then said that they would settle for $2.60 or $2.65 and a 53 percent index. Discussions and bargaining between the White House and the AFL-CIO, with Ray Marshall acting as go-between, preoccupied the White House during much of May. Both Schultze and Blumenthal were strongly opposed to big increases. Finally, on July 12, the president described the compromise agreement with the AFL-CIO at a breakfast with the Democratic congressional leadership. The hourly rate was to go to $2.65 with subsequent increases to a 52 percent indexing base in January, 1978, and a 56 percent base in January, 1979, which would bring the minimum wage to $2.90.[36]

This one case of microeconomic policy making in the Carter administration demonstrates, above all, that the EPG did not work well. It provided little analysis, was not able to limit the number of options going to the president and did not subject competing options to scrutiny. The contending parties within the administration seem never to have tried developing a common position on behalf of the president. Rather, Ray Marshall was an advocate for the labor point of view in contrast to the Department of Treasury, CEA and OMB positions. Carter wished to raise wage levels but with minimal impact on inflation. Schultze and the CEA provided him with the necessary analysis to guide his choices and Eizenstat provided helpful strategies for seeking a middle ground. Eventually, Marshall fell into line. However, the administration was at odds with the AFL-CIO from the beginning. Both sides were perhaps to blame, since labor made its demand without consultation and the president responded in kind. The subsequent negotiations produced agreement but the unions gave Carter no credit for it; he had given them half a loaf. At no point was he accorded respect by organized labor. The Carter White House and the AFL-CIO were simply not part of the same family.

WAGE AND PRICE GUIDELINES

A second case study, the implementation of guidelines to hold back inflation, provides somewhat broader illustrations of the difficult politics of the administration's microeconomic policy. Decisions made in particular sectors of the economy affected all sectors and thus the inflation rate—the number one macro problem.

At the postelection meetings in Plains on economic policy, Charles Schultze had favored specific wage and price guidelines even though he had opposed standby wage and price control authority for the president. He wanted to use guidelines to control inflation as the economy recovered, with the idea that business, labor and consumers would all gain if voluntary agreements could keep inflation from soaring. At this time, the new Treasury Department officials and Bert Lance opposed specific guidelines, and Ray Marshall and the AFL-CIO were adamantly against them. Schultze subsequently felt that the administration proposed guidelines too late and too timidly, primarily because its major constituency, organized labor, was against them.[37] But the "conservatives" in the administration also withheld support.

In April, 1978, the president announced the appointment of Robert Strauss as inflation adviser, though no program proposals accompanied the announcement. In due course, Barry Bosworth, director of the Council on Wage and Price Stability, proposed "deceleration," which meant that business and labor would seek fewer price and wage increases in the year ahead; Strauss's role was to persuade them to comply, on moral grounds. The administration was concerned about food inflation and energy supplies. In July, 1978, Secretary of Labor Marshall sent a memo to the president suggesting that the administration set some kind of guidelines to be used as a standard for prices and wages with the government taking specific sanctions, such as denial of government procurement contracts to firms, against those who exceeded the standards.[38] Some of Secretary Marshall's top assistants had urged him to advocate voluntary standards since 1979 would be a major collective bargaining year in which the Teamsters Union, auto unions, electrical and rubber workers would bargain for new contracts. High settlements would spur inflation and hurt the administration politically. Marshall's memorandum generated strong enthusiasm, though the idea of mandatory controls of any kind had little support within the administration. The memo had suggested that the government could relax import restrictions to control prices. And one possibility for controlling wage levels would be to reduce regulation of the trucking industry if the Teamsters got too high a wage package. The deputies' group of the EPG concluded, however, that the presidency did not have the latitude to take such actions, which would often require changing the law or gaining congressional approval. Still, administration planners set to work to develop a program. The EPG deputies' group worked out the details of standards through bargaining among the Labor Department, which wanted a high ceiling for wages, and OMB and the Council on Wage and Price Stability, which wanted a low figure. Eventually, a 7 percent figure for annual wage increases was agreed upon and approved by the EPG and the president. No disagreement surfaced over price standards, and companies would be expected to keep average price increases 5 percent lower than their average in the 1976–1977 base period, up to a limit of 9.5 percent.[39] In October, 1978, the plan was ready and President Carter's speech to the nation set out the guidelines and announced the appointment of Alfred Kahn as chairman of the Council on Wage and Price Stability and adviser to the president on inflation. At the same time Carter signaled an increased determination to reduce federal deficits through tighter fiscal policy.

The President's economic advisers did not see galloping inflation on the horizon in late 1978, though they wanted a slight pullback to deter inflation, especially in the form of excessive wage increases. Of course, this policy did not anticipate the shock to the economy of the 1979 OPEC oil increases which made it very difficult to hold labor to the wage guidelines.[40]

The Council on Wage and Price Stability (CWPS) was responsible for administering the guidelines. Its members were essentially the same as the EPG, with a separate staff under Kahn and Barry Bosworth. In the Fall of 1979 it was apparent that voluntary guidelines were too weak to hold back wage demands in response to OPEC II. The administration had intended that management enforce the guidelines by keeping wage increases within acceptable limits. The White House did not want a confrontation with labor. When it became clear that management was going to give in to higher wage settlements and that inflation was running away, Vice-President Mondale, William Miller and Ray Marshall negotiated an "accord" with organized labor. The accord created a Pay Advisory Committee and a Price Committee to advise CWPS. The Price Committee, chaired by Harvard economist John Dunlop and consisting of fifteen members eventually divided between organized labor, business and the public, was active. The eventual result was tension between CWPS and the Pay Advisory Committee, with the committee speaking for organized labor much of the time. Still, the White House knew that the guidelines would not work unless labor supported them, and the acceptable level for wage increases thus rose to 9.5 percent.[41]

CEA economists by this time felt that the guidelines were worthless, because of numerous loopholes resulting from concessions the Pay Advisory Committee and the EPG had granted in particular cases. They judged that organized labor had gone on the committee to kill the guidelines and that the administration had virtually abdicated authority for policy to the committee.[42]

By February, 1980, the inflation rate had hit 18 percent and the administration introduced its antiinflation program of selective credit controls, a balanced budget for fiscal 1981, higher taxes on gasoline and an increase in CWPS activities in monitoring wage and price increases. However, because wage standards had been permitted to rise and price standards had not, businessmen were less supportive of the guidelines program then they might otherwise have been. The actual efforts to enforce the standards were not carried out by CWPS but by the selective involvement of the president in meetings with industry groups arranged by Alfred Kahn in Spring, 1980. Little was accomplished and this activity stopped as summer came. Since President Carter had always opposed wage and price controls, had accepted the voluntary program reluctantly and, furthermore, did not enjoy "jawboning," he did not relish being involved in these meetings. Political prudence also inhibited him from risking his prestige on such an uncertain crusade. In early 1980 the CWPS staff had suggested that it be empowered to delay or rescind price increases. But this was not politically possible for the president when Senator Edward Kennedy, who was running against him, advocated mandatory wage and price controls. Thus the consensus of those in the administration is that, in 1979 and 1980, Carter viewed the guidelines program primarily as a means to keep the support of union labor for the 1980 presidential election.[43]

Schultze felt that the incomes policy had helped moderate inflation to a limited extent in 1979 and 1980. American workers did not try to recapture oil price increases in their wage to the same extent European workers did. But Schultze also believed the program to have been too little, too late. In retrospect, Alfred Kahn thought the guidelines had helped slow down union efforts in 1979–1980 to recoup through wage settlements the inflationary effects of the OPEC oil shock. Nationally the catch-up attempt in those years was less than in 1974–1975 after the 1973 oil shock. The guidelines, he speculated, might have held inflation down by a point. Kahn participated in the 1979 negotiations that led to the accord between organized labor and the administration and continued to talk regularly with AFL-CIO leaders and John Dunlop, chairman of the Pay Advisory Committee. It was Dunlop's belief that the administration was lucky to get agreement on a 9 percent wage increase ceiling at a time when the inflation rate was going from 13 to 18 and back to 13 percent.[44]

Kahn was quite aware of the political constraints within White House councils on a rigorous antiinflation effort on microeconomic policy. When the vice-president or Eizenstat would argue that social security benefits could not be touched or unemployment among auto workers could not be tolerated, they were perceiving the external political constraints accurately. Kahn and his assistants saw Mondale's staff and his people on the DPS as being dedicated to looking out for the traditional Democratic constituencies. For example, one of Mondale's assistants told one of Kahn's aides that he would have to convince her that holding the line on agricultural subsidies would knock a percentage point off the Consumer Price Index. If this could not be demonstrated, the administration would lose more politically than it would gain economically. On another occasion a DPS leader told one of Kahn's staff to stop pushing anticonstituency proposals, particularly on medical matters. Kahn and his staff found the general approach defensive rather than creative.[45]

These two cases reveal relations of the Carter administration with organized labor early and late in the four-year term. In the minimum wage case the president was trying hard to impose some discipline upon the claims of a politically important interest group. He achieved his policy goal but at a high political cost. The story of guidelines reveals an administration with its mind not only on inflation but on the coming 1980 election. Political considerations were much stronger than in 1977. One can see parallels with domestic policy making as the search for comprehensive programs, such as welfare reform, gave way to incrementalist policy and politics, as in the creation of the Department of Education.

MACROECONOMIC POLICY

Jimmy Carter campaigned in 1976 on the theme of getting the economy moving again and criticized the Ford administration for tolerating unacceptably high levels of unemployment. In the minds of many Democrats this was surely a repeat of John F. Kennedy's 1960 promise to restore health to the economy. In 1976, the unemployment rate was over 7 percent, inflation was between 5 and 6 percent and the federal government was running a $66 billion deficit. Carter promised to set all this right in one term; by 1980 he would reduce unemployment, curb inflation and balance the budget.[46] Carter and his advisers expected the return of economic growth to not only provide new jobs but reduce the deficit gap. There seemed no danger of reviving inflation so long as unemployment was so high.

In 1976 the economy was in the early stages of a recovery, with inflation remaining low as recovery reduced unemployment. The hard task, then, was to keep from overstimulating the economy, a prelude to inflation. Herbert Stein contends that the Ford administration had not won public support for a policy of reviving the economy gradually to keep inflation at bay. People forget about inflation as times get better, and Carter appealed to the desire for fast recovery—with the accompanying danger that expansion would bring inflation. Carter's 1977 stimulus would combine spending programs with tax cuts and, through the cooperation of the Federal Reserve Board, increase the money supply so that interest rates would fall and thus stimulate recovery. Slack in the economy would inhibit inflation. At this point the analogy with the Kennedy period breaks down. Kennedy became president after a period of stable prices in the Eisenhower administration. But Carter followed ten years of Johnson-Nixon inflation and a mixed and unhappy experience in the Nixon years with wage and price controls. Inflationary forces were, therefore, stronger in 1977 than in 1960 and economic recovery carried a greater risk of inflation.[47]

DEVELOPMENT OF THE 1977 STIMULUS PACKAGE

The official advisory group on economic policy during the Fall campaign was headed by Lawrence Klein, a University of Pennsylvania economist. The group put together an economic white paper that was the basis for the economic stimulus package developed after the election. The plan was very much the creation of professional economists, especially the designated chairman of the Council of Economic Advisers, Charles Schultze, who was appointed and went to work on the package before the secretary of the treasury was selected. Schultze was the only one of the president-elect's economic advisers with sufficient governmental experience to know how to develop such a plan. Bert Lance and Ray Marshall had not served in the federal government and Michael Blumenthal's previous experience had been in the State Department.[48] On December 1, after the main outline of the stimulus plan had been completed, the president-elect met in Plains with Schultze, Klein, Blumenthal, Cooper, Andrew Brimmer, a Harvard faculty member and former Federal Reserve Board member, and two former CEA chairmen, Walter Heller and Arthur Okun. They advised Carter that to heed the great slack in the economy and introduce a stimulus package would permit real growth of 8 percent in 1977 and reduce unemployment to slightly over 6 percent with only a 2 percent increase in inflation. The slack in the economy was the safeguard against greater inflation. The alternative to stimulus, they said, was recession.[49]

The four parts to the stimulus package were a temporary tax cut in the form of a fifty dollar rebate to every taxpayer, public works, public service employment, and a small, permanent reduction in taxes. The rebate was Schultze's idea—a means of giving the economy a shot in the arm without limiting the government's capacity to collect revenue for balancing the federal budget in future years. The idea of a rebate grated on Carter, who thought of it as something for nothing. But Schultze talked him into it. Carter then used the argument for a rebate to counter appeals of congressional Democratic leaders for increased public works; the economy needed a quicker, more direct stimulus, he told them.[50] Carter's economic advisers recommended keeping the public works part of the package at a $2 billion level. However, in a second meeting with Tip O'Neill, Jim Wright and other Democratic leaders, Carter agreed to add another $2 billion in contingency funds in case the recovery was slower than anticipated. Ray Marshall sold Carter on the idea of Public Service Employment, which Schultze opposed.[51]

The main elements of the plan were decided upon at a January 6 meeting in Plains, with Carter, Mondale, Schultze, Lance, Cooper, Marshall, Blumenthal, and the secretaries of commerce, agriculture and transportation designate—Juanita Kreps, Bob Bergland and Brock Adams—attending. The next day the group presented the economic program to the House and Senate Democratic leadership, and after that meeting Schultze and Blumenthal held an informal press conference to outline the main elements. Spending programs would involve the expansion of Public Service Employment under the Comprehensive Employment and Training Act (CETA) by approximately $2 billion over existing levels. The existing accelerated public works program would be expanded from $1 billion to $2 billion. CETA job and skill training would be expanded to include on-the-job training incentives, a youth employment service corps and special programs for veterans. The countercyclical revenue-sharing program would be expanded by $1 billion a year in the form of Public Service Employment jobs. The tax side would require raising the standard deduction, an investment tax credit for business, and a one-time tax rebate to all citizens. The program would cost $12 billion to $16 billion in fiscal 1977 and $13 billion to $16 billion in fiscal 1978. The standard deduction change would cost $2 billion in fiscal 1977 and $6 billion in 1978. Business tax cuts would cost $7 billion to $11 billion in fiscal year 1977 and nothing in fiscal 1978.[52]

The congressional leaders told Carter that it would be hard to hold public works to intended levels and that the rebate plan would be un-popular with Congress and the public. At that point Carter argued against a massive public works program—there were limits, he said, to how many people could be usefully employed in that way—and defended the rebate as a quick stimulus to the economy. Charles Schultze strongly supported the president on the need for the rebate.[53]

The pressures on the new president and his advisers for a big stimulus were very strong. In early December Carter had met with a group of corporation executives who told him that a stimulus of less than $20 billion would be ineffective. A week later he met with representatives of the National League of Cities and the National Conference of Mayors who asked for a much larger stimulus package than the one intended, including almost $8 million in rebates to low income people in addition to an urban development bank. Carter told these groups that he was going to operate under tight budget constraints but pledged to try to reduce youth unem-ployment. In early January, before he was inaugurated, Carter, Marshall and Eizenstat met with AFL-CIO officials who also had a much grander stimulus plan than the administration's. They were opposed to tax cuts and favored a large public works program and other direct employment efforts. In early February the new president met with black leaders who were critical of the scope of his stimulus plan, fearing that it would not bring full employment and asking specifically for an additional $2 billion for black teenage employment. They also complained about lack of consultation with black opinion in the making of policy.[54]

Carter may have felt some ambivalence about stimulating the economy. He had promised in the campaign to get the economy moving and was responsive to the requests of congressional leaders and Ray Marshall, within the constraints set by Schultze. But, as he said at the first cabinet meeting, on January 24, he intended as well to be a restraining influence on the spending of a Democratic Congress, particularly on the leadership's desire for higher expenditures than those provided in the stimulus pack-age.[55] He had also resisted the requests of labor, the mayors and black groups for a larger stimulus package. One of his more "conservative" advisers reports that Carter was ambivalent about the stimulus package from the beginning, and he did later withdraw the rebate and identify potential inflation as the most severe long-term economic problem the administration would face. According to this observer, even after all of Carter's economic advisers called for a stimulus program at a post-election meeting in November, Carter said privately that he was reluctant to go so far. By December, as the package was being developed, he became skeptical about whether the economy was really in a recession. "The President's first instincts were not to go the route on the stimulus. That was his own gut instinct; that was not followed. . . . He got beaten down in December by his own people. . . . And we ended up doing it and got in the embarrassing position of having to withdraw the thing [rebate] by spring." In the view of this aide, Carter would have done better had he followed his own assessment that the economy was improving and developed a long-term strategy against inflation. But he lacked the confidence to override his own economic advisers. Carter and Bert Lance were the only two people who did not want to go along—Lance because he was conservative and Carter because he did not think the economy was in such bad shape.[56]

A continuing theme in Carter's decision-making style, observed this aide, was the degree to which the president listened to advice as opposed to following his own instincts.

In the campaign, when Jimmy Carter did not want to do something, come hell or high water, he would not do it. . . . All through the campaign he would follow his instincts when he decided he was right. . . . We began to see a different pattern start to emerge [after he became president], when he would just get weighed down with all this advice. Part of it was the character of the President, and part of it is the inexperience of being President-elect. And another part of it is the lack of long-term strategy, not coming in with a sense of what our problems were going to be, what we were going to face right away. . . . We were doing it all in a relatively ad hoc fashion.[57]

Charles Schultze confirms Carter's ambivalence by recalling that the new president was unhappy about increasing the deficit with the stimulus program and saw his political advisers and the congressional leaders as pushing him beyond where he wished to go. Carter acted with more conviction, Schultze remembered, when he waged a campaign for fiscal restraint in his last two and one half years. Even though it was harder to do politically, in contrast to stimulating the economy, it suited his views.[58]

THE REBATE

The significance of the disagreements within the new administration about the tax rebate, which Carter finally dropped in April, went beyond the manifest question of whether the rebate was any longer necessary in a quickly improving economy. Carter, of course, decided and announced that it was not necessary, but several other issues of importance for the future were entangled with the decision. One was the question of whether inflation was a greater enemy than recession. Another was that of constancy; the president's advisers were divided on whether such reverses in policy were politically prudent. And the debate also revealed the major divisions among Carter's economic advisers.

Neither Lance nor Blumenthal had liked the rebate idea and both continued to question it after the stimulus plan had gone to Congress. By early February Blumenthal was telling the president that the economy was recovering faster than had been thought, with the implication that less stimulus was needed. Congressional leaders had never been for the rebate, at least partly because they preferred more substantial, visible, long-term programs and opposed a one-shot action. Hubert Humphrey told Carter that it was immoral to be dropping fifty dollar bills around.[59] However, despite their preferences the leadership supported the rebate, and the general view in the White House throughout March and early April was that it was important for recovery. By this time the president's advisers were in two camps, with the vice-president, Schultze and Eizenstat favoring the rebate and Blumenthal and Lance in opposition. In early April, Carter began to have doubts. Retail sales had risen, and he began to ask his advisers if the rebate was still necessary. Mondale and Eizenstat argued that his political reputation would suffer if he appeared to be suddenly shifting course. The issue was thoroughly discussed at an April 13 White House meeting in which Carter was skeptical, Lance and Blumenthal in favor of reversal, and Mondale, Schultze and Eizenstat in favor of retaining the rebate. The real question, the president said, was whether he had to worry about inflation or a dormant economy; later that day he told the vice-president that he was going to withdraw the rebate. He announced his decision the next day but failed to tell the secretary of the treasury, who defended the rebate in a noon speech at the National Press Club. Carter appears to have been preoccupied with the merits of the issue rather than its politics, although he may have been responding in part to congressional grumbling about the rebate, even from those like Senator Edmund Muskie who were leading the charge for it. Schultze perceived Carter's concern about inflation to be a reaction to the 1977 rise in price levels, which Schultze labeled an inflationary flurry primarily due to the increases in food prices after a temporary drop in late 1976 as farmers sold off their herds. Carter seems to have heeded messages from Lance and Blumenthal that the rebate might be inflationary and that inflation was his real problem—a worry he had had in November and December when the stimulus package was first considered.[60]

In retrospect, Carter saw the debate over the rebate as a fundamental issue for future economic policy.

Bert [Lance], Mike Blumenthal and I were more conservative than anybody else among my advisers. . . . The test came with the fifty dollar tax rebate. When we went into office, there was a unanimous commitment to an immediate creation of jobs and we had anticipated that the fifty dollar tax rebate could be implemented by April. We were going to pass it in February and March and it was going to be an immediate thing. Well, it didn't happen that way. It went through the House quickly without any delay. It got to the Senate and a lot of opposition was being aroused to it because the economy seemed to be stimulated more than we anticipated on its own. Bert and Mike Blumenthal and I felt that the fifty dollar tax rebate should not be implemented and we had a squabble among our economic advisers, an inevitable squabble but not anything ugly. We finally prevailed, and we just aborted it.[61]

Carter understood that more was at stake than the single rebate issue, as he records in his memoirs.

From then on [after rebate withdrawal], the basic course was set, but my advisers were right about the political damage. The obvious inconsistency in my policy during this rapid transition from stimulating the economy to an overall battle against inflation was to plague me for a long time. But I knew I had made the correct decision; for more than three and a half years my major economic battle would be against inflation, and I would stay on the side of fiscal prudence, restricted budgets, and lower deficits. Discretionary domestic spending, in real dollars, increased less than 1 percent during my term in office.[62]

In early 1977 Carter was fighting with important members of Congress about his elimination of a number of water projects from the 1978 budget, which he saw as saving $5 billion that would not be well spent. This position paralleled his rebate turnabout in its espousal of the conviction that budgetary restraint was the chief weapon against inflation—a conviction that brought political difficulties.

I wish some of you could have sat in on some of our leadership meetings and just seen the stricken expression on the faces of those Democratic leaders when I was talking about balancing the budget . . . [which] was anathema to them. . . . That wasn't something a Democratic president was supposed to do. So even in that early phase, I'm talking about the spring of '77, I was already getting strong opposition from my Democratic leadership in dealing with economics. All they knew about it was stimulus and Great Society programs.[63]

The accounts of the stimulus package and the rebate set the stage for the strategic problem in economic policy which plagued the Carter administration for four years—how to revive the economy without inflation. Democratic presidents, with their constituencies, find this difficult to do, and both Carter and John F. Kennedy were going against the grain in their parties. Kennedy had to persuade Democratic congressional leaders that a tax cut and deliberate deficit spending, in accordance with Keynesian theory, comprised intelligent policy. Many were skeptical, as was the president himself at first. But in time the threat of a "Kennedy recession" and the growing strength of social reform forces in the Democratic party gave Kennedy the impetus to ask Walter Heller, chairman of the CEA, to prepare the tax cut plan which passed the Congress in 1964.[64] President Carter was fighting against the political legacy of that success in altogether different economic conditions. He was convinced that the problem of inflation called for budgetary restraint, but his own party leaders knew only the politics and economics of growth.

The problems of economic policy in the 1970s were less tractable than in the Kennedy years. The Great Society entitlement programs gave a Democratic president, in 1977, very little room to maneuver in reducing the budget, particularly if defense expenditures were also to be increased, as Carter came to believe they should be. And then economists failed to appreciate fully the underlying strength of inflationary forces in the economy. A mistake in government policy on the inflationary side was not easily reversed. The accompanying concern, of course, particularly among Democrats, was that actions taken to dampen inflation might tilt the economy toward recession. It is not clear that economists knew how to halt inflation without the country paying a severe price in the form of recession.[65] The tasks of political and economic leadership were interlaced, and this strategic problem of coping with both the political and economic obstacles to an explicit presidential war against inflation was a central economic policy problem of the Carter presidency.

The central macro policy story was the shift in emphasis in annual administration budget proposals to Congress between goals of economic expansion and contraction. Administration economists were the intellectual and political heirs of the belief among Democratic economists that government fiscal policy could fine tune the economy to achieve growth without inflation. Thus fiscal policy could be loosened if recession appeared to be a possibility and the budget, as an instrument of policy, would either contain tax relief or spending programs, so that expansion might negate recession. But if economic indicators, studied by the CEA, showed signs of inflation, the budget might be tightened to draw money out of the economy. All of the insights and tools of economic science were used to try to keep a balance between the extremes. At each critical juncture the president chose expansion or contraction, through fiscal policy, depending on what his economists saw on the horizon.

During the Carter years the economy grew faster than its long-term potential. For example, Gross National Product (GNP) increased by 5.5 percent in 1977 and 4.8 percent in 1978 with a consequent drop in unemployment from 7.5 percent in early 1977 to 5.8 percent by late 1978. But the productive supply of capital, labor and technology grew at only 2.5 percent to 3 percent each year. The slack could hold inflation down only for a time; with economic recovery it revived in due course. As unemployment fell, wage inflation increased. High GNP growth rates in the United States helped tighten commodity markets, particularly food and oil, with higher commodity prices entering the country through international trade and finance.[66]

Throughout the four Carter years, the inflation rate steadily climbed. The January, 1981, *Economic Report of the President,* prepared by the outgoing CEA, gave the figures.[67]

Year	Changes in GNP	Unemployment Levels	Consumer Prices
1977	5.5%	7%	6.5%
1978	4.8%	6%	7.7%
1979	3.2%	5.8%	11.3%
1980	1.2%	7.1%	13.5%

The subsequent research literature offers a number of explanations for the increase in inflation along with the increasingly depressed state of the economy. These are cited here as contextual factors without an assessment of their relative importance.[68]

1. The administration's stimulation of demand processes in the economy in 1977 and 1978 produced a buoyant economy but also strengthened underlying inflationary forces and expectations present since the Johnson inflationary period. Expectations about wage and price increases became part of a psychological and institutional momentum that was very difficult to stop.

2. The cumulative effect of federal entitlement programs passed by Con-

gress in the 1960s, most of which were indexed to inflation, and the occupational safety and health consumer protection and environmental regulatory programs passed in the 1970s, increased inflation.

3. The unanticipated, abrupt decline in productivity that began in 1978, perhaps associated with young people and women expanding the work force, held back growth that might otherwise have stayed ahead of inflation.

4. The growth of the money supply from 1977 to 1979, a result of Federal Reserve Board actions, contributed to the rapid expansion of consumer demand.

5. Administration policy decisions to increase the minimum wage, raise milk support and sugar prices and reduce farm acreage for grains added to inflation.

6. The value of the dollar declined in international markets in 1977 and 1978. The dollar lost 20 percent of its value relative to other currencies, which pushed up the prices of goods imported into the United States.

7. The 1979 OPEC oil price increase, comparable to the 1973 shock, caused oil prices to nearly triple between 1979 and 1981.

The president's early worries about inflation surfaced at a press conference on March 24, 1977, when he announced (to the great surprise of his aides) that a "very strong" antiinflation package would be presented within two weeks. When the program was unveiled three weeks later, it simply presented the goal of a balanced budget, a commitment to disciplined government spending and a plea for voluntary cooperation on wage and price restraint.[69] On April 4 the president told his cabinet that congressional budget committees were recommending $6.5 billion more spending than he had requested. Unemployment could not be reduced without controlling inflation and his strategy for its control would center on tight budgets and informal agreements with business and labor. Carter again addressed inflation at the regular breakfast with congressional Democratic leaders two days later, stating that he could easily have supported a higher minimum wage and farm price supports had he not been trying to curb inflation. Charles Schultze agreed that inflation would accelerate unless the line was held. In making a major issue of inflation control, the president added, he would have to change the Democratic image of big spending; if he could do this Republicans would lose a political weapon. On April 8, at an EPG meeting, Secretary Califano described the tone of the president's proposed antiinflation statement as conservative and outside the mainstream of the Democratic party. Carter replied that he had promised to make the antiinflation statement and that many senators felt it necessary in order to pass the rebate, which had not yet been withdrawn. His role, he believed, was to be an educator and not claim to know all the answers. Indeed, there were no magic answers, and solutions could only come about through the cooperation of business and labor. At a staff meeting on May 28, Carter reiterated his concern about inflation and said that an increase to a rate of 8 or 9 percent would be devastating politically.[70]

It is not clear from the record whether Carter was watching indicators that triggered his worries about inflation, or whether he was simply following the instincts which told him that inflation would come with recovery. At this time his economic advisers were not worried but instead were trying to stimulate economic recovery. Bert Lance, whose economic intuitions were akin to the president's, had already warned him at the close of 1976 that if inflation increased by 1980 he would not be reelected. Lance advised Carter to find a way of turning down an expanding economy to abate inflation long before the election, so that by 1980 trends would be moving in the right direction.[71] That time didn't come until the very end, and such thinking was not compatible with the actions and rhetoric of economic recovery. According to one report, the general view within the higher levels of the administration was that the president's promise to balance the budget was purely symbolic.[72] But Carter spoke too often of the inflation threat to make this interpretation a likely one.

For estimates of economic trends the Council of Economic Advisers relied on several econometric models provided by private firms. These models reported great slack from the 1975–1976 recession and thus encouraged the inference that expansion could go quite far without the threat of inflation. In fact, the models failed to forecast strong inflationary forces because they did not capture the slow growth in productive potential in relation to growth in GNP. And the models did not fully capture the inflationary prices of international markets.[73] Schultze and his staff were fully aware that models only analyze the assumptions put into them, and they therefore skeptically analyzed all projections. What was missing at the time was an appreciation of the difficulty in correcting any actions made in favor of inflation, since—as was to become apparent in subsequent wage-price settlements and other areas of the economy—inflation did not decline easily, if at all, in response to corrective actions. Strong institutional factors in the American economy held it up.[74]

One antiinflation strategy that was available in 1977 was to attempt to increase the value and strength of the dollar in world markets. However, in the cause of economic recovery the administration had urged Germany and Japan to allow their currencies to appreciate against the dollar, to make American goods more competitive in world markets and to stimulate the economy.[75] But this also contributed to the cost of what Americans purchased abroad. When the dollar suddenly fell below European and Japanese currencies in November, 1977, because of fears in financial markets of renewed United States inflation, Carter reaffirmed his commitment to cutting deficits.[76]

However, the budget the president sent to Congress in January, 1978, was expansionary, proposing increases in many domestic programs as well as requesting a $25 billion tax cut and tax reforms.[77] The January report of the Council of Economic Advisors called for a stimulus package and forecast an economic slowdown by late 1978. In fact, 1978 was to be a boom year and CEA economists were to realize that they had underestimated the strength of the economy. They had probably added a point or a point and a half to the inflation rate by continuing to stimulate the economy.[78] Although the OMB at this point was arguing for a more stringent budget, the dominant thinking in the White House was that a tight budget could not be sent to Congress in an election year. Administration economists also believed that the remaining slack in the economy meant that the task of containing inflation could be handled by slowing down the economy at appropriate points. Inflation was not seen as fundamentally a demand problem, and the idea was to place a "speed limit" on recovery so that inflation would not get out of control. The White House did not at the time see the expansionary budget of 1978 as inflationary. In fact, the fear of recession was stronger.[79]

But by March OMB was reporting to the president that its projections for the fiscal 1980 budget, which would be sent to Congress in January, 1979, foresaw a $55 billion deficit. The query that accompanied the report was whether it was wise to let the deficit rise almost 40 percent in a time of increasing inflation. Such reports prompted the president to discuss the economy and budget with his cabinet in May and to stress his deep concern that inflation not be permitted to get out of control. He said that he had decided to propose an austere budget the following January. Because cabinet officers are department heads in charge of spending programs, the response was mixed and the dominant mood was political; the president should not be trying to simultaneously cut taxes and balance his budget, and the Democratic party could not plausibly become the party of fiscal stringency. This strain was compounded by Carter's 1977 decision to increase defense spending at an annual level of 3 percent beyond inflation, an increase that could only be accomplished by cuts in domestic programs. By the Fall of 1978 the budget to be introduced in January had become a political issue in Washington because the OMB budget figures had been leaked. The midterm Democratic party convention in Memphis, Tennessee, became the occasion for Democrats to charge that Carter was deserting the historic missions of the Democratic party. Senator Edward Kennedy delivered a rousing speech against Carter's budget policies, opposing any cuts in social programs. The gulf between Carter and Kennedy at this point began to visibly open, a breech that deeply affected the second half of Carter's term because the rallying of the "liberal" wing of the Democratic party around Kennedy made it very hard for the president to build a centrist coalition for budget restraint. Carter was increasingly caught between Kennedy and the Republican criticisms that his programs were too "liberal."[80]

The administration took one decisive action in November, 1978. Blumenthal convinced the president that it was necessary to immediately shore up the value of the dollar, which had been declining and therefore feeding inflationary psychology at home. In November the United States adopted a policy of "managed floating" of the dollar and the maintenance of a strong dollar became Carter administration policy. United States intervention in foreign exchange markets and the cooperation of the Federal Reserve Board with higher interest rates were designed to keep the dollar up.[81]

The other big economic policy initiative of 1978 was the tax reform bill. Senator Russell Long and Congressman Al Ullman, chairmen of the respective finance committees, had asked the administration not to send a tax reform measure, Congress having just passed one in 1976. The president, however, felt a strong campaign commitment to reform a tax system that he had called a "disgrace to the human race." Congress was not interested and converted the reform bill into a reduction of the capital gains tax, which Carter almost vetoed because he felt he had been double-crossed. In retrospect administration economists realized that a veto of the bill, even for the wrong reasons, would have brought greater fiscal restraint, more unemployment and less inflation in 1979. But they did not encourage a veto, and the resultant tax cuts may have stimulated the economy at the wrong time. Carter had not focused on the importance of using tax incentives to stimulate industrial productivity as a long-term instrument against inflation because his tax reform crusade had been a Populist one against the "three martini lunch" and other tax loopholes.[82]

By late 1978 the desire of the president and his advisers for a more formal antiinflation program led to the appointment of Alfred Kahn and the establishment of the wage and price guidelines. Administration economists still apparently disagreed about the seriousness of the inflation problem. The inflation rate had increased from 6.5 percent to 7.7 percent in one year but the real question was the potential for growth in underlying demand factors. Heineman and Hessler write that, by late 1978, Carter economists knew that they had miscalculated and that inflation was rising dangerously.[83] An OMB economist remembers great disagreement among economic advisers in 1977 and 1978 over the degree of restraint necessary in fiscal policy. However, he notes that after late 1978 little internal disagreement remained on the need for fiscal restraint. The problem from that point on was that administration economists had to combat White House domestic policy advisers and those cabinet officers who opposed restraint.[84] The CEA view in late 1978 appears to have been that the rate of unemployment had been brought down too fast and had thus created excess demand, though CEA did not consider inflation out of control. They thought that administration stimulus policy plus some micro decisions, such as the increase in the minimum wage, might have added a point or two to the inflation rate.[85]

In January, 1979, President Carter submitted a budget for fiscal year 1980 of $532 billion in spending and $503 billion in revenue. The projected $29 billion deficit was approximately the same figure he had publicly set the previous November in announcing the new antiinflation campaign. The domestic budget, including grants to state and local governments, fell in real terms and he recommended reductions of $600 million in medicare and social security. Defense spending was projected to grow 3 percent in real terms.[86]

The January, 1979, budget predicted economic growth of 3.2 percent, inflation of 6.3 percent and unemployment of 6.2 percent. A year later, in January, 1980, the forecast for the year ahead was much darker, with projections of 1 percent economic growth, 10.4 percent inflation and 7.5 percent unemployment. The darkened projections were responses to the shocks of 1979—the sudden, unexpected dip in productivity, the growth in unemployment and, above all, the unanticipated inflation that came with the Iranian revolution, the cutoff of Iranian oil to the West and the OPEC pricing decisions that raised inflation levels by at least three percentage points in 1979.[87]

The intentions behind the restrained 1979 budget were for a slight slowdown of economic recovery. The *Economic Report of the President* implied that recovery may have come too fast and admitted that unemployment could not get lower than 6 percent without stimulating inflation. In late 1978 and 1979, Carter's economic advisers also thought that the Federal Reserve Board, under Chairman William Miller, was too easy in its money policies, and in December and January Blumenthal and Schultze gave background press interviews designed to get Miller to tighten up. But the president stopped the campaign with a critical note to Schultze, for despite his fiscal conservatism he did not like high interest rates.[88]

At this time the CEA did not see an upsurge in core inflation but were still hoping that the guidelines program would keep wage increases within bounds. The OPEC price shock, however, blew the guidelines sky high. Organized labor was no longer interested because its members were absorbing the oil price hikes through increased inflation.[89]

In mid-1979 the CEA suggested in its reports that the oil shock might precipitate not a "natural" recession but one caused specifically by the inflation increase oil prices had generated. It did not seem appropriate to combat OPEC inflation by forcing a recession, and in fact, administration economists never considered the possibility. Thus the administration's implicit decision was to rely on incomes policy through the wage and price guidelines rather than forcing a recession to reduce inflation. No one was prepared to argue that the unemployment rate should go up.[90] The Iranian revolution and OPEC decision brought a 120 percent increase in oil prices and set in motion a chain of events which required the administration to react to crisis through damage control. Had it not been for OPEC, economists speculated, the 1979 inflation rate might have been contained at 8 or 9 percent instead of 12 or 13 percent. Administration policy makers did not regard this OPEC-induced inflation as a consequence of flawed economic policies.[91]

Other forces which exacerbated inflation included a decline in productivity that denied the possibility of economic growth as a way of keeping ahead of inflation. Oil imports had not been reduced because the president and Congress failed to agree on pricing policies for oil as part of the overall energy program. In mid-1979 the president used his authority to begin a phased decontrol of oil prices, and this contributed to the inflation rate. Energy policy and the macroeconomic policy directed toward inflation did not appear to be coordinated.[92] Furthermore, spending for entitlement programs soared in 1979 because the programs were indexed to inflation. Because the president had pledged a 3 percent increase beyond inflation, defense budgets also increased.[93]

Paul Volker was appointed chairman of the Federal Reserve Board in the early Fall of 1979, after William Miller moved to the Treasury Department, in order to calm the reaction of New York financial markets to Miller's departure. A conservative was put at the Fed to reassure the financial world.[94] In October and early November, 1979, Chairman Volker chose a monetarist strategy of dealing with inflation by limiting the supply of money rather than directly setting interest rates. Schultze opposed Volker's strategy, preferring a raise in interest rates. He believed that once set monetary targets were hard to change because credibility depended upon sticking with the goals.[95]

The fiscal 1981 budget introduced in January, 1980, was printed in green on white, the Carter reelection campaign colors, signifying that it was an election year budget. It contained many good things for Democratic constituencies. Income security programs and proposals for selective increases in health, education, employment and urban development programs were projected to grow by 11.3 percent in the coming year. But the principle of fiscal conservatism was also emphasized. Total federal spending would rise by 9.3 percent in fiscal 1981, the predicted inflation rate. Expenditures were projected to be $615 billion and revenues $600 billion for a deficit of only $15 billion in contrast to the $29 billion deficit originally projected for fiscal 1980. This was to be possible because taxes were not to be cut. Inflation would drive up income tax payments and additional revenue would come from increased social security taxes and the windfall profits tax on oil companies. Administration officials saw the budget as "restrained." They had resisted the temptation to reduce taxes in order to stave off a possible recession. In addition, Carter kept his pledge to increase defense spending 3 percent beyond inflation with proposals totaling 12 percent.[96]

At the same time, Carter revised his fiscal 1980 budget to reflect later forecasts. The revision projected a $40 billion dollar deficit for fiscal 1980 instead of the original projection of $29 billion.[97]

Neither of these budgets inspired the confidence of the financial community. Bond prices fell and interest rates rose, with the prime rate hitting almost 20 percent. Inflation reached 17 percent. Herbert Stein's interpretation of the Wall Street reaction is that the budget was not convincing as an antiinflation program. The incomes policy seemed to be on the ropes, productivity was not going to improve in the short run, the expenses for entitlement programs were soaring and defense estimates were unrealistic.[98]

It is clear that Carter and his advisers had sought a "steady as you go" economic policy for fiscal 1980, keeping at bay the specters of inflation and unemployment with a budget that was neither too expansionary nor too austere. Carter was not happy when his economists told him in late 1979 that no major dramatic moves were available to him in dealing with the shocks received by the economy.[99] The revised 1980 budget and the fiscal 1981 plans reflected the logic of a Democratic president who leaned toward fiscal restraint but who was not, in the final analysis, a conservative prepared to launch a period of austerity.

However, the administration immediately recognized that the financial community did not accept its estimates and that adjustments would thus have to be made in the fiscal 1981 budget. The revised projection of the fiscal 1980 deficit, the inflation rate and the president's announcement of increases in defense budgets after the Soviets invaded Afghanistan were all seen by Wall Street as foreboding signs for the economy. One presidential adviser concluded, after the fact, that national financial markets direct a government's economic policy as much as they are led by that policy. Private investors reveal their confidence in the president's economic course through their actions. A Democratic president who pursues even modest stimulative policies in inflationary times cannot sustain such policies if the market undercuts them by reacting negatively. Carter and his advisers decided that a new, more restrained budget for fiscal 1981 would have to be prepared. In March, White House officials began a lengthy set of negotiations with congressional leaders, and by the end of that month reductions of $3 billion in the 1980 budget and $17 billion in the 1981 budget were announced.[100]

Schultze detected a psychological mistake in the preparation of the 1981 budget in that insufficient attention was paid to the budget getting out of hand in the face of inflation. The administration may have then overreacted but, on balance, he believed the process of congressional bargaining that reduced the budget to have been a good one. In his view, the entire exercise was primarily one of "damage limitation" in which the American government did better than its European counterparts in keeping the rate of inflation down.[101] Some optimism seems to have seeped into the White House at the time, as Carter remembers Schultze and Blumenthal telling him in March and April that the inflation rate would be down to 5 or 6 percent by October.[102]

President Carter's interpretation of the events of March, 1980, and subsequent developments was that he and his aides had negotiated a balanced budget for fiscal 1981 which he announced on March 31. He saw this action as an extension of his persistent efforts to balance the budget and impose fiscal restraint. As part of the agreement he had promised congressional leaders to impose a fee on oil imports as a revenue measure, a politically unpopular commitment. However, he was disappointed with the ultimate congressional response to the balanced budget goal. For example, in June Congress overrode Carter's veto of a vote overturning the oil import fee. Carter felt that many congressional Democrats had experienced a failure of nerve under pressure from organized groups with stakes in federal programs.[103]

According to Schultze the one big mistake, made in the March negotiations, was the decision to reduce consumer buying by invoking selected controls on credit through the Credit Control Act. Paul Volker, who participated in all the meetings with Congress, was opposed to the action and Schultze was lukewarm. This decision produced the steepest GNP decline in any quarter in American history. The American people stopped using credit to an extraordinary extent. The "quickie recession" that resulted, Schultze determined, did not help bring the economy into balance. And although this recession occurred in the second quarter of 1980, its full effects did not become apparent until the next quarter, right before the election.[104]

President Carter was, in part, responsible for the onset of the recession, aside from the action on credit controls, because of his strong drive for a balanced budget. While Edward Kennedy and Ronald Reagan were calling for tax cuts to prevent recession, Carter was pushing Congress hard on the issue of a balanced budget. David Calleo believes this to have been undue optimism on the president's part because the recession, along with falling revenues and the rising cost of indexed entitlement programs, would have unbalanced the budget no matter what Congress did. And, of course, energy prices were rising in response to administration policy.[105] Carter's economic advisers wanted him to insert a contingency possibility of a tax cut for business in the midyear projection of the budget that would go to Congress. The president, overruling all his advisers, refused to consider tax cuts or any other fiscal action because of the fact and fear of inflation. His commitment to fiscal soundness caused him to fight a conservative, non-constituency-oriented Fall presidential reelection campaign, in Schultze's judgment.[106]

The tax cuts for business had been discussed in the administration since 1979 as a means for providing additional investment and thus attacking the productivity problem. Administration economists feared, however, that implementing tax incentives for business would tempt Congress to pass a large, inflationary tax cut for individuals. In the late Summer of 1980 the president did address the issue of productivity by proposing that the next Congress enact a tax package of investment incentives, an action all administration economists supported.[107]

In late October, just after the end of the 1980 fiscal year and a week before the presidential election, the final figures for the 1980 fiscal year were announced. Expenditures were $579 billion, an increase of $47 billion over original estimates, and the deficit was $59 billion, about twice the $29 billion projected figure. Ronald Reagan attacked the figures as evidence of economic mismanagement. The restrained budget of 1980, upon which Carter had used political capital and incurred the anger of Democratic groups, did not bear political fruit for him.[108]

By 1980 there seemed to be no way for Carter to improve his situation. His economic advisers may have been correct when they told him in late 1979 that nothing dramatic could be done. He could not urge the Federal Reserve Board to clamp down tightly with monetary restraint because the result would be high interest rates, recession and unemployment. Drastic fiscal restraint would have required deep cuts in social programs, and much of the Democratic party, in and out of Congress, would have opposed such initiatives. Tax cuts to stimulate employment would have risked the increase of inflation.[109] Ronald Reagan addressed the same problems differently in 1981 but he was not a Democratic president who had, by the logic of his political coalition, to combat inflation without inducing recession. The Carter administration struggled with the problem for four years and speculated that without the OPEC oil price increases of 1979 they would have won the battle.[110] Regardless of what might have been, the administration was surely blamed at the polls for inflation and the impending recession.

From the first day of his administration, Jimmy Carter believed that inflation was the country's most serious economic problem. Despite this insight, which he arrived at ahead of his advisers, inflation was one of the principal causes of his defeat in 1980. What stood between the president's insight and its successful implementation in policy?

The economic policies he was expected to pursue as a Democratic president were incompatible with the problems he faced. Presidents Kennedy and Johnson were able successfully to introduce policies to stimulate the economy without inflation because the Eisenhower administration's fear of inflation had created great slack in the economy. Carter faced the economic legacy of the Vietnam War and the failure of the Nixon and Ford administrations to repeat the Eisenhower performance. He also had to face OPEC. But his political constituency, in Congress and the country, did not appreciate these new conditions. Democratic expectations for economic policy were back in the 1960s.

The economists who advised President Carter were intellectually rooted in the 1960s experience of stimulating the economy, especially with the successful tax cut of 1964. As good Keynesians, they knew that too much expansion too fast would be inflationary. They also knew the tools for direct control of inflation, such as guidelines and wage and price controls, to be deficient. But they believed that the pace of recovery could be controlled, through fiscal policy, to achieve recovery without inflation. They did not fully realize that they faced two problems too powerful for the available fiscal tools. The first was OPEC. The second was the combination of strong institutional and psychological forces in the society that fed inflationary expectations. Patterns of collective bargaining, popular anxiety about the future effects of inflation, even though people were enjoying current prosperity, and the voracious demands of interest groups on government were all too strong in the Carter years for the theories of liberal economists.[111] The only instrument available to bring down soaring inflation was a major recession, a possibility not even considered, much less rejected. Fine tuning through fiscal policy on the pattern of the 1960s was weak medicine.

A few strong fiscal conservatives, such as Lance and Blumenthal, might have favored challenging the Democratic coalition with restrained economic policies. Even the president seemed, at times, to be of this persuasion. Others, such as the vice-president and Secretaries Marshall and Harris, urged expansionary policies. But neither of these groups was dominant. Rather, the president stood with the centrists, principally Schultze and Eizenstat, who believed that it was possible to combine careful expansionary economic policies, which could be qualified to control inflation, with political appeals to the Democratic groups to restrain their demands. Administration economic and political strategies were not in conflict but instead reinforced each other. The conflicts emerged when it became apparent that many Democratic groups did not want to play by the administration's rules. They had higher expectations of a Democratic president, and when Carter did not meet their expectations Senator Kennedy was happy to do so.

What appeared to be a policy of zigzag in both microeconomic and macroeconomic affairs was actually a coherent strategy of balancing opposites. This meant splitting the difference in decisions of micro policy between group demands and the requirements of economic sense. It meant weaving back and forth in macro policy between expansionary and restraining actions. The difficulty was not absence of coherence, but absence of a constituency behind the policy. As the four years progressed, political camps became increasingly polarized and the president was caught between the Kennedy Democratic challenge and the Republicans smelling blood. Carter's economists could not give him a policy strategy for the inflation problem that he could pursue as a Democratic president. The centrist political strategy did not work, either with Democratic interest groups or with diffuse publics.

Carter's centrist advisers contend that had it not been for OPEC II in 1979 the policy of balancing opposites might have worked, both economically and politically. Rates of inflation might have stayed at 8 or 9 percent through 1980 and the prosperity that had come with recovery, after a mild recession, would have been undeniable.[112] In 1978 when a modest antiinflation program was announced with Alfred Kahn's appointment, administration economists believed that a middle way was possible. They hoped to impose fiscal restraint without drastic and dramatic budget cutting and thought it possible to avoid recession without incurring undue inflation. In short, their policy insights informed their political strategy. But OPEC II torpedoed both centrist policy and politics. In his last year, the president openly proclaimed himself to be the fiscal conservative he had been all along, but it was too late to stop the inflation. And his actions, to balance the budget, increase oil prices, tax oil imports and refuse to cut taxes, all hurt him politically as the economy began to go into a tailspin.

There was a great need for tax policies that would stimulate business investment and increase lagging productivity. But Carter missed his opportunity by his Populist approach to tax reform. In 1979 and 1980, when his economic advisers began to see the need for a different kind of tax policy, the president could not have gotten Congress to enact selective taxes for business without a general, and inflationary, tax cut. This issue was left for the next president.

Critics complained, after the fact, that administration energy policies were not well coordinated with macroeconomic policies.[113] Indeed, actions required by energy policy in 1979 and 1980 increased inflation. But such criticism assumes that presidents are seers. No one could foresee when Congress would decide to pass the president's energy program. Nor could it be predicted that success on that score would coincide with OPEC II. Carter wanted his energy policy and pushed ahead regardless of the political consequences.

Carter did not like the alternatives he received from his economists because, although acute in the diagnosis of dilemmas, they prescribed little in the way of decisive action beyond muddling through.[114] He was skeptical of economists, because, he said, they disagreed among themselves and had little to tell him.[115] Some of his closest advisers thought his distrust came from not understanding macroeconomics well and not finding that way of thinking congenial. These two explanations are compatible. He might have been more attentive if the payoff in the investment had been clearer.

Keynesian economic theory and analysis was found wanting in a period of simultaneous inflation and recession. Prescriptions for economic policy, by Schultze and other economists, were so hedged with qualifications and uncertainties that the engineer president, who liked to get his teeth into problems and solve them, was deeply dissatisfied with the advice he received. Yet he followed the advice. Unlike his successor, he was not inspired by a higher dogma that would permit him to disregard conventional economic analysis. Carter had no theory but he did have goals. He wished to limit inflation without recession. He relied on his experts to tell him how to do this and as they walked a narrow path, he walked with them. It was only at the very end, when his advisers were urging him to stimulate the economy in hopes of averting a recession, that he consulted his own values and refused.

5
FOREIGN POLICY MAKING

The two broad foreign policy perspectives Jimmy Carter brought to his presidency were a determination to attack and resolve a number of difficult and outstanding problems, such as strategic arms limitation, a Panama Canal treaty and a Middle Eastern settlement, and an allegiance to an idealistic, "Wilsonian" world view which valued peace and human rights. The impulse to tackle the most intractable problems—which motivated his domestic policy initiatives as well—inclined him toward comprehensive approaches that would manifest the Carter stamp. In his memoir, *Keeping Faith,* he does not discuss strategic foreign policy objectives in terms of a theory of the enduring relations among nations but rather introduces specific problems to be solved.

Cyrus Vance writes that when negotiating a treaty with Panama or seeking stability in the Middle East, "Carter did what he thought American values and interests demanded, even though he was keenly aware of the political risks." Vance mentions this willingness to take political chances when the cause was just also in regard to South Africa: "President Carter was determined that we might do what was in our long term national interest and not what was politically expedient or good for his ratings in the public opinion polls."[1] Carter was intrigued by and moved to solve the big problems, and such problem solving required neither a philosophical framework nor any particular set of priorities.

Nonetheless, Carter also appears to have brought a coherent world view about foreign policy into the presidency, though one too loosely joined to be called a philosophy and too normative to be called a strategy. It was a set of predispositions and values that might be called "Wilsonian" in the sense that peace, human rights, self-determination and cooperation were paramount. These values were articulated in his book *Why Not the Best?*

The time for American intervention in all the problems of the world is over. But we cannot retreat into isolationism. Ties of friendship and cooperation with our friends and neighbors must be strengthened. Our common interests must be understood and pursued. . . .

Our ultimate goal should be the elimination of nuclear weapon capability among all nations. In the meantime, simple, careful and firm proposals to implement this mutual arms reduction should be pursued as a prime national purpose in all our negotiations with nuclear powers—present or potential.[2]

In *Keeping Faith* Carter argues that American foreign policy should be based on the democratic idealism of Jefferson and Wilson. Idealism, he contends, is more practical than realism and provides the strongest basis for American power and influence in the world. He wanted human rights to be "a central theme for American foreign policy" because "it was time for us to capture the imagination of the world again. As President I hoped and believed that the expansion of human rights might be the wave of the future throughout the world."[3] This democratic idealism, his lieutenants agreed, was deeply rooted in Carter. According to Zbigniew Brzezinski, Carter's personal philosophy was the point of departure for his foreign policy, and the central theme was a religious impulse to make the world more human. He had an "intense and instinctive desire to go down in history as the peacemaker," and though he might agree with his national security adviser that he needed to be Truman before he could be Wilson, "emotionally he thirsted for the Wilsonian mantle." Consequently, although Carter was tough, "reliance on force was not instinctive with him."[4]

Another adviser remembered, "It's part of the President's background, his evangelism, that he did believe when he came to office that he could make the lions lie down with the lamb, that you could sit down and reason with people and get them to do what they ought to do and that you could pursue six or eight noble objectives all at once. And it was only fairly late in the day that he would subordinate one to another."[5] Another senior aide characterized Carter as "fundamentally the Christian warrior" and a "Wilsonian" who was much closer to Vance than to Brzezinski in his world view. And he was "terribly innocent and naive," with a "do good view of the world."[6]

In the first few weeks of the Carter presidency a set of foreign policy goals was developed that were, to some degree, extensions of Carter's values but incorporated as well the work of the Trilateral Commission, which Brzezinski had directed while Carter and Vance were members. But the blend of Carter's own values with Trilateral Commission themes as a basis for the new administration's foreign policy must first be understood in terms of the previous period of foreign policy making and the reaction against the Henry Kissinger era.

For two years before his election Carter campaigned against the excessive assertion of American governmental power, whether in Vietnam or later in the Watergate and CIA scandals. He devoted particular criticism to secrecy in foreign policy, singling out the Nixon administration's reputed efforts to undermine the government of Chile and then the Ford administration's attempts to intervene militarily in Angola. Carter attributed government by secrecy to the influence of Henry Kissinger and promised that his administration would carry on open diplomacy and government and would emphasize the moral values of human rights and democracy in its dealings with other nations. It was logical for such appeals to deemphasize the Cold War rivalry with the Soviet Union and call for greater United States attention to Third World nations. Such appeals were also anti-Washington and anti-power politics in general. Carter charged that the United States had become a status quo power concerned primarily with its position in a series of bargaining arrangements with the Soviet Union. It should, in contrast, seek to be a revolutionary force for good in the world beyond the confines of power politics. It is interesting in this regard that Carter was critical of SALT I for not doing enough to reduce arms on either side. He felt that the achievement of some stability in United States-Soviet relations had caused the Americans to ignore other outstanding world problems, such as human rights and nuclear proliferation.[7] This articulation of the need for a new framework that downplayed the rivalry between the two superpowers was consistent with Carter's interest in tackling hard, unresolved problems like the Arab-Israeli conflict and the Panama Canal treaty.

ORGANIZATION OF FOREIGN POLICY ADVISERS

During the 1979 campaign Carter had expressed his opposition to the highly centralized system of decision making in the Nixon White House; he was especially critical that Henry Kissinger, when assistant to the president for national security, had appeared to be directing the departments. This view was in line with his often expressed belief that the president was to make decisions which the departments would then implement. But Carter in no way indicated that he intended to delegate the formation of foreign policy to department heads. "I knew full well that Carter would not wish me to be another Kissinger," writes Brzezinski. "At the same time, I also felt confident that he would not let Vance become another Dulles. He wanted to be the decision maker, and even more important, to be perceived as one."[8]

Just before the inauguration Carter charged Brzezinski with developing a National Security Council (NSC) organization. Adhering to the president-elect's injunction that there be no "Lone Ranger" in the administration, Brzezinski and his deputy David Aaron designed a plan for seven NSC committees, four of which would be chaired by department secretaries and three by the assistant for national security—the latter being areas such as arms controls, intelligence and crisis management that cut across departments. Carter rejected the plan, saying that there were "too many committees" and asking for "a simple, cleaner structure." He was trying to reduce the number of government agencies and the size of the White House bureaucracy. The president and Brzezinski then developed a plan for two committees. A Policy Review Committee (PRC) for broad issues was to be chaired by the appropriate secretary depending upon the topic for discussion. It was assumed that the secretary of state would preside most of the time. The Special Coordination Committee (SCC), to be chaired by Brzezinski, would have responsibility for arms control, intelligence and crisis management. Carter was anxious for cabinet officers to attend committee meetings and, perhaps in consequence, gave Brzezinski cabinet status. The president-elect's idea was to get cabinet members accustomed to working as teams in committees.

At a preinaugural cabinet meeting on St. Simon's Island, Carter surprised Brzezinski, and certainly Cyrus Vance and Harold Brown, the secretaries of state and defense designate, by announcing that he and Brzezinski had worked out a new NSC system, which he then outlined in brief form. Since it was clear that he had helped to design it, no one challenged it. Brzezinski returned to Washington and drafted more specific plans including the procedures the committees would use. These were cast as a presidential directive and signed by Carter on the eve of his inauguration, without being seen by Vance and Brown. After they received copies Vance complained to Brzezinski that he had not been consulted and, later, he objected to the assignment of SALT, which he considered the province of the secretary of state, to the SCC. Brzezinski countered that the secretary of defense's claim to SALT was as great. When Vance also laid claim to crisis management, Brzezinski answered that the president would manage crises and that he, Brzezinski, was only a surrogate.[9]

It seems clear that Carter's objective was to design a highly collegial system with himself at the center of separate streams of advice. We cannot know whether Brzezinski's thoughts about how he might be influential in the system were apparent to Carter. Brzezinski perceived at the time that Carter wanted a foreign policy-making system "that would be simple and responsive to his personal control," and he concurred, since he felt "that this would permit the NSC to play the central role." Knowing that Carter intended to be the decision maker, Brzezinski records that he sought "an institutional arrangement whereby I could help to shape those decisions," adding, "I was determined to maintain an active and personal dialogue with the President on foreign policy issues because only then could I assert my own authority in a manner consistent with his views."[10] The two thoughts here are the assistant's hopes that proximity will permit him to influence the president and his awareness that his authority in the administration must reflect the president's views. This is something more than the policy coordinator who sees his role as that of policy analyst, neutral arbiter, or "custodian" of the president's options. The custodian and advocate roles are different.[11]

In an October, 1976, memorandum to Carter on policy and organization Cyrus Vance asserted the preeminence of the State Department in national security policy making because it was important that military instruments be viewed as the means, rather than ends, of foreign policy. But, he added, his department's authority could not be maintained without special supporting machinery in the White House, since the Defense Department had a vast and powerful domestic constituency which the Department of State lacked completely, a situation that could not be changed. Therefore, Vance argued, a strong national security adviser with an NSC structure under his chairmanship and under the wing of the president was essential for State Department primacy. For such a system to work, Vance continued, cooperation must be close between the secretaries of state and defense and the national security adviser. It was important that the senior officials in the Department of State be able to operate as a team, both within the department and, with the help of the NSC staff, throughout the administration.[12]

In Vance's mind then, as evidently in Carter's, the key to the smooth operation of such a tightly coupled, collegial system was the willingness and ability of the principals to work together in harmony. Carter had asked Vance in November if he objected to the appointment of Brzezinski to the White House post and Vance had said that he thought they could work well together. He set the conditions that he, Vance, would be the administration's spokesman on foreign policy and that he must be able to present his views to the president, without filtering, before decisions were made. Carter agreed with these conditions. Vance also told Carter that it was appropriate for Brzezinski to give independent policy advice; in fact, the president should seek a variety of views.[13]

The NSC apparatus Carter and Brzezinski set up eventually included the weekly foreign policy adviser breakfasts which became Carter's most preferred working forum. This group demonstrated the collegiality Carter so valued, Carter himself set the agenda with his questions, and the group could actually make decisions that would stick—three themes vital to the NSC structure in general. The NSC's decision-making system was to be highly centralized, with the president and his cabinet level advisers engaged in day-to-day debate. Collegiality would be the rule, yet Carter intended to make the final decisions. "There have been presidents in the past . . . that let their Secretaries of State make foreign policy. I don't," he remarked in October, 1980.[14] But Carter enjoyed the debates and wanted full discussion before making decisions. He encouraged frankness, was not upset by disagreement and did not seek to be shielded from hard facts. His advisers felt that he would often permit debate to go on too long and, as Vance put it, would "absorb every detail and nuance before making a decision." His tendency to immerse himself deeply in the subject before making decisions at times caused him to become too involved in a continuing issue after a decision had been made. According to Brzezinski, "He would at times overrefine his approach and occasionally alter it by simply sticking with it too long. At times, I thought he was like a sculptor who did not know when to throw away his chisel."[15]

Senior officials had many opportunities to present their views to the president in this NSC system—at cabinet meetings, full NSC meetings, NSC committee meetings, the weekly foreign policy breakfast and one private hour each week with the president for Mondale, Vance and Brown. There was always freedom to write a personal note to Carter as well, and Vance sent him one each night. Officials could record their views in the frequent Policy Review Committee and Special Coordination Committee meetings, and the president received verbatim minutes of those meetings so that he might make judgments independent of interdepartmental recommendations.[16]

Carter appears to have been satisfied with these arrangements. In his memoirs he writes that, understanding the inherent differences between the NSC staff and the State Department, he "attempted to tap the strongest elements in each as changing circumstances demanded." He saw himself as the active agent, picking and choosing between advice from two predictable entities. In Carter's perspective Brzezinski and the NSC staff were best suited for the production of new ideas and the critical analysis of old ones. They were free of bureaucratic baggage and he encouraged them to present new ideas, even though many had to be rejected as impractical. The State Department, on the contrary, was a repository of institutional memory which, though not in the least innovative, could test the workability of new ideas. Brzezinski was provocative; Vance, with his intelligence, experience and soundness, reflected the virtues of his department. Carter clearly felt well served by his advisers and the advisory structure: "The different strengths of Zbig and Cy matched the role they played, and also permitted the natural competition between the two organizations to stay alive. I appreciated those differences. In making the final decisions on foreign policy, I needed to weigh as many points of view as possible. When Brzezinski and Vance were joined by Fritz Mondale and Harold Brown, plus others as required to address a particular issue, they comprised a good team."[17]

Carter's retrospective assessment of Brzezinski was couched solely in terms of his value as a personal adviser, with no mention of any other governmental role that the assistant for national security might play. Carter knew of Brzezinski's "exuberance" before he appointed him to office and was warned that he might not be "deferential" to a secretary of state. But, he says, "the final decisions on basic foreign policy would be made by me in the Oval Office and not in the State Department." He describes Brzezinski as a companion, conversationalist and tutor who brimmed over with interesting ideas. Carter also describes Vance as an adviser but gives him the additional institutional role of diplomat and the State Department that of implementer of foreign policy.[18] Brzezinski's intellectual qualities appear to have especially attracted Carter. William Quandt, the National Security Council Middle East expert, remembered: "If Vance was the steady, patient negotiator, Brzezinski was the theoretician and manipulator. He operated on two distinct levels. More than anyone else in Carter's entourage, he had a talent for providing a general frame of reference for policy debates. Formulations came easy to him, and Carter found this useful in integrating all the discrete pieces of information that flowed in his direction."[19]

Others close to Carter report that he was satisfied with the advisory and decision structure throughout his time as president. Hamilton Jordan recalls that Carter saw no conflict between the Vance and Brzezinski roles. Brzezinski would be the idea man, Vance the diplomat and Carter the decision maker. Another senior adviser observed that Carter enjoyed Brzezinski as a source of ideas, had the usual presidential view of the State Department as tradition bound, and ultimately aimed to set his own foreign policy agenda. Brzezinski was better informed than anyone Carter knew, said yet another adviser, but lacked Vance's judgment. The important point is that Carter saw his own decisions as the key element of foreign policy making. Brzezinski records that because Carter found contradictory advice from those on the inside of government useful, he underestimated the political damage of press reports about disagreement. And because Carter dominated the process "he did not feel touched by the disagreement."[20]

The president's two principal advisers, however, had quite different views of how the decision-making system should work. Vance had made clear in his October, 1976, memorandum to the president-elect that the principal role of the NSC and the assistant for national security was to support the secretary of state and the diplomatic point of view in the councils of government. Vance saw the State Department as *the* agency for execution of presidential policy.

[I wanted] to bring the Foreign Service more fully into the process of developing and implementing policy. I believed deeply in the necessity of "institutionalizing" foreign policy. To be enduring, our policies have to be rooted in the institution charged with implementing them. However skilled, a diplomacy that depends on the talents of a single individual is bound to be ephemeral. The United States needs a firm, consistent foreign policy, understood and supported by its professionals, if we are ever to bridge the gap that exists between the formulators of policy at the political level and the professional executors of that policy in the Foreign Service.[21]

Vance was expressing a widely held view among foreign policy "professionals" that coherence, consistency and continuity of foreign policy are best achieved if the president uses the Department of State as the principal agency for both formulating and implementing presidential policy. In this view policy and operations are inevitably joined. The United States government speaks with one voice—the State Department being the president's agent in this regard—and the NSC is a coordinating mechanism for both policy making and implementation. The assistant to the president for national security, in this view, is properly a "custodian," the guardian of free discussion, rather than an "advocate."[22]

It is perfectly clear that Brzezinski did not share this view. He thought it possible to pursue the "custodian" and "advocate" roles in his position, and he did so. He also, on occasion, consciously cultivated the secretary of defense's support against the secretary of state.[23] Initially, though, he eschewed the advocate role, going so far as to say at the press conference announcing his appointment that he saw his job not as a policy-making position but as one of helping the president facilitate decision making.[24] Still, from the beginning he wished to be near the president in order to influence policy choices. "The issues were too important for me to be passive," he said.[25]

Brzezinski acted as a broker of agreement much of the time, holding weekly luncheons with Vance and Brown to settle issues that might be taken to the president in agreement. He also used his NSC authority to facilitate decisions on which there was basic agreement, such as human rights, the Panama Canal treaties, the SALT talks, and the Middle East negotiations. But he reports that he was an advocate on key issues, particularly on using the normalization of relations with China as a lever against the USSR, on checking Soviet military intrusion into the Horn of Africa, on the need for buildup of strategic weapons and a Rapid Deployment Force and on the necessity of encouraging the Shah of Iran to retain his throne by military force if necessary.[26] Brzezinski reported three periods in his relationship with Carter. For the first six months of the administration he acted as an occasional tutor, with Carter referring to him as his "eyes and ears on the world." The two of them sometimes had informed in-depth discussions on the historical and geographical background of current crises. The second period, which lasted until mid-1979, was one of balance and parity with Vance, in which Carter actually was closer to Vance than to Brzezinski in policy choices. The third period marked the decline of Vance and his ideas and the ascendancy of Brzezinski and coincided with the time of troubles in which Brzezinski's predictions about the difficulties of dealing with the Soviet Union appeared valid to Carter.[27] Above all, Brzezinski felt that the president never questioned his personal loyalty and would thereby protect him against all opposition. Carter confirmed such a strong bond, remembering that Brzezinski "didn't have to protect his turf" for fear Vance or Brown would come between the president and his assistant for national security.[28]

It seems clear that Carter did not accept Vance's thesis that the State Department should be the principal agency for policy formulation. He did see it as the agency for policy implementation, a view he held of all the cabinet departments. The White House was to stay out of implementation. The high priority that Carter gave to presidential decisions—and his willingness to make them in a collegial setting of advisers with different views—meant that no single subordinate would have preeminence. The secretary of state was not to be first among equals; the State Department had a valuable institutional perspective but a partial one.[29]

EARLY POLICY DIRECTIONS

During the 1976 campaign Carter asked both Vance and Brzezinski to formulate specific goals and priorities for a Carter administration foreign policy. The ideas the two advanced at that time were very similar, reflecting Trilateral Commission themes. Vance's memorandum began with the idea that the United States should stay strong in relation to the Soviet Union, defend vital American interests but work to reduce tensions. American-Soviet relationships should not be permitted to dominate foreign policy. Other goals included good relations between the industrialized and developing nations, human rights, and partnership between the new administration, the Congress and the people in the making of foreign policy.[30]

Brzezinski's memo, written with Henry Owen and Richard Gardner, was used as a basis for campaign speeches, according to Brzezinski, and after the election Carter asked him to articulate administration objectives in a more formal memorandum. Brzezinski, by then appointed assistant to the president for national security affairs, set NSC staff members Samuel Huntington, a Harvard political scientist, and William Odom, an army officer and former Brzezinski student, to work on what became a forty-page memo setting out ten major objectives, all to be achieved in four years. Carter liked the memorandum and asked Brzezinski to show it to Mondale and Vance. Copies were later given to Secretary of Defense Harold Brown and CIA Director Stansfield Turner. The president regarded the document as the basis for administration foreign policy.[31] Only a few differences in emphasis and tone distinguished Vance's October paper from the NSC staff's ten objectives. The staff paper objectives included engaging Western Europe and Japan in close political and economic relationships with the United States, the creation of a worldwide web of bilateral political and economic relations with key developing nations, the development of more accommodating North-South relations among nations, a push for arms control negotiations with the Soviet Union aimed toward extensive arms reductions, normalization of United States-China relations, obtaining a comprehensive Middle East settlement, efforts to move Southern Africa toward biracial democracy, restrictions on the level of global armaments, enhancement of human rights around the world and maintenance of a defense posture capable of deterring the Soviet Union on both strategic and conventional levels, which would require modernization of United States defense readiness.[32]

Vance and Brzezinski differed on certain specifics. Vance was more cautious about the possibility of a Middle Eastern settlement under the aegis of the United States and advised Carter to feel his way slowly through diplomatic channels. He took the same view toward normalization of relations with China, suggesting that the ground be carefully prepared through diplomacy. He favored negotiating on SALT II on the basis of the agreement President Ford and Leonid Brezhnev had reached at Vladivostok in 1974, with the unresolved questions being saved for SALT III. Vance called for studies of American military preparedness and suggested that combat readiness might be a problem, though he did not call for a defense buildup. His estimates of the prospects for agreement between the United States and the USSR were cautiously optimistic; the Soviets, he observed, had an aging leadership, were plagued by bad harvests and low economic growth and were desirous of pursuing detente and the SALT talks.[33]

These early discussions provide several clues as to how Carter would approach foreign policy. His optimistic hopes for good relations with the Soviets coincided with Vance's. After a long post-election meeting with Carter in Plains, Vance felt that the two basically agreed on the main issues facing the new government. However, Carter made clear that he hoped any SALT II agreement would include deep cuts in nuclear arsenals. Carter always preferred a "bold, comprehensive" approach to any problem rather than a more "incremental building on past agreements," Vance observed, and he was thus more likely to call for daring departures in contrast to Vance's caution.[34] However, Carter's rhetoric, as seen in his 1977 speeches, was perhaps closer to Vance's views about international politics than to Brzezinski's in the sense that the Soviets were depicted as cooperative and the quest for global community was the central theme. As his administration began, Carter was clearly relying on his two principal advisers, but the world view he brought to the presidency set his strongest commitments and identified him as his own man in setting policy objectives. The desire of the activist problem solver to attack hard and specific problems complemented the broad Wilsonian framework of hopes for peace and human rights.

After the election and before the inauguration Carter decided to move aggressively for a Middle Eastern settlement, seek final agreement with Panama about a treaty for the future of the canal, normalize relations with China and move quickly to conclude a SALT agreement.[35] And his chief advisers appear to have supported the president-elect's desire to seek "bold, comprehensive" solutions to these issues.

CARTER PLAYS TO HIS STRENGTHS

Foreign policy was Jimmy Carter's element. Most presidents find it absorbing, since the problems are important, crises must be faced, political constraints are perhaps fewer than in domestic policy (though surely increasing in recent years), and the possibility of political credit for achievement is greater than in domestic policy. But presidential styles of leadership in foreign policy vary. For Carter national security issues were a perfect way of playing to his strengths as a leader. Leaders try to play institutional roles in ways that maximize their strengths and avoid or downplay their weaknesses.[36] Carter's deliberate pursuit of hard problems to solve, often contrary to his advisers' prudent warnings, reflected his will and skill in facing and overcoming difficult obstacles. He thought it very important to confront issues like the Panama Canal treaties and the conflicts between Israel and the Arab nations, since these issues, if not addressed and resolved, would later erupt and damage American interests.[37] Attempts to normalize United States relations with China and to negotiate a SALT II treaty with the USSR were not guaranteed to be successful, but they provided scope for Carter's ambitions for peace. Two other issues he considered part of his political legacy were global human rights and the curbing of international nuclear proliferation. Carter was not required to push either of these hard issues but he did so without equivocation. He subsequently saw his major foreign policy achievements as the Panama Canal treaties, the Camp David agreement, establishment of diplomatic relations with China and SALT II. All played to Carter's inclinations and strengths for problem solving, his articulation of the national interest and his hope for political reward through policy achievement. However, the last factor seemed least important, since he realized, before and after the resolution of each problem, that the political damage might be greater than the credit because such issues were not inherently popular domestic matters.[38]

An analysis of these four stories will illustrate Carter's style as a foreign policy leader and diplomat and also reveal certain limitations inherent in that style. One may also see strengths and weaknesses in the organization of national security policy making.

A major failure was the inability of the Carter administration to save the Shah of Iran from revolution in 1979 or to establish good relations with the revolutionary regime that followed the shah. The initial debacle of the fall of the shah illustrates the operation of the national security decision system at its worst because of the breakdown of collegiality. This case provides a contrast to the four success stories and underscores the degree to which the strengths of the Carter system were also potential weaknesses.

PANAMA CANAL TREATY

This story, not recapitulated here in detail, illustrates Carter's ambition for achievement and thus serves as a point of departure for the more detailed case studies that follow. One variety of conventional political wisdom would have had Carter delay the issue of the canal, which was sure to be unpopular with Americans, until a SALT agreement, which would be popular, could be concluded. Then a president riding high with a popular success would have political capital with which to attack the messy Panama treaty issue. In rebuttal Carter points out that the canal issue was ripe for resolution and SALT was not. Soviet leaders rejected the alternative SALT proposals that Secretary Vance took to Moscow in early 1977 and therefore dampened Carter's hopes of having both Panama and SALT agreements in his first year in office. He did not think in terms of emphasizing one over the other as a question of political strategy but pushed hard in both directions; Panama was responsive to his push and the Soviets were not.[39]

Carter's way of doing business was to capitalize on opportunities when they arose for fear the opportunity would not come back. Mrs. Carter attempted to persuade him to delay the canal issue until a second term but he refused, saying that if he did so for political reasons and was not re-elected, he would have fewer achievements to his credit.[40]

Carter and his advisers agreed even before the inauguration that the canal negotiations should be an immediate priority. If the United States did not successfully complete negotiations, which had been going on since the Johnson administration, the government of Panama might create conflict in the zone that would require drastic American action.[41] Both Vance and Brzezinski give Carter credit for tackling the issue, for although he was taking a political risk, the consequences of inaction, they believed, were worse.[42]

This was Carter's kind of issue. He saw the opportunity to break a deadlock and also do the morally right thing. He writes in his memoirs that he sought a treaty with Panama to correct an old injustice, to avert sabotage and to remove a wedge between the United States and all Latin American nations. He knew that Congress and the public would be opposed but believed that he could win their support by presenting the facts.[43] Brzezinski reports Carter's exhilaration at the signing of the treaty in Washington in September, 1977: "Carter clearly enjoyed his role as the political emancipator of a downtrodden people. For him, this occasion represented the ideal fusion of morality and politics: he was doing something good for peace, responding to the passionate desires of a small nation and yet helping the long range U.S. national interest."[44]

The administration's strong, intensive drive for Senate ratification of both treaty documents featured the president as persuader.[45] Carter's emotional response after the second treaty was ratified provides some clues to his handling of issues in which he had made a strong personal investment. He was "increasingly exasperated" over the time ratification was taking, he notes, and was "exhausted" and "exhilarated" when it was all over; it had been "one of the most onerous political ordeals of my life." At times discouragement made him wonder if the result would justify the political costs but "I decided that we simply could not afford to fail." Had he foreseen early in 1977 what a battle he would face in Congress, however, he would have been tempted to avoid the issue in his first term.[46] These thoughts suggest that Carter underestimated the difficulty of the task, something he often did in such cases. They also reveal that he relied heavily on homework, personal effort, will power and moral persuasion to carry the day. He had decided that the issue was important and he could not afford to fail. This is not the thinking of a politician who calculates the high probability of victory before he takes a leap.

EGYPT-ISRAEL MEDIATION

Carter writes that during the 1976 campaign and after the election most of his advisers urged him to stay out of Middle Eastern conflicts because the chances for success were slight. But his intuitions appear to have been similar to those about Panama: "I could see growing threats to the United States in the Middle East, and was willing to make another try, perhaps overly confident that I could now find answers that had eluded so many others."[47] Securing peace between Israel and the Arab nations required the resolution of such intractable issues as the Israeli occupation of the Egyptian Sinai, the political future of the Palestinian population in the West Bank area under Israeli rule, the occupation of the Golan Heights area which Israel had taken from Syria, the future of Jerusalem and guarantees for the security of Israel. In January and February of 1977 the new administration resolved to take the initiative for peace, an action both Vance and Brzezinski favored.[48] Carter and his advisers agreed that unless the president intervened personally it was unlikely that either Arab or Israeli leaders would be bold enough to take the necessary risks.[49]

The administration's initial policy was to work toward convening a conference of the contending nations at Geneva under United Nations auspices to be cochaired by the United States and the Soviet Union.[50] Little progress was achieved on this score with any of the parties.

In the first year Carter paid little attention to domestic political consideration in his pursuit of a comprehensive peace settlement. However, the search for comprehensiveness meant that the issue of a homeland for the Palestinians had to be addressed. Carter lost political capital with American Jewish groups during that year by stating publicly that something would have to be done for the Palestinians. When the Israeli government and the friends of Israel in both domestic political parties publicly criticized his statements, Carter shifted to quiet diplomacy. He also began to realize that a comprehensive peace agreement was not possible with the Arab states so divided and jealous of one another and the Palestinian issue so far from any possible resolution.[51] However, an altogether different line of development emerged as a result of the close personal friendship that Carter and Anwar Sadat forged. This friendship was the key to all subsequent positive steps. The two leaders discovered at their first meeting in Washington in April, 1977, that they liked and trusted each other. Both Vance and Brzezinski observed this friendship and reported how greatly Sadat "valued loyalty and friendship" and how Carter regarded Sadat as virtually a member of his family. Sadat apparently decided that his friendship with Carter could become the basis of a new Egyptian tie with the United States, an attitude Carter encouraged.[52] Consequently, at crucial moments in the next years Sadat felt that Carter supported the risks he took and Carter was able to win Sadat's support for the risks he wished to take in bargaining with the Israelis.

Conversely, Carter's first meeting with Menachem Begin in July, 1977, produced no such friendship or agreement. Nor was the administration successful in persuading the nations involved to publicly accept a plan for a meeting at Geneva. In October, 1977, Carter wrote Sadat asking him to publicly endorse such a step, even though Sadat had already indicated to Carter that it might be preferable for Egypt and Israel to negotiate directly with each other. Sadat's response was to announce his dramatic plan to visit Jerusalem—a bold move which Brzezinski felt was in direct response to Carter's plea for help. Sadat already had such action in mind, however, though Carter's support, which he gave immediately, may have provided necessary strength.[53]

The task of turning Sadat's initiative into concrete negotiations between Egypt and Israel fell to the United States, and more than six months of diplomatic floundering followed. During that period State Department and NSC experts worked on plans for a Middle East settlement, apparently without internal conflict.[54] During a period of discouragement in 1978, Carter suggested to Brzezinski that they invite Begin and Sadat to meet at Camp David, but because of the press of congressional business they set the idea aside. Instead it was decided that the two leaders would be invited to visit the president separately, for Carter was determined to get an agreement. His diary note of February 3, 1978, recorded some tension with his aides:

We had quite an argument at breakfast with me on one side and Fritz, Cy, Zbig, and Ham on the other. I think we ought to move much more aggressively on the Middle East question than any of them seem to, by evolving a clear plan for private use among ourselves . . . discussing the various elements with Sadat, one by one, encouraging him to cooperate with us by preventing any surprise in the future, and by inducing him to understand Begin's position. The plan that we evolve has got to be one that can be accepted by Begin in a showdown if we have the full support of the American public. . . . I don't know how much support I have, but we'll go through with this effort.

Carter added that the bone of contention was whether the administration should develop an "American plan" and try to sell it to Sadat and Begin. "In effect," he said, "I decided on this course of action."[55]

Brzezinski records that at that time "Carter's mood grew more and more impatient." He told his aides that he was disappointed with the slow progress and with what they were recommending to him.[56] By this time Carter realized that he was racing against the political calendar of presidential politics, for if a Middle East agreement could not be concluded in the second year of his presidency he might lack the political capital to continue pursuing the issue. The second half of his term would be taken up with reelection politics.[57]

When Sadat met with Carter in Washington in early February, 1978, he was pessimistic about Begin's desire for an agreement except on his own terms. Carter appears to have persuaded Sadat to hold back his criticism and support a plan for compromise that the United States would present Begin when he visited in March. Carter, however, found Begin to be unyielding, and he stunned the Israeli delegation by telling them that he did not think they wanted a diplomatic solution to their problem. After that meeting Carter was momentarily ready to abandon the entire quest. He and his lieutenants decided to hold back their views and hope for a change in Israel, though bilateral consultations among the three nations continued. After a meeting of the three foreign ministers in England in July, Vance and his chief aides concluded that the two parties would not be able to develop a peace plan by themselves; the United States would have to do it. Harold Saunders, the assistant secretary of state for the Middle East, at that point began to draft a plan very similar to what eventually became the Camp David accord. But negotiations were stalled. Carter then returned to the earlier idea of inviting Begin and Sadat to a September meeting at Camp David, thinking he might be able to bring them to agreement if he could present a moderate compromise. Vance regarded this decision as a "daring stroke" which both he and Brzezinski strongly supported.[58]

In June Carter had met with a small group of "wise men," former Democratic administration officials, and had been advised against his continued involvement in the Middle East issue because it was a losing proposition. "At that time," he records, "I could not think of any reason to disagree with them, but there was just no way I could abandon such an important commitment unless the situation became absolutely hopeless." At the same time Democratic members of Congress and party officials were telling the president that his Middle Eastern peace effort was hurting the Democrats with American Jews. Carter discussed the question with his wife Rosalynn and "finally decided it would be best, win or lose, to go all out." He would bring Begin and Sadat together for a three-way negotiating session. After he had announced plans for the meeting he was deluged with warnings from close advisers and friends about the possibility of failure. Nonetheless, he says, "I slowly became hardened against them, and as stubborn as at any time I can remember."[59]

At a strategy meeting in July, the Fall, 1978, congressional elections were on everyone's mind, and Vice-President Mondale recommended to the president that he pull back and rebuild the American Jewish community's confidence. Hamilton Jordan was strongly in favor of Carter pressing forward in the view that only an agreement would give political reward now. Carter, too, was hoping that the dramatic impact of a successful summit meeting would help him politically.[60]

Carter, Vance and Brzezinski have all described in detail the successful negotiation of the Camp David accord.[61] Carter applied all of his intelligence, capacity for detail, and moral zeal to achieving an agreement between two men who did not like each other. There were several ingredients to his success. He was finally able to prevail, when matters seemed hopeless, by getting President Sadat to trust him to work out an agreement with Begin. Carter became discouraged often and thought on several occasions that failure was certain, but he did not give up. And although tenacity is no guarantee of success, on an issue of this kind it is the first requirement. According to all reports the American delegation of principals and experts functioned smoothly as a team. The cooperation of State Department and NSC officials enabled Carter and Vance, as the principal negotiators, to be ahead of the Israelis and Egyptians on technical and negotiating issues and thus to keep the initiative. This close collaboration of White House and State Department colleagues had always existed on Middle Eastern issues.[62] Friendly critics have contended that the settlement tilted toward Israel, particularly in its ambiguity toward the future of Palestinian political rights on the West Bank. Given American domestic politics and Israeli intransigence there was perhaps no alternative.[63] Some of Sadat's advisers argued to the very end that too much had been given away to Israel, but Sadat trusted Carter to help bring the agreement to reality.[64]

Carter had originally favored a comprehensive solution of the outstanding disagreements between Israel and the Arab states. But as time went on he began to see that the most feasible possibility was an agreement between Israel and Egypt on specific issues. William Quandt, the NSC Middle East specialist, in retrospect saw that Carter understood better than his advisers Sadat's willingness to accept vague agreement on the future of the West Bank and a future homeland for the Palestinians versus Menachem Begin's unwillingness to make any concessions on the issue. However, to compensate Sadat would have to negotiate the return of the Sinai Peninsula to Egypt, territory Israel had held since the 1967 war. Carter was disappointed in the briefing books Vance, Brzezinski and their aides had prepared for Camp David because the papers expressed hope for agreement on the principles to guide future negotiations on all issues, particularly the West Bank. The president wanted a written agreement between Israel and Egypt on specific issues.[65]

Sadat had come to Camp David expecting that he and Carter would gang up on Begin, particularly on the West Bank issue. For though Sadat was always more interested in the Sinai, he was under heavy pressure from his lieutenants to win concessions for the Palestinians in order to keep Egypt's credibility with the other Arab nations. But Begin's rigidity on the West Bank was stronger than anything either Carter or Sadat had to offer; he was willing to leave Camp David without an agreement. In the end Carter pressed Sadat to accept vague language about the West Bank, with most of the issues left open to future negotiations, because this was the only way to get an agreement on issues that could be mediated. Quandt writes that Carter had two choices as the meeting drew to an end with no agreement in sight: agree with Sadat on all issues and publicly blame Begin, or get Sadat what he most wanted, the Sinai, at the price of avoiding the hard question of the West Bank and other territories occupied by Israel in the aftermath of past military conflicts. The first choice would be politically risky at home and the second would keep the peace negotiations on track and be popular at home. Carter chose the second alternative. Sadat told his advisers that when he threatened to leave Camp David because nothing was being accomplished, Carter said that he needed an agreement to ensure his reelection. Quandt believes that Carter was the architect of the settlement, which returned the Sinai to Egypt with guarantees to Israel about its security in relation to the Sinai. Carter also thought that the agreement on terms for future negotiations about the status of the West Bank precluded new Israeli settlements during the five-year period of negotiations. Begin later denied such an agreement, insisting that settlements were to be delayed only while the Camp David treaty was being negotiated. Quandt believes Carter's memory to be accurate.[66]

The Camp David negotiations were artificial in the sense that the control Carter exercised there would be impossible once Begin and Sadat went home. Few political situations permit such control, and Carter's negotiating skills were enhanced in this tightly controlled framework where homework, tenacity and appeals to goodwill were more likely to be effective than in highly fluid, decentralized settings. After Camp David Carter lost control for a time and was forced to visit the Middle East in 1979 to restore agreement. It appears likely from the descriptions of events provided by Vance, Brzezinski and Carter himself that the reconciliation process would not have continued without Carter's visit. Sadat was with Carter all along, but Begin remained difficult, though the efforts of other Israeli cabinet ministers, in response to Carter's urgings, appear to have made the difference.[67]

Brzezinski describes a meeting of the president and his colleagues in February, 1979, to discuss what to do about the continuing Egyptian-Israeli impasse over the West Bank. Vice-President Mondale advised staying away from the issue because there was no political return. Brzezinski speculated that Carter, who was to meet with Begin the next day, might have taken Mondale's advice if his perception of Begin's "toughness and bluntness" had not made his "adrenalin flow." He adds, "I could tell from Carter's account that he was stirred up and challenged." At a later meeting Carter said that to lead and act like a president he must develop a bold stroke. He then decided to go to the Middle East.[68]

After his presidency Carter attributed his successful interventions in the dispute between these two nations to his tenacity, which, he said, might also have contributed to some of his political failures. But something more than tenacity was at work in the second round of negotiations, with Carter as mediator, in 1979. The Shah of Iran had fallen from power in the meantime and Carter was concerned about America's strategic position in the Middle East and about scoring a policy success which would erase the domestic political damage caused by the shah's fall. Quandt reports that Carter knew the political calendar was working against him in 1979. He would not have the domestic political capital to take any risks in diplomacy as he entered the long reelection campaign.[69]

NORMALIZING RELATIONS WITH CHINA

In June, 1977, an NSC-State Department working group produced a paper on normalization of relations with China that called for full diplomatic recognition. In subsequent discussions, differences in emphasis between Vance and Brzezinski appeared. Vance wished to go slowly with China in order not to risk a delay in the SALT negotiations that might arise from Soviet hostility to a United States-China understanding. He thought such a move would hurt relations with Russia and Japan.[70] Brzezinski and to a lesser extent Harold Brown saw the new tie with China as a counterweight to the USSR. It was agreed that Vance would visit China in August, 1977.

At a July 30 meeting of Vance, Brzezinski, Brown, Richard Holbrooke, assistant secretary of state for the Far East, and Michael Oksenberg of the NSC staff, Carter abruptly decided to pursue normalization and instructed Vance to take up the issue with the Chinese. As Brzezinski describes it, "He said his entire political experience had been that it does not pay to prolong or postpone difficult issues."[71]

However, the president pulled back after Mondale said that it was too much to ask the Senate to handle the Panama Canal treaty and new agreements with China at the same time. Vance was thus told not to be explicit about normalization, and his visit to China was inconclusive. Over the winter of 1977–1978 Brzezinski worked to persuade Carter to renew the initiative. He cultivated relations with Chinese officials in Washington, solicited an official invitation to visit China himself, and lobbied with both Mondale and Brown to support his trip in discussions with the president. The State Department was opposed to such a visit because Vance was still focusing on SALT as the priority. In the Spring of 1978 Carter decided that Brzezinski would visit China but would not be authorized to negotiate about normalization. He explains that in early 1978 Averell Harriman, who had just met with the Soviet leaders, reported that they wanted a SALT II agreement very much. Carter was determined not to delay SALT II negotiations and so decided to send Vance to Moscow and Brzezinski to Peking as soon as the Panama Canal treaties were ratified. Vance did not like it, fearing that the United States would be seen as having more than one spokesman, but he accepted Carter's decision. Brzezinski's and Carter's accounts disagree as to whether Brzezinski actually discussed normalization with the Chinese. Brzezinski says that he was authorized to negotiate and did so; Carter says that he was not there to negotiate but did a good job of laying the groundwork for the agreement that was reached in December.[72]

In the Summer and Fall of 1978 Carter negotiated the terms of normalization directly with the Chinese through the United States ambassador to China, Leonard Woodcock. Carter gave personal attention to every line of the messages going to Woodcock, and secrecy was so great that Vance came to the White House to read the communiques. In December Carter sent word to Deng Xiaoping, the dominant figure in China, inviting him to visit the United States as soon as the agreement was concluded. He also told Deng that the United States and the Soviet Union had resolved all major SALT II issues and that the date for a summit meeting between himself and

Brezhnev would soon be set. When he asked if Deng was prepared to agree to normalization in the terms that had been negotiated, the Chinese leader quickly signaled his concurrence. Carter evidently regarded normalization and a SALT II agreement as mutually reinforcing. Some senators known to be doubtful about SALT II had expressed the hope that the United States would develop stronger ties with China, he writes, and he "believed that congressional support for better relations with both the Soviet Union and the People's Republic of China would be strengthened if the two peaceful moves could be combined—a SALT II treaty with the Soviets and normalized relations with the Chinese."[73]

Carter's diary from the previous May 16 records that all of his advisers, including Vance, had agreed that a better relationship with China would "help us with SALT."[74] Vance's misgivings about timing seem not to have been expressed strongly enough to influence the president, who, in any event, had turned to Brzezinski as his principal assistant on normalization. He later called his national security adviser the driving force behind normalization, saying, "Whenever I wavered, you pushed me." And Brzezinski makes clear that he pulled the staff work for the normalization negotiations into the White House and away from the State Department. Michael Oksenberg led the effort and coordinated State Department counterparts. When it became clear to Brzezinski in 1978 that he wanted more rapid movement than Vance, he held staff meetings in his office and State Department officials dealt directly with him.[75]

Later disagreements were about tactics and timing rather than substance. Vance was annoyed in May that Brzezinski had made provocative public statements about the Soviets after his return from China and had allowed his trip to be characterized as a counterbalance to the Soviet negotiations. It had also been Vance's understanding that the normalization agreement would be announced in January, 1979, after Vance and Andrei Gromyko had met in Geneva in December, 1978, to put the finishing touches to SALT. This agreement was made with the president in October before Vance went to Moscow for the final round of formal SALT negotiations. However, Carter was so surprised and delighted by Vice-Premier Deng's quick response to the normalization terms that he decided to surprise Deng in return by proposing that the agreement be revealed in two days, as soon as Vance could return from the Middle East. Carter wished to make the public explanation in its totality and not give time for piecemeal leaks.[76] He asked Vance to come home immediately for the announcement, and when Vance requested that the announcement be delayed until January, about a week after his meeting with Gromyko, Carter replied that he feared negotiations might become unraveled through delay. Vance was still concerned about a negative reaction from the Soviets and further charged that at a critical moment Brzezinski had blocked Deputy Secretary of State Warren Christopher and Richard Holbrooke out of administration decision making so that they had been unable to inform him of Carter's plans.[77]

Gromyko held up the SALT agreement when he and Vance met in Geneva, protesting that the announcement of the new United States-China tie contained critical references to the Soviet Union, particularly in a criticism of any power that sought "hegemony." According to Vance the Soviets did not object to the substance of the announcement but to its timing and tone. It took another six months to reach agreement on SALT. Brzezinski did not accept Vance's interpretation, arguing that SALT was delayed by unresolved issues. Strobe Talbott reports that after discussions with Anatoly Dobrynin, Soviet ambassador to the United States, and with American officials who had been in Geneva, Brzezinski reluctantly came to agree with Vance that the timing of the China announcement, together with the news that Deng would visit the United States, had indeed complicated SALT.[78]

The new element in this foreign policy story is that with Brzezinski turning from objective monitor to advocate Carter himself became custodian of the decision-making process. Moving in response to his own imperatives, he provided a strong lead which his lieutenants followed. But when his two chief lieutenants disagreed on timing and tactics Carter sided with Brzezinski and made him his agent. Although the language about "hegemony" to which the Soviets objected was Brzezinski's, Carter accepted it. By using Brzezinski as his agent, particularly in Vance's absence, Carter left himself unprotected from any adverse consequences of Brzezinski's advice. By acting as an advocate Brzezinski could not scrutinize the timing and wording of the announcement with the sensitivity of a more neutral "custodian." Carter saw that normalization might adversely affect other issues and on Mondale's advice had delayed discussions with China until the canal treaty was ratified. But he believed that China normalization and SALT reinforced each other, as well as reinforcing his vision of the Wilsonian president reaching out for peace with all nations.[79]

SALT II

In November, 1974, President Gerald Ford met Leonid Brezhnev at Vladivostok just to get acquainted. But the meeting, which Secretary of

State Henry Kissinger also attended, produced general terms for a SALT II treaty. Ceilings were set on the number of total strategic nuclear launch vehicles along with a subceiling for vehicles with multiple warheads. The Soviets could keep their total number of missiles and continue to add multiple warheads to them. The United States could increase their number of missiles and warheads up to the ceilings. The two unresolved issues were whether a new Soviet plane, the Backfire, was an offensive bomber (if so defined it would be included in the agreement) and whether the American Cruise missile, which was not mentioned, would be considered a missile in terms of the Vladivostok agreement.[80]

Assuming the possibility of agreement on the Backfire and the Cruise, a SALT II treaty based on the Vladivostok meeting would have stabilized the arms race but not reduced weapons arsenals. Limits were set on future development with the goal of parity. In October, 1976, Cyrus Vance recommended to Carter an early conclusion of the SALT II treaty on the basis of Vladivostok, including an agreement about Backfire and Cruise. SALT III could then begin in the Fall of 1977, just as SALT I expired.[81] During the campaign Carter had told Brezhnev, through Averell Harriman, that if elected he would move quickly to negotiate SALT II based on the Vladivostok accord if the unresolved issues could be settled. In November, 1976, Brezhnev appealed for an agreement based on Vladivostok, but without reference to the unresolved issues.[82] However, Carter was of two minds because he also wanted deep cuts in the total number of missiles on both sides. As the new president he immediately instructed the NSC staff, the Department of State and the Department of Defense to push the "limitation" talks into "reductions," with a fallback option.[83]

Carter believed that SALT obstacles might be reduced through communication with Brezhnev. However, their initial correspondence was disappointing. Brezhnev's reply to Carter's first letter was to make clear that the Soviets wanted a quick SALT agreement based on Vladivostok, with the Cruise missile included and Backfire excluded. Carter in turn suggested that SALT II could be concluded without Cruise or Backfire but that it might be possible to move toward SALT II with deep reductions in existing forces. He also expressed the hope that the Soviets would speak out for human rights. Brezhnev's response was cold; SALT II had to be based on Vladivostok with Cruise and without Backfire. He ridiculed the human rights argument and took exception to a letter Carter had written to the Soviet dissident Andrei Sakharov. Brezhnev's letter was a jolt to Carter.[84]

The options the Departments of State and Defense developed from the Vladivostok agreement did not please Carter, Brzezinski or Secretary of Defense Harold Brown. For Carter they were not ambitious or imaginative enough, though he was perhaps feeling this way because he had endorsed the idea of a quick agreement minus Cruise and Backfire at a February 8 press conference. Harold Brown and David Aaron, Brzezinski's deputy, were concerned that the Vladivostok agreement perpetuated Soviet heavy missiles. They wanted deep cuts in those forces, as did Senator Henry Jackson, whose support Carter wanted for any agreement. By mid-February the Special Coordination Committee, with Brzezinski and Aaron presiding, had developed a plan for deep cuts in forces on both sides. The president, making this his priority at a March 12 meeting, said he hoped for "real arms control" through "a fundamentally new kind of proposal." He was impatient with "merely staying within the Vladivostok framework" and felt that the bureaucracy had been "sloughing off." Brown was perhaps the key person in selling this plan to Carter, who, however, was clearly already thinking along these lines.[85] At March 19 and March 22 meetings three options were developed for Vance to carry to Moscow with him that month. The preferred model was one of deep cuts. The alternative was Vladivostok without Cruise and Backfire. And a third, which Carter instructed Vance not to mention, was a compromise position of less drastic reductions in force.[86]

Vance writes that in early 1977 the Soviet leaders were uneasy about Carter's well-publicized desire for sharp reductions in nuclear weapons. They were also concerned about Carter's letter to Sakharov and statements about human rights—issues Vance would have saved for quiet diplomacy. By March, 1977, Vance's preference was to negotiate an agreement based on the Vladivostok formula without the Backfire and Cruise items which Kissinger had been unable to get agreement on in 1976. Such a SALT II would form a "stable foundation for U.S.-Soviet relations" from which a more comprehensive SALT III might be developed. He therefore urged Carter to let him take a second proposal based on the Vladivostok plan to Moscow. In agreeing, Carter warned him to make clear to the Russians that he preferred the proposal for deep cuts.[87]

Just before Vance left for Moscow Carter outlined his objective of comprehensive arms cuts in a speech to the United Nations General Assembly and in a press conference. The president saw this as "openness" and felt it important to publicly describe his goals because of the need for public and congressional support for a treaty. At the press conference Carter gave the Soviets an opening to reject all United States proposals and wait for something more to their liking when he said, "If we're disappointed [by the Soviet response], which is a possibility, then we'll try to modify our stance."[88]

Brezhnev rejected the proposal for deep cuts and again insisted that SALT II be based on the Vladivostok agreement with Cruise included and Backfire excluded. Vance was thus not able to raise the fallback position of less drastic cuts. The Soviets did not seem ready for an agreement on any conditions except ones unacceptable to the United States. And though they later accepted constraints on both Backfire and the Cruise missile as part of the SALT II agreement, a long internal debate within the Soviet government may have been necessary before they could depart from their version of Vladivostok. Vance doubts that American rhetoric about human rights abuses in the Soviet Union made a big difference in the Soviet response to his proposals. But he does think that the Soviet leaders distrusted Carter's boldness, interpreting it as an effort to put one over on them. Carter's public rhetoric about comprehensive arms reductions apparently struck the Soviets as propaganda and pressure. Talbott's interviews within the administration in the aftermath, when everyone was asking how such a diplomatic mishap could have occurred, produced agreement on the following main reasons for the Soviets' rejection of Carter's plan: they wished to test the new president's toughness, they resented open American diplomacy, they resented the effort to change the rules from Vladivostok, they resented efforts to put them on the defensive, they resented American rhetoric about human rights in the Soviet Union, and, most important, they saw the proposal for deep cuts as favoring the United States because it could require the Soviets to dismantle weapons while the Americans only desisted from development.[89]

The president—as impatient as ever for results and as willing to be bold—clearly dominated the decision-making process. We have seen the successes of such a style. Its debits are in acting without sufficient caution or thoroughness and getting out on a limb that is then sawed off. When a president has his mind made up in cases of this kind, his lieutenants may influence details but generally not the direction or speed of action.

Carter's own testimony is that his exchange of letters with Brezhnev before the Vance trip had revealed that the Soviets did not want rapid change, which was why Vance took two options. Carter would not have done that differently. But with hindsight he would have approached the Soviets more slowly, with greater preparation and less publicity. He understood that the Soviets resented his publicizing his views before Vance had the opportunity to present them privately. He did not think his preaching on human rights was an obstacle, but even if it had been he would still have preached. He also records a characteristic response to frustration. When it became apparent that the Soviets wished to move slowly and incrementally, he says, "I was angry . . . and disappointed because we would have to set back our timetable for an agreement."[90]

Basic agreement between the two nations on SALT II was achieved in April, 1979, and final differences rounded out at the Carter-Brezhnev summit meeting in June. Carter was centrally involved the entire time and appears to have impressed the Soviets with his knowledge and seriousness, particularly in a September, 1977, meeting with Andrei Gromyko in Washington. The Soviets altered the pace of SALT talks according to their happiness or unhappiness with other United States actions, such as the emerging American tie with China. United States opposition to Soviet interventions in Africa may have been another cause for slowdown. Finally, principals and staff within the administration appear to have worked cooperatively to resolve differences. Brzezinski describes his role as working through the SCC to resolve interagency disputes, particularly between the State Department and Defense Department. The State Department, however, had the lead in conducting the negotiations and appears to have received no serious interference from other quarters. Carter approached the meeting with Brezhnev with hopes that the SALT agreement could be the basis for greater accommodation between the two nations on a broad variety of issues. He chided his advisers for not being sufficiently bold in their planning papers. But when he raised such issues with Brezhnev he received little response.[91]

THE IRANIAN REVOLUTION

When the Iranian revolution began in mid-1978 Carter administration policy makers were already overloaded with the Panama Canal treaties in the Senate, the post-Camp David negotiations between Egypt and Israel, negotiations with China and the continuing SALT talks. It was almost impossible for the people at the top to give Iran the attention it deserved. The first meeting in the White House was not until November 2, after months of turmoil in Iran. The difficulty of responding effectively was compounded by the poor information about Iran available to the American government.[92]

The Nixon administration had virtually mortgaged United States policy toward Iran to the shah by giving him open-ended control over arms purchases and by restricting the operation of intelligence activities in Iran for fear that contacts with political opposition groups would upset the Persian monarch. As a result neither the State Department nor the CIA was able to provide reliable information as the crisis developed and passed from one stage to another. Perhaps more importantly, there was virtually no appreciation in Washington of the Ayatollah Khomeni's vision of an Islamic republic that would radically transform the society.[93] A genuinely creative revolutionary movement cannot, by definition, be fully understood at its beginning. Something new is to be created in history.

A third problem for intelligent policy making in response to the Iranian crisis was the deep split between the NSC staff and the State Department over the appropriate United States policy. These differences, characterized by hostility and failures of communication, were never resolved, nor was much effort made to resolve them.[94]

The American government may never have had a realistic course of action. The shah's efforts to respond to the crowds in the streets by palliative reforms and, eventually, a centrist coalition government, were weak. But the United States could not force the shah to be a different person. The idea of a new government composed of national leaders who would be a bridge between the shah's regime and the new revolutionary forces was stillborn and probably came too late to be a realistic possibility. It was eventually established that a military government that would save the monarchy or establish a new regime that would put down the Khomeni forces was not possible because the military was not under unified control and its leaders lacked the will to act. Finally, eventual American approaches to the imminent revolutionary regime revealed that they considered the United States their enemy. Thus historical forces may have been inexorable and critics have not, in retrospect, come up with a plausible course of action.[95]

However, having said this, it is also the case that the policy-making process employed during the Iranian revolution was chaotic. Any opportunity the president might have had to influence the situation in behalf of United States interests was systematically denied him by a sloppy bureaucratic process. These events are therefore of interest in helping us understand a poor decision process, particularly in comparison to the centralized and efficient process with which the Carter government managed the hostage crisis.

The first problem with the decision process was that Jimmy Carter did not play a central role in it. He did not set out United States objectives at the outset, beyond the clear desire to keep the shah on the throne. He did not participate in meetings to any extent. He did not throw himself into the substance of the issue in order to master the details as he always did when he had a strong personal investment. He stayed aloof and was content to set general guidelines. One can speculate on the reasons for this posture. He may have had the realistic perception that there was not much he could do to influence events. Carter chose his policy initiatives carefully and this was perhaps not the kind of problem that engaged his talent for creating new possibilities. His strongest vision was moral. He was a peacemaker and reformer who was neither comfortable with strategic questions about the balance of power in the Persian Gulf nor sympathetic to the use of military force.[96] The crisis forced these unwelcome issues on him, requiring him to assess the strategic importance of Iran and decide whether the United States should support a coup by the Iranian military. Carter was consistent from beginning to end—he supported the shah—and when that policy failed he hoped for the best from the new regime. But his fairly passive role during the crisis dramatized the need for a strong coordinating hand in the White House to pull together options for the president. Without this service Carter had to process advocates' competing claims without the benefit of central analysis and refinement of those claims. In some cases, such as SALT and energy, he integrated the disparate advice into policy options for himself. But his blind spot was his failure to see the need for a custodian who could play a neutral role in developing options for him. The custodian seemed less necessary when Carter was acting as his own desk officer on issues in which he made an investment. He surely knew that he was not well served on other issues, but his style of authority which rejected intermediaries prevented him from overcoming the difficulty.

Brzezinski was an advocate in this case from start to finish. He saw the stakes in Iran in larger geopolitical terms and regarded it as a disaster for the United States if Iran should leave the Western orbit. He and Energy Secretary James Schlesinger were the only two top officials who saw the issue in such global terms and Brzezinski thus encouraged Schlesinger to enter as a player. Brzezinski believed that a military solution in Iran was the only way to avoid a revolutionary regime and he pressed for that choice until the end when it became apparent, even to him, that the Iranian military lacked the will and capacity to act. He was opposed to the State Department view that the shah might be able to save himself through a new centrist government and, when that failed, to State's proposals for discussions with Khomeni. He encouraged the president to bring in George Ball as a special adviser on Iran, hoping that Ball would agree with him. When Ball argued for a Council of Notables to govern in behalf of the shah as a transition regime Brzezinski opposed him. But it was apparent to Brzezinski all along that the president did not find his ideas congenial. He perceived Carter as believing that it would be morally wrong for the United States to encourage the shah or the generals in Iran to use force against the revolution. Brzezinski, however, saw the fall of the shah as a personal calamity for Carter, which would undo his effective leadership at Camp David, weaken the credibility of his opposition to the Soviet invasion of Afghanistan and hurt his image as a world leader. Brzezinski saw major stakes for the president and the nation in this crisis and therefore believed that he should act as an advocate. The issue was too important for him to remain neutral.[97]

As a consequence he used his position as chairman of the Special Coordinating Committee, which was to manage crises, to advance his own position and deny the State Department opportunities and information. State Department officials charged that they were being excluded from meetings, and without their knowledge Brzezinski opened his own back channel to the shah through the Iranian ambassador in Washington. This was closed after the shah complained that he was receiving contradictory advice through different channels and Vance protested to Carter.[98] The president had sent a military emissary to Iran, on the advice of George Ball, to talk with the Iranian military leaders. This reporting channel gave a different picture than that provided by Ambassador William Sullivan and the confusion that prevailed was not counterbalanced by an NSC staff effort to clarify matters.[99]

Secretary Vance was out of the country much of the time during the first months of the crisis because he was preoccupied with the Middle East and SALT. Therefore, in the early stages the State Department working staff members were no match for Brzezinski.[100] In due course Vance did enter the picture and put the State Department behind a policy of supporting the shah's efforts to create a centrist government that could weather the crisis.

When this failed Vance got presidential approval to talk with Khomeni. Brzezinski opposed this move but Carter sided with Vance.[101] Apparently neither he nor his secretary of state were thinking in geopolitical strategic terms but rather were intent on protecting the United States from charges of undue intervention in the affairs of another nation.

A more effective policy process would have been one in which the president imposed himself on the process in the active search for options, the assistant for national security and his staff oversaw that search, and bureaucratic politics was channeled constructively through the development of options. But even had such a process been at work the president would have had difficulty finding a course of action that could have worked to United States advantage in Iran.

However, the contrast with the organizational response to the hostage crisis a few months later was very great. Here the president was clearly in charge and sat at the head of the table in a command-post posture. The secretary of state and his department provided the policy lead and all parties involved cooperated with minimal friction. Information coming from various parts of the government was good and reached the White House. Domestic advisers were brought into the meetings to enhance the political management of such a sensitive problem. The most important difference between the two decision processes was that in the second the president was in charge and was communicating his demand for options.[102]

Jimmy Carter could have attempted to put the hostages on the back burner to protect himself politically, but this was not his nature. He later said in an interview that the hostages were on his mind day and night without relief. He had the same sinking feeling in the pit of his stomach, he said, as in his early years as a businessman when he feared that the bank might foreclose on him.[103] Those who observed him dealing with the hostage problem report that he was totally absorbed by the substantive problem of how to get the hostages out. He gambled that an intensive campaign of pressure and diplomacy would free them, which failed and perhaps undermined the initial public support he had on the issue.[104] But this was Carter the problem solver at work. He would have loved the political credit attached to their release, but his first goal was to get them out and he did not appear to be concerned with his credibility problem if he failed.

These cases show Carter to have had a consistent style of coping with diplomatic problems. He deliberately took on hard cases, often against the advice of politically cautious advisers. Such boldness was served by tenacity and homework in the pursuit of achievement. He was quite explicit about his hope that achievement would bring domestic political benefits, but he was prepared to accept domestic criticism. One does not get the sense that he would have desisted from his goals because of their domestic unpopularity. Yet he was willing to settle for second best in order to achieve something and win domestic credit for presidential achievement.

One sees the same pattern as in domestic policy of first seeking comprehensive solutions and then, if necessary, pulling back to an achievable plan. The theme of undue optimism, which caused impatience, also appears. Quandt writes that Carter had great difficulty understanding the depth of the historic antagonisms between Jew and Arab in the Middle East and persisted in seeing the issues left unresolved by Camp David as technical and legalistic when, in fact, the disagreements were deep.[105] The same impatience and tipping of the presidential hand marred the first overture to the Soviets about a comprehensive SALT agreement. Undue optimism and impatience may also explain the failure to clearly acknowledge the effect of one issue on another; thus the timing of the agreement with China may have delayed the SALT agreement.

The president had constructed a system of national security decision making that worked well when he gave a strong lead and his advisers were in agreement. In those instances the task of analysis was shared cooperatively between NSC and State Department staffs and the principals cooperated. Brzezinski acted more as "custodian" than "advocate" but was free to advise the president as a foreign policy expert. The first sign of weakness in the decision system came when, in the Chinese case, Brzezinski became both advocate and diplomat, with the president's consent. Although Carter believed Brzezinski's role to have been constructive, his advocacy of a strongly held position deprived the president of the neutral and objective voice that would have helped him sort and analyze options. And by engaging openly in diplomacy the assistant for national security ran the risk of appearing to be in public opposition to the views of the secretary of state. These weaknesses took extreme form in the case of the Iranian revolution, when the United States government was caught off guard and, moreover, was deeply divided. In retrospect, it is difficult to outline a course of action that might have either saved the shah or created ties with Khomeni. But the open conflict in the NSC system and its inability to provide coherent options for the president surely reduced any opportunity he might have had to act intelligently. In this case, unlike the others, he was poorly served by the system he had created.

An undercurrent in these cases is the issue of whether Brzezinski was custodian or advocate. He seems to have been both, at different times. When Carter made his goals clear and took a strong personal lead Brzezinski appears to have worked well in harness with Vance and others, primarily as a policy coordinator. In the Camp David case and, to a lesser extent, SALT, Carter, Vance and Brzezinski agreed on goals and strategies of action. Brzezinski moved to advocacy when he thought the president was uncertain or mistaken. In these situations he risked conflict between himself and Vance rather than confining himself to the guardian role of fashioning options for the president out of policy disagreements.[106] The origin of this problem was Carter's use of Brzezinski and his staff as personal advisers instead of neutral policy analysts and custodians. The collegial model of competing streams of advice was sure to show strain if advisers were at odds on fundamental issues. Brzezinski interjected a strong personality and advocacy element into the national security system that was not found in domestic and economic policy making. But Carter appears to have had a blind spot about Brzezinski and about the possibilities of the custodian role.

The President's Reorganization Project midterm study of the National Security Council raised hard questions about whether Brzezinski and his staff were fully serving the president's needs for the development of policy choices. The inquiry was begun in December, 1978, by Peter Szanton, deputy director of the PRP, a veteran of the 1967 studies of the Heineman Commission on executive organization and the 1970 Murphy Commission on the organization of foreign policy making and coauthor of a book on the organization of foreign policy decision making.[107] Szanton recruited Philip A. Odeen, a former Defense Department and NSC policy analyst, to direct the study. The charge asked whether executive branch organization and processes for making foreign policy decisions permitted such decisions to be consistent with each other and with national priorities. Could issues requiring interagency or presidential consideration be identified early? Did NSC decision making reflect the full range of relevant considerations and to what degree did the NSC oversee the implementation of policies for internal consistency?[108]

Odeen assigned senior staff officers on loan from agencies to do case studies and conducted eighty interviews himself. Carter had originally authorized the project in August, 1977, but Brzezinski managed to delay its start until December, 1978.[109] Once Odeen began it took several months to complete the work, and it was March, 1980, before the administration agreed on features of the Odeen report to be implemented.

Odeen's principal finding was that Carter put "particular emphasis" on the personal advisory role to the president of the assistant for national security and his staff. Carter looked to these advisers for fresh ideas, new policy approaches and, in some cases, independent analysis.[110] There was general agreement that Carter was being well served by the NSC staff, which was "providing him the staffing, recommendations and analysis he desired." Particular examples of effective staff work were the cases of SALT and the Middle East peace negotiations. The Odeen interviews revealed a favorable view of the policy development process through the PRM device. But considerable criticism surfaced over apparent "incoherence" in policy and the appearance of inconsistency. This inconsistency, the study determined, existed because the administration philosophy of "open" decision making paraded disagreement, because policy initiatives in human rights and arms exports seem to have been muted as they encountered the "realities" of the world, and because changing international conditions of increased superpower rivalry had led to significant policy shifts.[111]

Odeen also suggested that a price was being paid for the use of the NSC as a personal presidential staff. The management of decision processes to ensure the greatest possible consideration of options and realistic alternatives was underdeveloped. Coordinated interagency papers were too infrequently used as the basis for PRC and SCC meetings. The real issues were often not clear because policy papers were usually the product of one department with little integration of agency views into options. This may have been due, Odeen suggested, to the "conscious effort to give the agencies more responsibility." But, in their lack of synthesis, the materials developed for the president's review often did not aid his decision making. For example, during his final review of the fiscal year 1980 defense budget Carter had to work from three separate books supplied by the Department of Defense, OMB and the NSC staff. The facts did not agree and the issues were not uniformly presented. Odeen suggested that the reduction in size of the NSC staff could be a reason such issue management had received insufficient attention but added that "inadequate process management may also be a price the President has paid for asking the NSC to devote a major portion of its time to personal staff support."[112]

Another negative consequence of the focus on decision making was a failure of the NSC staff to clearly communicate presidential decisions throughout the government and oversee their implementation.[113] Again it was a question of staff resources, which may or may not have been a problem. In retrospect NSC staff members remembered the institutional obligation to oversee implementation, admitted its difficulty because of the day-to-day press of policy decisions and claimed that implementation was primarily the business of the departments and agencies.[114] One might infer that implementation by presidential staff would not be a high priority, for Carter had made it clear at the outset of his administration that White House staff members would not tell others in the executive branch what to do and that the job of implementing policy lay with the departments.

The Odeen analysis may have exaggerated the degree to which any analytic staff can manage to develop comprehensive policy alternatives on a wide range of issues. Three former NSC staff members acknowledge and explain the difficulty of "coordination," the last with specific reference to the Odeen report.

Sometimes lack of coordination was the case. I myself contributed to some of that confusion. . . . Brzezinski himself would sometimes lose interest in something and not follow through in a close procedural way. People who were used to working in a highly structured environment would be horrified by the lack of structure and the lack of routinization on the NSC staff. . . . We were pretty lousy in some regards on coordination in some areas and in others we were pretty good. . . . It depended on the policy and it sometimes depended on the staff member supporting it, and it depended on Brzezinski's own interest.

You think you're working on the world's most important thing and all of a sudden the world's really most important thing comes to your desk and you set that first one aside and the coordination that we've been working on then all of a sudden disappears.

Let me explain a couple of things that became very clear to me early in this administration. The President picked a thirty four year old young man to be his chief of staff. He gave the appearances of decentralization of power. We were going to get rid of that centralized Kissinger system. There was a Policy Review Committee that would be chaired by State and Vance as appropriate. Brzezinski was left with one NSC committee to chair. Each one of the secretaries were to have direct access to communications daily and weekly. He got rid of that Haldeman-Ehrlichman image. No strong chief of staff and all that. Everybody was pleased at this decentralization.

The press's view was that it was an excessive decentralization. In fact, the President was his own chief of staff. In fact, you had an extraordinary amount of centralization. In fact, Brzezinski had to coordinate things that were minute and almost embarrassingly small at times. I think the President, because of his ability to handle lots of minutiae and because he was a workaholic, actually enjoyed it. The Odeen report could not change this arrangement.[115]

This last comment suggests that Carter himself was responsible for the arrangements criticized by the Odeen report. He used Brzezinski and the NSC staff as personal advisers, in neglect of the custodian role and with the result that policy options were often not sufficiently analyzed. One might suggest that the problem was compounded by Brzezinski's "advocate" style, which the president also supported.

SHIFTING POLICIES IN THE COLD WAR

The utility of the generalizations extracted from foreign policy episodes might be confirmed by matching them to one prolonged issue, Carter's management of United States relations with the USSR, in which he was also managing Vance and Brzezinski. The management of policy, persons and process came together because Vance and Brzezinski were increasingly at odds over how to deal with the Soviets, and Carter tried to manage this disagreement in ways consistent with his goal of cooperation between the powers.

Carter shifted his ground in the last year of his administration. The Soviet invasion of Afghanistan moved him from Vance's side of the balance to Brzezinski's more aggressive posture. The evidence suggests that Carter was always in charge of policy, but his management of the process created two problems. First, he was not sufficiently attentive to the impact of the Vance-Brzezinski disagreements on his professional reputation. Second, the style of ad hoc decision making, in which each issue was decided on its merits, gave Carter control over policy but also gradually undermined the initial promises and appeal of his policy of cooperation between the United States and the USSR. When he shifted abruptly from cooperation to competition he gave the impression that his policy of cooperation had been overtaken by events.

Vance's influence declined and Brzezinski's rose not because either man's effectiveness had altered but because Carter's mind was changing in response to events. Carter's primary goal in regard to the Soviet Union was the SALT treaty. He had a general strategic conception that United States-

Soviet relations consisted of both cooperation and conflict and in the first two years emphasized his hopes for cooperation. Such a conception was too general to be a guide to action in specific cases and therefore Carter responded to situations according to whether he thought a cooperative or a competitive response was appropriate. The pattern gradually shifted from cooperative to competitive, on Carter's part, in response to the Soviet Union's increasingly provocative actions. Carter was determined to move on SALT and supported the concept of detente. He also thought that the Soviets had abused detente under previous administrations by making trouble in the world, yet he hoped that increased cooperation would be possible.[116] In two major foreign policy speeches in 1977 Carter stressed cooperation. At Notre Dame in May he argued against the preoccupation with Soviet activities around the globe in favor of policies for stabilizing Third World countries in the interest of the United States aside from any rivalry with the Russians. In Charleston, South Carolina, in June he called for increased cooperation between the two great powers.[117]

Carter and Vance were very much in agreement on this world view. Vance also set SALT II as his highest priority and was much opposed to reading East-West rivalry into every situation of conflict that developed around the world. He also opposed the idea of "linkage" in which American cooperation on SALT required "good" Soviet behavior in other spheres of action, particularly in the Third World.[118] There was little disagreement between Vance and Brzezinski during the first year because of cooperation on Panama, SALT and the Middle East and because Brzezinski gave his talent and support to issues about which both he and Carter felt strongly— United States arms sales, human rights and nuclear proliferation, all issues on which Brzezinski had attacked Henry Kissinger. Vance concurred, although he favored a muting of human rights zeal as a practical matter because of the need to deal with individual nations differently.[119] In fact, it became apparent in the first year that Vance and Brzezinski were both more cautious than Carter on a number of questions, largely because of experience. Both opposed the president's determination to withdraw United States troops from Korea. Both favored incremental increases in defense spending in contrast to Carter's early announcement that he planned to cut the defense budget. Both were surprised by Carter's early announcement that he would seek the demilitarization of the Indian Ocean.[120]

Brzezinski saw Vance as too optimistic about the Soviets. Both advisers thought detente had been oversold but Vance was hopeful that a SALT treaty would be a means of improving relations whereas Brzezinski regarded SALT as a way to reduce the Soviet military buildup. From the very beginning Brzezinski tried to push policy in the direction of improving American military strength. He wanted to put off summit meetings with the Soviets until the United States defense effort had borne fruit and the "China card" had been played.[121] But he had to move cautiously because the president was not thinking that way.

At the beginning of the administration Brzezinski asked Samuel Huntington and General William Odom to oversee the preparation of a Presidential Review Memorandum on the relative strengths of the United States and the USSR. A number of interagency task forces examined and compared the military, economic and political capabilities of the two nations in the major regions of the world. The general conclusion was that the United States was superior to the Soviet Union in political and economic capabilities and equivalent in military strength. However, an unfavorable military balance was emerging because of the decline in United States defense expenditures and the steady increase in Soviet military development. Huntington and Odom also identified the Persian Gulf, especially Iran, as the area of the world most vulnerable to Soviet pressure and specified the high strategic stakes the United States had in the region. They concluded that United States defensive capabilities required strengthening, particularly the capacity to respond rapidly to fast-breaking situations around the world. "Military equivalence" with the USSR was suggested as the appropriate criterion for defense policy.[122]

The State Department was not altogether happy with the memorandum's conclusions and, according to some reports, influenced the tone of the presidential directive based on it so that the commitment to defense increases was muted. For example, although Presidential Directive 18 called for an increase in defense spending of 3 percent per annum, the base on which the increase was to be calculated was not specified.[123]

One NSC staff member who worked on the paper and the ensuing directive saw the administration acting at cross purposes in its first months because major presidential directives were inconsistent. Specifically he believed that the new policies discouraging arms transfers and nuclear nonproliferation were applied indiscriminately in ways that weakened the emphasis upon enhanced strategic capabilities called for in the presidential directive. For example, the administration moved quickly to reduce the flow of arms to the Persian Gulf and the Indian Ocean and to press Pakistan to reduce its arms buildup. The net effect, in his view, was to convince American allies in the region that the United States was withdrawing from a major strategic role there. He blamed the State Department and ascribed to Secretary Vance the view that the Soviet Union had no military designs on the region. "For the next two years," he said, "based on the kind of analyses we had done in PRM 10 [the Huntington-Odom paper], we had to work slowly to bring the realities to the eyes of the President, the eyes of the Secretary of Defense, Secretary of State and make them realize that he had to tackle some of those policies from very fundamentally different directions."[124]

The first noticeable conflict between Vance and Brzezinski came in late 1977 and early 1978 over the question of the appropriate American response to Soviet logistical support given to Cuban and Ethiopian troops fighting against Somali guerrillas in the Ogaden region of Ethiopia. Brzezinski wanted the United States to make a show of force by sending an aircraft carrier task force into the area. Vance and his advisers agreed that the Soviets were seeking to exploit a local situation but did not interpret the issue as one of United States-Soviet rivalry. They preferred to deal with the Egyptian-Somali conflict on its own terms and, in fact, saw the Somalies as the aggressors. Carter sided with Vance, but the fundamental differences between Vance and Brzezinski had become apparent. It was by then also clear that Brzezinski saw his role as advocate and bureaucratic player. He says,

I think once disagreements surfaced, then all of the institutional rivalries and resentments which always are there, particularly when a small elite staff dominates a department, also intensified. . . . The press got onto it, and I think the press pumped it up a great deal. Then gradually things began to get more competitive, and in a way, one was almost driven to keep score to see who wins and who loses, and that's probably never good in a power setting, especially if you feel strongly that you are right. If there is something very important at stake, you feel you have to make sure that your point of view prevails, and on some issues I felt that way. I felt very strongly that way, that if we don't become tougher sooner two things will happen: detente will fall apart, because the American people won't support it; and the President's standing will fall apart because the country won't support a President it perceives as weak.[125]

The more fundamental disagreement between Brzezinski and Vance, aside from how to deal with conflict in the Horn of Africa, was whether Soviet behavior in such spots should be linked to SALT II negotiations. Vance, being opposed to "linkage," did not want SALT II to be held hostage to every Soviet action in the world; Brzezinski wished to use the promise of SALT II as a constraint on Soviet actions. He continued to press the issue and even though he was overruled at a meeting of senior officials in February, 1978, with both Vance and Brown against him, he made a public statement on March 1 that Soviet actions in the Horn of Africa would complicate the SALT talks. Carter then had to deny that the United States intended to link the SALT negotiations to other issues. However, the president did admit that Soviet actions might harm the chance of getting the Senate to ratify a treaty.[126] Carter never embraced the concept of linkage as a means of influencing the Soviets, except by acknowledging that Soviet actions could kill potential agreements.

By the end of his first year in office Carter faced a dilemma. He could have silenced Brzezinski as a public figure and supported the secretary of state as the central foreign policy official. Or he could have taken the public lead himself, with the national security assistant as his executive officer and the secretary of state as an implementer. He did neither. Both Vance and Brzezinski appeared to be spokesmen and the press began to question where the president stood. This problem was exacerbated when Carter began to encourage Brzezinski to speak up on behalf of administration positions because Vance seemed reluctant to do so. In his memoir Carter explains his disappointment that Vance was not inclined to assume a sustained role in the education of public opinion. Carter would ask Vance to make a public statement on a given subject and then see Hodding Carter, the State Department press spokesman, handling the matter at the State Department news briefing. So he used Brzezinski as a public advocate, though not nearly as much as Brzezinski was willing to be used. And according to Carter, with one or two exceptions Brzezinski's statements agreed with his own views. Carter was quite aware that Vance and the State Department were unhappy to have Brzezinski speaking at all, but the president did not feel that he could hold press conferences three times a week and he wanted statements in support of administration positions going to the public regularly. By default Brzezinski assumed the role, even though Carter was fully aware that his manner was provocative.[127]

The year 1978 was one of foreign policy success for the Carter administration. The Panama Canal treaties were ratified, the Camp David accord was achieved and normalization of relations with China was negotiated. But by the Spring of 1978 Brzezinski and Vance and their staffs had taken sides on the fundamental question of how to deal with the Russians. At that point the SALT talks were moving very slowly, the Soviets were active in Africa and were developing massive SS 20 missiles. Brzezinski, who thought United States-Soviet relations were at a stalemate, wanted to engage the Soviets in a broad dialogue on a wide range of issues. Vance wanted to get the SALT agreement.[128]

Carter appeared to waver. In March he gave a speech at Wake Forest University warning the Soviets about their actions around the world. In April Brzezinski gave the president a memo on steps for putting pressure on the Soviets, particularly in regard to United States defense development and the negotiation of technology-sharing agreements with China. Carter liked the ideas and instructed Vance to discuss overall relations with the Soviets when he next met with them. Brzezinski drafted Vance's instructions. He recalls that he was actively trying to "influence the President's thinking on this subject." In May it became clear that the Soviets were backing one of the sides in the Angolan civil war and that Cubans were fighting there. But on May 25 Carter publicly said that SALT was too important for the United States to practice linkage, though if the Soviets continued to abuse human rights and send Cuban troops to Africa it would be more difficult to conclude and ratify a SALT agreement. Carter was clearly trying very hard to balance the themes of cooperation and competition but the tension between them was sharper than it had been a year before.[129]

In May Vance sent a private memorandum to the president expressing distress at the increasing hostility to the Soviets in the United States and asking Carter to avoid the renewal of Cold War tensions. Vance explained that although some Americans opposed a Soviet role in Africa and disapproved of Soviet human rights violations, the Soviets thought the first to be legitimate foreign policy and the second to be a strictly Soviet domestic concern. Increasing talk of linking SALT with such issues, Vance warned, was confusing the Soviets and making them uncertain whether the United States still wanted a treaty. Vance recommended that Carter prepare and circulate clear policy guidelines for his advisers in order to overcome the impression that the administration was divided and uncertain. He recommended commitment to a prudent defense buildup, conclusion of a SALT II treaty, moderation in human rights rhetoric toward the Soviet Union, avoiding playing China off against the Soviets, only indirect opposition to Soviet and Cuban adventures in Africa and a show of consistency in policy. To that end he asked the president to give a speech describing United States policy for regulating a "basically competitive relationship with the Soviet Union."[130]

This became the Annapolis speech Carter gave at the Naval Academy in June, 1978. Both Vance and Brzezinski provided the president with drafts, but he wrote the speech himself. The speech balanced themes of cooperation and competition, calling first for cooperation and then warning the Soviets that cooperation would be harmed by excessive competition on their part. Vance felt that Carter, in drawing material from both drafts, had split the difference between the two poles of advice he was receiving and thus "the image of an inconsistent and uncertain government was underlined." Brzezinski, evidently more pleased with the speech than was Vance, disagreed. Carter had written the speech in the context of a very unsatisfactory May meeting with Gromyko on SALT, and the tough language about the Soviets was his own. Gromyko did not appear to understand that Soviet adventurism in the Third World was imperiling SALT, and Carter therefore decided to send a message to the Soviets through the Annapolis speech. In the talk he stressed that detente required restraint from both nations in troubled areas, he called for increased United States ties with China, Eastern Europe and the USSR and for equivalent nuclear strength between the two great powers, and he challenged the Soviet Union to seek cooperation rather than confrontation. Carter had not abandoned the cooperation/competition theme but he had acknowledged the tension and had given the Soviets a warning. This was what Brzezinski wanted and what Vance had warned against. However, Carter comments in his memoirs that even though the Soviet reaction to his speech was hostile, the SALT talks continued to make headway that summer. He was operating on the hope and assumption of cooperation.[131]

Brzezinski admits that the Annapolis speech did not set a clear direction for United States policy. Issues had to be fought one at a time, and the next one to erupt was that of the proper response to the Soviet decision to put two well-known dissidents, Anatoly Shcharansky and Aleksander Ginzburg, on trial. Carter's domestic advisers urged him to respond strongly and negatively, presumably for domestic political reasons. Brzezinski chaired a meeting of key advisers without Vance present, in which it was agreed that the United States should deny the Soviets the opportunity to import specific technologies. Vance later opposed such a step. Secretary Brown agreed with sanctions but Secretary Blumenthal, representing a Treasury Department point of view, was opposed. The president was severely cross pressured by his own advisers and also had to consider the impact of a sanction on SALT. He eventually decided to impose a set of specific restraints on the importation of American technology to the Soviet Union and became quite angry when he later discovered that the Treasury, Commerce and State departments were dragging their heels on implementation. A further controversy over the issue between the secretaries of commerce and energy found its way into the newspapers, and Brzezinski reports that Carter was furious.[132]

The problem was greater than a specific issue of technology transfer. According to a senior NSC staff member the fundamental division within the administration was "over whether the Soviet Union was a status quo power."[133] The president was trying very hard not to come down on either side of that issue but to warn the Soviets that cooperation was better for them than conflict.

Brzezinski appears to have regretted the fact that he and Carter did not share a grand strategy in the manner of Nixon and Kissinger. Since neither Carter nor Vance thought in broad conceptual terms, in Brzezinski's view, he had to work to influence the president on specific cases. In a December 28, 1978, diary entry he stated, "The President on specific issues tends to be tough, and sides with me when there is a showdown, but at the same time he is very much tempted by the vision of a grand accommodation with Brezhnev."[134]

An analysis of the speeches of Carter, Vance and Brzezinski in 1979 reveals different views of the world. Carter generally shared Vance's optimism about the stability of the international system, with Soviet actions causing occasional eruptions of pessimism. His speeches were most concerned with the Middle East, China and SALT. Brzezinski, in contrast to Vance, described the USSR as the cause of increasing global instability.[135] NSC staff members recalled that they could predict Carter's position on issues on which he had convictions such as human rights and SALT. But in the last two years they found they could not predict his response to events such as Iran, the discovery of a Soviet brigade in Cuba and the Russian invasion of Afghanistan.[136]

Brzezinski was acting much more explicitly as an advocate by 1979, with Carter's approval, he believed, since "events bore out my grimmer assessments of the Soviet role and because increasingly the administration needed an articulate voice to explain what it was trying to do."[137] Carter, however, bounced back and forth between Brzezinski and Vance until the end of the year and the Soviet invasion of Afghanistan when he shifted permanently in Brzezinski's direction.

Brzezinski used NSC staff work and his chairmanship of the SCC to win support for new policies from the president and his cabinet colleagues. The early identification of the Persian Gulf as an area in which the United States had strong security stakes did not initially lead to action in developing corresponding military capabilities. Brzezinski and NSC planners were distressed at the Soviet display of military force in the strategic air and sea lifts to Ethiopia in 1977 and 1978 but could not evoke much concern within the government. Huntington and Odom had attempted to get people in the State Department and Defense Department to look at Iran in 1977, particularly in regard to the stability of the regime. But NSC staff members who worked with State Department colleagues on Iran perceived that such an analysis could be done only over the department's opposition. In the Spring of 1979, as events began to overtake the shah's government, Brzezinski got the SCC to recommend to the president that United States military capability in the Persian Gulf region be equivalent to that of the USSR. This led to a push by Brzezinski for the development of the Rapid Deployment Force, an idea agreed to in 1977 but never implemented. The Soviet invasion of Afghanistan gave real impetus to this effort, and Brzezinski used the SCC to push his cause. The president was brought into discussions and eventually a presidential directive went to the Defense Department asking for the development of a Rapid Deployment Force. The NSC staff members who initially had identified the Persian Gulf as an area at risk felt vindicated.[138]

Brzezinski increasingly regarded Secretary of Defense Harold Brown as an ally in influencing Carter. At first Brown had been on the fence in the strategic geopolitical disagreements between Brzezinski and Vance, displaying little interest in such general questions. He also failed to support Brzezinski in regard to Soviet actions in Africa or the need for a military coup in Iran. But in 1979 and thereafter Brown joined with Brzezinski in pressing the president to increase United States defense capabilities. Carter often resented Brown's insistence and asked Brzezinski to have his staff give Pentagon budgetary claims increased scrutiny. Carter, however, reversed himself on defense, primarily to obtain the Senate's ratification of the SALT treaty. He announced plans to develop the MX missile before signing the SALT treaty even though, according to a June diary entry, the decision ran against all of his instincts. Senator Sam Nunn and others believed that

Carter was not sufficiently committed to a strong defense, citing his decision not to build the B1 bomber. The MX decision and the commitment to increases of 3 percent after inflation in the defense budget were Carter's responses.[139]

The internal debate within the administration in August and September after the discovery of a Soviet brigade in Cuba made Carter appear indecisive, though in fact his response reveals his determination to do nothing to weaken the chances of SALT ratification. In July an intelligence surveillance Brzezinski had requested uncovered the existence of the Soviet troops. Brzezinski then used the information to illustrate Soviet adventurism in Africa, Yemen and in support of Vietnamese aggression in Cambodia, urging Carter to make an issue of the troops in the context of the larger pattern. A public response was necessary because news of the brigade was out and some members of Congress were calling for strong action and saying that SALT was in danger. Brzezinski reports that Carter was prepared to make a speech on the Cuban brigade with special emphasis on Soviet activities in the Third World. But Democratic Senate majority leader Robert Byrd and Soviet Ambassador Anatoly Dobrynin conveyed to Carter their shared view that the brigade was a red herring. It had been there since 1962 and was a training rather than a combat unit. Byrd told Carter that making a major issue of the brigade would risk SALT ratification, which was Vance's view as well. In due course Carter spoke on television, labeling the existence of the brigade unacceptable (a term he later regretted) but also denying that it was a major problem. Brzezinski considered resigning because the speech did not focus on Soviet adventurism. But the issue eventually died down and the SALT hearings continued. The accounts of Carter, Vance and Brzezinski in their memoirs do not always coincide. Brzezinski gives the fullest and most dramatic version. But despite the deep split between Vance and Brzezinski, Carter pursued his primary goal, which was to get SALT ratified. In this sense, he was still closer to Vance than to Brzezinski.[140]

The Soviet invasion of Afghanistan in late 1979 had a more profound effect on Carter than any other unanticipated event in his administration. He felt personally betrayed in his efforts to win ratification of SALT II. The invasion changed Carter as a person, one of his closest aides thought; it steeled and toughened him and made him more forceful, as seen in his retaliatory actions of suspending high technology sales to the Soviets, the grain embargo and the boycott of the summer Olympics.[141] The balance of influence within the administration permanently tipped in favor of Brzezinski, a fact which Vance admits: "Before Afghanistan, these differences, though sharp at times, were containable at the cost of not having a truly coherent policy. Afterward, however, it became increasingly difficult to hold the [internal] coalition together." Vance saw himself and the policy of a regulated competition with the Soviet Union as the losers. Confrontation was the new policy, although in his opinion the confrontation "was more rhetorical than actual." For Brzezinski the Soviet invasion was a perverse vindication of his early warnings that United States failure to challenge the Russians in Ethiopia would give the impression of American weakness and embolden the Soviets for other aggressive actions. The invasion gave Brzezinski the opportunity he had been seeking for three years, beginning with the Huntington-Odom study, to establish a new foreign policy on the presumption of East-West conflict. Brzezinski's consoling remark to Carter, as the president postponed the ratification of SALT, was that he would have to be Harry Truman and contain the Soviets before he could be Woodrow Wilson and bring the peace.[142]

The collapse of SALT, the Iranian revolution and the Soviet invasion of Afghanistan were all disappointments for the State Department policy of balancing cooperation and competition with the Soviet Union, and Carter was reported to be dissatisfied with Vance as these events engulfed the administration. Vance's resignation in opposition to the Iranian rescue mission grew out of his opposition to the use of force to save the hostages, but the immediate conflict also provided an opportunity to leave an uncongenial situation. In early 1980 Vance had asked Carter to let him talk with Gromyko about the increase in tensions and send Marshall Shulman, Vance's adviser on the Soviet Union, to talk with Brezhnev. Carter had refused, which perhaps says more about Vance's resignation than the rescue mission. Another factor must surely have been the controversy about whether Vance or Brzezinski was in charge of foreign policy. On April 17, the Odeen report was publicly aired at Senate Foreign Relations Committee hearings on the "role and accountability" of the national security adviser. Opinion polls then showed Vance trailing Brzezinski in the public's perception of who most influenced the president's decisions, and Vance resigned on April 28.[143]

Carter did not succeed in establishing unity in his foreign policy team after Senator Edmund Muskie became secretary of state. Vice-President Mondale had recommended Muskie because he believed that Brzezinski was hurting Carter politically and that the politically experienced Muskie could control Brzezinski, as well as help Carter in the election. Muskie received a promise from Carter that he would be the principal foreign policy spokesman for the administration and Brzezinski's public role would be somewhat curbed. But tension resurfaced in August when Muskie discovered that he had not been informed or consulted about the major change in United States nuclear strategy signified by Presidential Directive 59 which set out strategies for fighting a prolonged nuclear war. Muskie had become secretary too late in the day for him to do the necessary homework to keep up with Brzezinski. However, the fact that Brzezinski and Brown excluded him from important discussions also contributed to his lack of knowledge of the steps leading to the directive. By early fall the secretary of state was saying publicly that if Carter were reelected he would stay on only if major changes were made in the way foreign policy was managed. Brzezinski saw the challenge coming and was confident that he would survive it because he had the president's support.[144]

Why did Carter tolerate the increasing internal discord within his own foreign policy councils? A comparison with the domestic and economic policy-making systems suggests, first, that he thought of White House policy advisers and their staffs as his personal advisers with substantive views of their own rather than as the brokers suggested by the "custodian" role.

Carter initially gave Eizenstat and the DPS a modest advisory role with virtually no coordinating authority. A stronger position for the DPS and its chief in relation to the departments developed virtually out of necessity, though DPS authority vis-à-vis the departments was never strong. Their primary role was to match administration domestic policy proposals to the political world of Washington. Eizenstat thus made himself and his staff useful to the president without treading on the prerogatives of cabinet members and departments.

The Economic Policy Group lacked analytic staff and was poor at formal coordination of policy options. Carter's lack of interest in such a formal coordinating role caused him to tolerate this situation. However, in due course his senior economic advisers sorted themselves into a pattern in which their respective staffs analyzed choices for the president. Only a few macroeconomic decisions came up each year—having to do with budgets and taxes—and the CEA and OMB were efficient analysts of microeconomic policy alternatives. Policy disagreements were clearly present but were contained by the informal collegiality of the decision system.

The same situation might have prevailed in foreign policy making if

Brzezinski had played a more restrained role. It seems likely, however, that Carter's policies toward the Soviet Union would have shifted as they did in any case. Brzezinski's contribution was to increase internal conflict and make it appear to the public that the president was not in charge—an implication Carter tolerated. He may have allowed it because he *was* in charge of policy and the decision system worked well most of the time, as revealed in the major policy achievements described here. He liked Brzezinski and learned from him. He may have lacked sensitivity to the impressions of internal disarray that were perceived outside the administration, and he did not appear to understand the "custodian" role and what Brzezinski might have done for him by playing it. He wanted a personal adviser and regarded himself as his own custodian.

The central story of Carter policy toward the Soviet Union, however, is not these organizational issues but the collapse of the detente between the United States and the USSR negotiated by President Nixon and Henry Kissinger. It had begun to collapse in the Ford presidency when Kissinger was secretary of state. Nixon and Kissinger had mistakenly assumed that the inducements of arms reductions and liberalized trade with the United States would persuade the Soviets to desist from Third World adventures. As Kissinger moved to check Soviet interventions in Africa, the Middle East and Southeast Asia, he found himself caught in the cross fire between Republican conservatives who opposed detente and Democratic liberals hostile to United States interventions in Angola and other contested areas.[145]

Carter inherited this situation but initially addressed it with hope that detente could be revived. He adhered strongly to this hope for three years, basing his public rhetoric not on Cold War themes but on the hopes for peace, stability and human rights. His major achievements were guided by these hopes. In due course, however, he encountered Soviet adventurism—a great disappointment to him—and responded forcefully. After the blow of the Soviet invasion of Afghanistan and the consequent withdrawal of the SALT II treaty from the Senate, Carter was forced to engage in Cold War rhetoric which was not his style and may have been uncomfortable for him. But his hopes that cooperation would contain competition had been dashed. A president with more foreign policy experience and greater historical knowledge might have seen it coming, but Carter had made his rhetorical and political investments elsewhere—in the Panama Canal treaties, the Camp David agreement, the normalization of United States relations with China and the negotiation of SALT II.

Carter's management of relations with the USSR and between the assistant for national security and the secretary of state broke down at the same time. His emphasis on cooperation and collegiality in policy making proved unsuccessful, and he was left with a policy and a policy process in disarray. But to have asked for a different policy and policy-making process would have been to ask for a different president. The process produced a number of important policy achievements. Like any political leader Carter had to play to his strengths, but in United States-Soviet policy and policy making his strengths were found wanting.

6
AN APPRAISAL OF STYLE

An American president seeks to fashion a unity among purpose, politics and process. Policy goals, calculations about the political resources available to achieve those goals, and the organization and management of executive processes by which goals are set and means are specified form a seamless web of interconnections created by the president. Continuing presidential actions create this web, and it sets the framework within which presidential lieutenants work. Advisers may influence its shape and direction within limits set by the president, but this setting of boundaries is a necessary ingredient of presidential authority. Other politicians, groups, observers and critics respond to this framework often without perceiving its interrelated character. They may fasten on a part of the whole—political strategies or management of policy making—without understanding the relation of the part to a larger pattern.

The fusion of purpose, politics and process is a creative action which is a manifestation of political personality. A president joins his values, needs, modes of thought and the skills that have developed from that combination into a style of leadership that emphasizes his strengths as he understands them. That political personality, in turn, seeks congruence and consistency among the elements of policy leadership—purpose, politics and process. The congruence and consistency are never perfect, but despite the sometimes inevitable tension and conflict presidents seek congruence as a way of coping with reality and the tasks of leadership. Alexander George cites a paradigm shift in cognitive inquiry from the conception of the person as a passive agent who responds to environmental stimuli toward a conception of people actively shaping their understanding of their environment through problem solving. As we acquire information we make sense of it by joining it with beliefs, norms and values and thus we develop a coherent way of understanding the world and relating that understanding to action. George supports the idea of congruence by linking individual cognitive style with managerial style. Thus, a person with a high tolerance for conflicting ideas may favor a form of decision making in which adversaries compete for his support; someone who seeks unity and order may prefer a highly structured model of debate and decision in which consensus prevails.[1] The idea of congruence among purpose, politics and process set out here is an expansion of George's conception of linkage to encompass the central elements of leadership style. Jimmy Carter thus sought to achieve public goods in the form of comprehensive programs through political appeals to diffuse goals rather than to specific interests and coalitions, and he developed such programs in a decision-making process that placed the highest priority on study and collegiality. The theme of achievement for a general welfare permeated purpose, politics and process. And that formulation of the task of leadership matched Carter's values, need for achievement, cognitive style and, therefore, his strengths as a leader as he understood them.

The congruent elements of leadership style are reinforcing and no one factor can be explained by the others. Thus one does not seek to explain policy purpose solely by the character of decision processes or strategies of politics although these surely influence goals. By the same token, policy goals may shape both political strategies and decision processes. We are talking about a loose, interactive system in which goals, calculations about politics and decision processes influence one another across time. In a stable system they also reinforce one another.

The conception of "policy leadership" encompasses presidential calculations about purpose, politics and process and is therefore broader than the simple notion of structuring and managing decision making. But it does not include leadership of Congress or public opinion in an active sense. The two companion volumes on Carter capture those two aspects of leadership.[2] The president's role as a diplomat, which in a strict sense reaches beyond policy leadership as defined, is included here because Jimmy Carter's actions in this area illustrate his problem solving bent better than does any other aspect of his presidency.

The central question in the appraisal of a president's effectiveness is to match style of policy leadership to the historical context of opportunities and constraints. Did the president make the most of his opportunities? Was his policy style well matched to the overriding imperatives for presidential leadership in that time?[3] To ask the question is to answer it in a few cases, such as Franklin Roosevelt's and Dwight Eisenhower's. Other presidents have clearly been out of place in their time. Herbert Hoover and Lyndon Johnson, for example, were not prepared for the crises that overwhelmed them. But most presidents struggle with ambiguous tasks in uncertain times. Jimmy Carter fits into this middle category, with the puzzle of his great successes and failures.

The effort to appraise an individual president in these terms necessarily leads to a broader and even more difficult question. How well does the policy leadership style of a given president match the requirements of presidential leadership set by the political system? This is a difficult question to answer because there is no widely accepted set of norms for presidential leadership. The dominant normative model has been that of the president as skillful bargainer with a sensitivity to power relationships. Richard Neustadt's 1960 portrayal of Franklin Roosevelt follows this model and is incomplete, because it emphasizes the fox and neglects the lion. More recent conceptions of the requirements of presidential leadership suggest that bargaining skills have taken second place to the presentation of self to the public, in a television age in which intermediaries between president and public have been weakened. And as a third variation on the theme, Greenstein presents Eisenhower as a combination of private political astuteness and public benevolence.[4] Different policy leadership styles seem to have been effective for varying times and tasks, which may explain the difficulty political scientists and historians have in agreeing on constant norms. The efforts to establish such norms continue, but in the attempt we are too quick to assume that all factors contributing to presidential success are unchanging except leadership skill. The political and institutional weaknesses of the presidency cause us to fall into this trap. We look for heroes who can save the republic by virtuosity. But presidents are effective or ineffective in part because of situational factors over which they have no control.

Yet we must not abandon skill as a gauge of effectiveness. The difficult analytic task is to assess the importance of skill in relation to historical opportunities and constraints. Skill and situation may reinforce each other positively just as ineptness may preside over hopeless situations. It is also possible for skill to overcome adverse conditions and for intractable conditions to swamp skill. The achievements and failures of individual presidents are best understood through contextual analysis.

Such a contextual approach does not resolve the question of whether there are better or worse ways to be president in all times. Comparative analysis within a common framework of skill, opportunities and constraints might yield some answers. But contextual analysis can help us appraise one president. At the end of this chapter we will examine Jimmy Carter's style and skill as a policy leader in relation to his times, not in a definitive way, but to raise questions for future work. The basis for such an appraisal must be a delineation of his style of policy leadership.

ELEMENTS OF STYLE

Jimmy Carter began his political career as an outsider who had to fight the machine to take his seat in the state senate. He invented a style of political leadership that combined his capacity for homework with the appeal to broad goals, and he thus reached beyond the normal representation of interests and politics of bargaining. This style of leadership was consistent with his commitment to good government as a southern Progressive and his personal interpretation of the social gospel of Protestantism. He made administrative reorganization the central theme of his governorship with normal legislative, bureaucratic and interest group politics the enemy. Even though he prevailed, his friends did not think that he could have been reelected governor because his style of leadership had not created a coalition to support him. He thought that in the wake of Watergate the combination of competence and morality he had brought to the governorship was perfectly suited for a race for the presidency.

An analysis of his operational code as governor and president reveals Carter to have been a nonpolitical politician who sought the achievement of "public goods" through a combination of homework and moral appeals and expected to be rewarded politically for them. He accepted conventional political advice from lieutenants about the stakes and interests of others and the requirements for bargaining, but he regarded these primarily as second best fallback strategies. His ideology, in all areas of policy, could be broadly characterized as centrist. He was not an engineer who lacked a philosophy and focused exclusively on solving problems. But his manner of making decisions through homework gave that impression. His executive style called for diversity of advice within a collegial setting emphasizing homework and knowledge. More than anything else he searched for hard problems to solve because he was good at problem solving and his world view required it. Purpose, politics and process were joined in a style of policy leadership.

This model of Carter's political personality is painted in broad strokes. Contradictions, tensions and inconsistencies in beliefs sometimes arose, and style varied according to problem and policy. But, even so, the coherence was remarkable. What is extraordinary and not easy to explain is how little understanding there was of his operational code. Deliberate strategies of leadership on his part were too often cited as instances of incompetence and inexperience. One reason may have been that Carter's critics, in politics, the press and universities, accepted bargaining models of political leadership as the norm for presidents and perceived Carter's rejection of such norms as ineptness rather than deliberate strategy. The chapters in this book on domestic, economic and foreign policy making reveal crosscutting themes of purpose, politics and process and illustrate the underlying coherence of Carter's policy leadership.

Carter could not be characterized either as a conservative southern Democrat who disliked spending money on social programs or as a consolidating Democrat who sought to tidy up social reform administratively. Nor was he a reform leader in the characteristic Democratic mode. He was guided by the insight that new social problems requiring fresh responses were emerging. The problem of overcoming bad national habits in the use of energy through new combinations of energy development and conservation was a prime example. The importance of tying work to welfare was another. He anticipated the need for tax reform and led the fight for deregulation in transportation and banking. The implicit theme in his domestic initiatives was the resolution of problems through efficiency and equity. He was not a political leader who sought to bring in a new era through political conflict. Rather, he sought combinations of new and old elements that would win broad approval. He was not at the end of a dialectic of thesis, antithesis and synthesis but perhaps at the beginning in that he addressed emerging problems. But this was one of his difficulties with the Democratic coalition. The ideological fervor may have gone out of the impulse for social reform but an abundance of "interest group liberalism" was the legacy.[5] Carter was sure to collide with the demands of Democratic interest groups for a number of reasons. He regarded group claims as selfish and antithetical to the general interest. In a time of new problems requiring fresh definitions of the public good they were beside the point. And his diffident style of public leadership prevented him from exploiting rhetorically, with claimant groups and their clients, the things that his administration did for them.

Carter's mandate to department heads that they would be the initial formulators of administration policies reflected his problem-solving orientation. When he turned to Schlesinger and Califano for leadership on energy and welfare reform respectively he was carrying out his view that responsibility and expertise should be joined. He set general guidelines, for example to join work and welfare or to make the Department of Education as comprehensive as possible, and relied on the responsible officials to develop the plan. The policy-making process was thus structured to produce public goods. Two problems emerged in short order. Substantive expertise was no substitute for political soundings, and cabinet officers could not coordinate each other. Carter's vision did not take sufficient account of legislative and bureaucratic politics. Remedies for these flaws evolved in the developing role of the Domestic Policy Staff, which took political soundings and coordinated the work of the departments without abandoning the commitment to designing comprehensive programs. But strategies for compromise on second-best plans were also part of the repertoire. Carter's machinery for policy making in the governorship had captured the same balance between ideal and reality.

The congruence among purpose, politics and process in economic policy making are clear. Centrist policies were designed to reach for support beyond the Democratic coalition without alienating that base. The decision process reflected this search for balance. Carter supported programs in health, education, labor and welfare within limits set by his concern about inflation. But too often he was caught between group claims and his own fiscal caution without a clear decision rule for resolution of the conflict. There is no easy intellectual guideline in microeconomics to limit spending on behalf of the larger concern for inflation sensitive fiscal policy. Nor were there clear political criteria for choice. So in most cases Carter split the difference, giving claimants half a loaf by invoking his goal of fiscal constraint. Sometimes he allowed more generous disbursements—unfortunate subsidies to maritime interests, for example, or the farm subsidies OMB analysts found excessive—but Carter never seemed to extract any political credit for such action and he caused himself political damage with organized labor and other Democratic groups when he threw back only half a loaf.

This tough-minded attitude toward group claims gradually moderated across the four years, as seen in the Chapter 4 story of the dilution of wage-price guidelines in response to the inflationary impact of the 1979 OPEC oil price increase. Organized labor abandoned its tepid enthusiasm for wage guidelines when its members had to struggle to keep up with the inflation caused by the oil shock, and the administration acquiesced. On the other hand, education and job-training budgets were cut in the last year in the second antiinflation budget submitted in 1980. So the signals to Democratic constituencies were mixed.

Macroeconomic policy began with the new president and the Democratic coalition pulling together behind the economic stimulus package, which came directly out of the campaign and Carter's criticism of the Ford recession. But even here Carter was cautious. He did not go as far as congressional and business leaders, organized labor and black groups advised. In fact, he had deep doubts at the outset about the necessity for a stimulus package because he thought the economy might be recovering on its own. Carter may have lacked the implicit Democratic reflexes for expansionary economic policy. When he later canceled the tax rebate proposal because of his conviction that recovery was on its way he also gave a clear signal to his associates that he regarded inflation as his, and the nation's, major economic problem. He was right. However, he gave mixed signals in macroeconomic policy, as in microeconomic issues. Annual budgetary strategy varied depending upon whether the specter to be warded off was inflation or recession. And in the last year when inflation soared Carter returned to his original antiinflationary resolve and rejected the advice of his economists to provide a quick stimulus to the economy and thus guarantee simultaneous inflation and recession. He had begun the term in harness with Democratic leaders and he left office fighting a lone battle against the same people.

Thus both microeconomic and macroeconomic policies were inconsistent across the four years, each exhibiting a zigzag pattern and at times in opposition to each other. This pattern reflected the difficulty of balancing between inflation and recession. But it may also have reflected uncertain management of the economic decision-making process. No single economic adviser pulled together options for presidential choice in terms of long-term policy priorities or strategies. Carter listened to diverse advice, much of it conflicting, and made decisions on the merits as he saw them in particular instances. It is difficult to separate the ad hoc, zigzag character of this decision process from the necessity of tacking and adapting to new circumstances.

The parallels of economic policy purpose, politics and process with the patterns of domestic policy are clear. Economic policy was centrist; it reached beyond Democratic constituencies toward a larger public while seeking to placate Democratic groups. Carter attempted to establish a new

Democratic identity for fiscal responsibility not unlike the efforts in energy policy and welfare reform. The themes were equity and efficiency. Economic decision making was limited to a small number of regular players in comparison to domestic policy because the process is more institutionalized, with the Treasury Department, the CEA and OMB sharing a division of labor and playing the central roles. Still, a loose collegiality and ad hoc decision making characterized both policy areas.

Carter's foreign policy sought international cooperation and the resolution of outstanding problems of conflict among nations. The agent was to be the president himself emphasizing his problem solving and negotiating skills with the support of a small circle of lieutenants.

Carter's idealism was more than a negative reaction to the realpolitik of Henry Kissinger. It was deeply rooted in his understanding of America's proper role in the world. Like Woodrow Wilson he saw the United States as a beacon for the ideals of democracy and human rights. This was also the religious Carter who cited Reinhold Niebuhr on the duty of politics to bring justice to a sinful world. He did not appear to be comfortable with military thinking and took pride in the fact that no American boy died in combat on his watch. Above all, he wanted arms reduction and thought of American relations with the Soviet Union in terms of that challenge. Problem solving, to reduce conflicts between the United States and Panama or Egypt and Israel, was an extension of this world view—a view that permitted Carter to use his skills to the fullest.

The politics of foreign policy achievement was an appeal to American idealism on an abstract level with the hope for credit from specific achievements like Panama and Camp David. Boldness in taking on problems was not inhibited by fear that there would be no political reward. There is an analogue to the introduction of comprehensive domestic programs here. Supporters cannot really bless the effort until it has succeeded. At the outset the proposed policy appeals to no tangible interests but rather holds the promise of a new condition beneficial to all.

Foreign policy making exhibited the most centralized collegiality of the three policy areas because Carter's role as decision maker and manager of the process was more central and decisive. Still, decisions had the same serial, ad hoc character, as Carter took one case at a time and responded to different advisory streams. This system produced the greatest successes of the Carter administration because the setting and conditions for success were most propitious. Carter could use his strengths of analysis and negotiation to fullest advantage. The negotiating process could be more easily controlled than in a wide-ranging conflict with Congress over domestic policy. When Carter gave a clear lead lieutenants were more supportive than in any other policy area. And the inherent intractability of economic forces beyond anyone's control was less a factor in diplomatic negotiations. It is little surprise that Carter put his energies here.

We see here, even more clearly than in domestic and economic policy, Carter's neglect of the coordinating role that staff assistants might play in decision making. Brzezinski did oversee a great deal of coordination but the evidence available suggests that neither he nor the president saw his central role as one of neutral custodian who would develop options for decision. The Odeen report simply confirms Brzezinski's self-portrait in his memoir and Carter's report of how and why Brzezinski was valuable to him. The absence of such a custodian, as in economic policy, helps explain the ad hoc character of decision making in American-Soviet relations. The central management of decision making in terms of larger strategic objectives was not a strong feature of Carter policy making.

Policy aspirations in all three areas were thus broad and idealistic. Carter hoped to move the nation forward to a new plateau of coherent social programs, a sound economy and international stability. This was more than consolidation of past trends. He was reaching for the vague outlines of a new era.

In politics Carter gave limited attention to coalition building. The norm was to go for the ideal first and then fall back to second best. The fallback was sometimes ungainly, as in the scramble to produce a budget and simultaneously fight inflation and recession in the last year and the Cold War rhetoric and response—with which Carter was clearly uncomfortable—to the Soviet invasion of Afghanistan.

Carter dominated the processes of decision making, imposing his priorities and acting as the integrating force among advisers. And for the most part he got the kinds of policies he wanted. The one clear weakness in the policy development process was that Carter did not manage the breakdown of collegiality well but simply took the extra burden of integrating conflicting advice on his own shoulders.

Carter's idealism and ambition for achievement lacked the dimension of political calculation, which caused him to make tactical errors and may have reflected deficiencies in his very idealism. One can see a progression across four years, in each policy area, from proclamation of ideal to acceptance of reality. Comprehensive domestic policies gave way to proposals for incremental change. Promises to balance the budget and restore economic expansion gave way in the last year to damage limitation measures directed against both inflation and recession. Hopes of international cooperation and arms control were replaced by a revival of Cold War rhetoric and actions. The approaching election of 1980 may have stimulated this realism, but a series of fallback actions was not the best way to gain public recognition for four years of achievement. The administration appeared to have been overtaken by events. The world had proved less tractable to problem solving than Carter had thought it would be.

A STYLE OF LEADERSHIP

Talented political leaders show a great range of skills in their work. They will turn from declamation to negotiation or from conflict to bargaining, varying their styles and strategies to match changing situations. Different ranges of skills may be available to them, but no leader can be effective with only one skill. However, at the core of a political leader's style, no matter how wide the range of skills, one will find a theme with which that leader defines himself as a politician and as a person. This core holds the fundamental strengths and weaknesses of a political man—both sides of the coin, for one does not have strong qualities without having the opposite. If a leader is to emphasize strengths, as self-definition requires, then the weaknesses will also become apparent. In playing to strength one grasps the aspects of reality necessary for success but neglects insights coming from one's less developed, weaker side. This search for fulfillment of self through political leadership may be a manifestation of the private, perhaps unconscious, person, so that one acts out one's sense of personal destiny in a political career. Thus, Harry Truman's love of making decisions, as a way of defining himself, caused him to turn this strength to a fault and decide too quickly at times. Eisenhower's gift for binding others to him precluded a politics of attack. Kennedy's cool detachment and logic inhibited rhetorical appeals. Johnson's capacity for building coalitions of support made it almost impossible for him to make divisive choices. Nixon's instinct for the bold advance was hostage to his fear of enemies.

Jimmy Carter had a range of style and skill that ran the gamut from the rhetorical to the analytical. When he campaigned he could be a preacher and before a knowledgeable audience he could be a lucid speaker in exposition of a complex problem. He used both moral appeals and knowledgeability in persuasion and negotiation and was capable of hard and dispassionate analysis in addressing problems. But the underlying theme was Carter's search for achievement. He would say during campaigns that he did not intend to lose, as if will itself were a key to victory. He would drive his lieutenants to persevere in a difficult negotiating situation, saying that he simply would not admit the possibility of defeat. He believed that correct answers to problems could be developed through study and analysis.

At the core of Jimmy Carter's political personality was the imperative for mastery. His life was to be a testing ground on which he would prove himself, and he was to do it alone. This was the source of his strength and his weakness as a political man. His great achievements—winning the presidential campaign and his foreign policy successes—were personal achievements. His failures came when he was unable to subordinate the intractable forces of history to his tenacity and perseverance. But he was alone in failure as in achievement.

The specific talents and corresponding failings clustering around the core of Carter's political personality can, when analyzed, help reveal the full dimensions of Carter the politician. First we have an enumeration of strengths, which were themselves complementary.

1. Carter's ambition to achieve what others thought infeasible gave him the staying power to overcome his own discouragement. The newly elected president introduced a comprehensive energy plan and fought for it for four years, with little encouragement from seasoned politicians. The final installment came only after an extraordinary appeal to the nation couched in moral terms few politicians would have been comfortable using. Carter's advisers before the talks with Begin and Sadat at Camp David were drawing up plans for an interim agreement on the terms of future negotiations. The president wanted an agreement on the issues at stake and, to a considerable degree, he got it. The drive to achieve and the tenacity to stay with the effort were a talent.

2. Carter was insightful about emerging historical situations that required solutions of the very kind he was inclined to propose. His mind searched for integrative packages of solutions through which old conflicts could be resolved and new problems faced. In a very real sense he had the solutions and was searching for problems to match to them. The theme of the solution was equity and efficiency. Thus welfare reform would provide fair national standards of income maintenance but would require work to give recipients the incentive and opportunity to get off welfare. He finally

proposed a plan for national health insurance that would extend coverage through insurance to those people without it but would balance that expense against careful planning to control cost inflation.[6] The archetypal quality to his thinking impelled him to search for equitable solutions to problems—the Panama Canal, the Palestinian question, parity in American and Soviet armaments, human rights abroad. The analogue to efficiency in cases of this kind was Carter's ingenuity in devising solutions that would overcome conflict.

3. Carter had great capacity to put all his abilities to work in problem solving. His ambition, optimism, tenacity and capacity for homework reinforced one another. Not many presidents would leap into difficult situations like the Middle East negotiations or day-to-day management of the hostage crisis and stay with them until resolution. This staying power was probably Carter's strongest talent as a political man.

4. He could create an atmosphere of unity and collegiality around his purposes. Lieutenants fell into line to help and cooperated easily with one another under his leadership. There appears to have been very little friction among Carter's lieutenants on major policy issues in which he made his goals and wishes clear. The record on Panama, SALT and the Middle East reveals a very high level of cooperation among the president's advisers, perhaps more so than usual in the councils of presidents. Carter's own drive and sense of purpose may have contributed to this unity. He also knew how to bring contending parties together in diplomatic negotiations, as evidenced most strikingly in the Panama negotiations and at Camp David.

The unavoidable weaknesses that corresponded to these strengths were the following:

1. Because of his ambition to solve problems Carter was not willing or sensitive to the need for careful political soundings about the feasibility of his ambitions. His very definition of himself as a politician ruled out the conventional politician's role—his "art"—of broker and compromiser. This lack was particularly apparent when Carter dealt with other professional politicians, whether at home or abroad. They sensed, correctly, that he was not operating by their rules. What appeared to him to be a superior kind of political leadership in which one sought public goods appeared to them to be a holier-than-thou attitude. This sometimes made it difficult for him to win the cooperation of other politicians for his ventures. He did not get along much better with foreign politicians than with members of Congress, except with leaders like Anwar Sadat who could be brought to share

his moral visions. This distancing of himself from other politicians was clearly a handicap, but it may have been the price paid for his ambition to achieve. His rejection of the conventional political arts caused him to make mistakes that gave him a poor professional reputation among politicians and observers of government. He seldom considered the effect of one issue on another; he made public statements that undermined his private negotiating position; he was insensitive to his own personal professional reputation. Carter could not be a calculating politician and play to his strengths for leadership as he understood them.

2. He saw clearly into the near future but had little sense of past history and therefore could easily make blunders by proposing impractical courses of action. He sought welfare reform because his experience as governor of Georgia convinced him that the federal welfare program was neither equitable nor efficient.[7] But knowledge of the deep political stalemate on welfare reform in the Nixon administration might have persuaded him that this was not a high priority issue in his own administration. However, he did not appear to value that kind of knowledge. Carter and his advisers all agree that he made a very great blunder in proposing deep cuts in arms, going far beyond the agreement reached for Ford and Brezhnev at Vladivostok, as his first overture on SALT II. Neustadt and May contend that this was an avoidable blunder had Carter understood his need for historical perspective on United States negotiations with the Soviets. A look at the history of arms control negotiations might have convinced him that the Soviet Union wanted the Vladivostok agreement as a sign of continuing detente, wanted above all continuity in relations and had never subscribed to an arms agreement in which they were required to reduce their strategic forces.[8] But Carter's ahistorical turn of mind may have been the counterpart to his capacity to envision solutions to emerging problems.

3. Carter so invested himself in the major problems, with great pride and self-confidence that he could solve them, that he stood alone when he failed. He was testing himself, and therefore he had to stand alone, win or lose. This may help explain why he did not use staff assistants as well as he might have. He thought that he could integrate a diversity of advice without special help from a neutral custodian. To have admitted otherwise would have denied the unspoken assumption that he was determined, as one of his assistants put it, "to have a sense of conquering the office in its every manifestation."[9] He took credit for major achievements, seldom sharing it. And it therefore followed that he would find himself alone with

failure. His management of the hostage crisis is perhaps the best example. If he had succeeded in winning the release of the hostages without harm to them during his term he would have received great public credit. But the way he made the effort, calling attention to himself and to the existence of the hostages, shows how failure left him alone on the public stage.

4. The success of collegiality in policy making was in large part a result of Carter's own capacity to unify. But he could not completely control the dispositions of others. When conflict overcame collegiality he lacked a strategy for dealing with it. Carter's tolerance for the insubordination of senior lieutenants was very great, which could be understood in part as an extension of his religious optimism that if he invested confidence in others they would respond in kind. To a great extent, he was right. But he did not know how to deal with Califano and others who crossed him, except by firing them. He had no intermediate course between tolerance and dismissal. Brzezinski was a problem he failed to confront because he liked the man and didn't regard him as a problem. He simply took on himself the extra burden of coping with deeply divided foreign policy advisers, which was consistent with his habit, as one of his assistants put it, of being much harder on himself than on others.[10] This commitment to collegiality may be another partial explanation for his failure to use staff assistants as custodians to the degree possible. A policy analyst who acts as custodian for a political executive must necessarily challenge the assumptions of operating officers. Carter's preference for debate among equals, with himself as the arbiter, may have made him resist an institutionalized adversarial system. He perhaps saw himself as his own policy analyst. One of his White House assistants joked that Carter really wanted Eizenstat's job because "he wanted to read all the papers."[11]

5. Much testimony points to Carter's inability to comprehend fully the depth of conflicting values and stakes in the issues he was trying to resolve. He did not understand that the conflicts over welfare reform were not technical but deeply ideological. He reveals in his memoirs that he regarded the issues of contention between Egypt and Israel after Camp David as technical and minor. As one critic put it, "Carter's chief weakness seems to have been an inability to appreciate the seriousness of the contradictions that confronted him, a belief that all good things must be compatible."[12] This may be true, but the strong desire to overcome contradictions was nevertheless the very core of Jimmy Carter's talent and strength as a political leader.

Critics have held Carter responsible for the failure of his presidency. One argues that Carter's difficulties were manifestations of problems of governance in a "no win presidency" characterized by weak parties, fragmented coalitions, voracious interest groups and unrealistic public expectations.[13] But most blame him for lack of skill following on inexperience and the refusal or inability to be a politician. Such criticisms are best assessed in the larger context of an awareness of Carter's strengths. If he was to be one kind of leader he could not be another. But one must also ask if Carter's strengths were sufficient for the tasks of the presidency and whether he made the most of opportunities. This final assessment must set Carter's strengths and skills within the historical context of possibilities for presidential leadership.

CARTER AND HIS CRITICS

Since the perennial criticisms of Carter correspond very well to the analysis of weaknesses as the obverse of strengths, one must ask whether the critics also appreciated Carter's strengths and whether Carter could indeed have been a more skillful and effective version of himself.

The strongest criticism of Carter as president is that as policy leader he was not a good politician. He failed to join his initiatives to thoughtful calculations about political strategies and resources. A central part of this criticism was the claim that he tried to accomplish too much without understanding the political constraints at work. With greater awareness of his limited political resources he would prudently have devoted more attention to fewer issues.[14]

Heineman and Hessler, who served in the Carter administration, set up the ideal of a "strategic presidency" in which policy goals, political calculations and policy-making processes are unified by the president's organizing intelligence. The central principle is that the president must choose goals and develop political strategies for achieving them in a way that does not waste time, energy and political resources. Policy making must therefore be structured to support major objectives. They believe this to be even more important in periods when historical forces are not creating a strong momentum for action, such as Franklin Roosevelt's second term and the Carter presidency. In terms of the politics of the possible the president must in such times be more careful about which goals to pursue, because the margin for error is greater than when the current of events requires action. They are therefore not prepared to let Carter off the hook with the argument that the Democratic coalition was in disarray or that the public appetite for government was satiated. They believe that Carter failed to set clear priorities and develop political strategies to achieve them. Thus, he sent too much to Congress his first year, he did not join policy to politics in his calculations about what to initiate, he launched major domestic initiatives in welfare reform and national health insurance without realizing how controversial those issues were, and he did not develop the extensive legislative campaigns necessary for success.[15]

Carter's lieutenants agree with this criticism and wish that he had been a better politician in conventional terms. One White House assistant and eventual cabinet officer remembered that Carter "liked the challenge of difficult tasks but had no sense of husbanding political capital."[16] A foreign policy assistant worried that the president did not think enough about foreign policy politically. Jordan and Mondale worried, but Carter—not wanting to subordinate his central objectives to political tactics—did not. And he believed in moving on a broad front with all his forces for all his objectives at the same time. But this strategy dissipated many of his resources.[17]

These insights help explain why Carter gave little attention to the timing of initiatives. It might have been more prudent to have achieved a modest SALT agreement in the first year, built up his professional reputation at home and then turned attention to the canal treaties and further progress on SALT. But Carter wanted more than a modest SALT treaty, and since the momentum behind the negotiations with Panama was strong he hoped to have both early on. By the same token, he believed that the timing of establishing diplomatic relations with China would strengthen the United States's position with the Soviets on SALT. He may have been wrong but he believed that one achievement would help another.

The Heineman and Hessler thesis is common sense. Surely a leader should calculate available political resources before taking initiatives. But Jimmy Carter's insight told him that conventional political calculations about the construction of coalitions led only to incremental achievements. One added up existing interests and achieved a slight change in the status quo. Carter wished to use the promise of fundamental policy change as a political resource to transform the politics of the situation. The policy promise itself would become the resource that produced changes—including people's understanding of their own interests. It is more difficult to take political soundings with this strategy because the promise of policy outstrips the immediate stakes of other actors as they understand them. Thus calculations about those stakes may fall short of what can ultimately be accomplished. The only way to find out is to present a vision of future policy and hope that the vision will transform the political situation.

The weakness of Carter's insight is, of course, the very one that Heineman and Hessler identify. Goals may be sought that cannot realistically be achieved. Even more telling, one must choose among goals, and the failure to do so in hopes that one of several initiatives will strike fire is to risk losing all. Also, as a practical matter a president can only give personal attention to a few major legislative battles during a four-year term. To present a number of major initiatives is to guarantee that some will receive the close presidential attention they deserve and others will not.

The energy and welfare reform stories illustrate the strengths and weaknesses of Carter's approach to policy leadership. He did not appear to take careful political soundings in either case. Incremental politics had failed in the Nixon and Ford administrations on both issues and the coalitions of interests were aligned against action. Carter conceived of transcending such coalitions by appeals to public goods; everyone, that is, would be better off if the new policy could be put in place. The policy vision was its own political resource. The strategy seems to have worked with the energy program, for despite a great deal of conventional bargaining with affected interests the vision of the whole was greater than the sum of the parts. The urgency of the national predicament may help explain the success of the strategy. There was no such sense of imperative in regard to welfare reform. Carter seems to have learned this after the first attempt and to have pulled away from a major investment of political effort.[18] This argument does not discount the Heineman and Hessler criticism, which indeed explains much of Carter's failure. But it does not explain his successes, which had more to do with his own theory of leadership in behalf of public goods, transcending coalition politics. And if one does not make an effort to understand Jimmy Carter in terms of his own insights into political leadership and his understanding of his strengths one misses the point.

Carter's lack of cultivation of the political arts, as understood by most political practitioners, meant also that he did not cultivate politicians. He did not like politicians, especially senators, because he thought they were selfish, seeking their own political advantage to the detriment of the public good.[19] As one of his aides put it, "To have a governing coalition you have to be prepared to work in harness with a lot of people who are not perfect.

He was not a generous man in that regard. He could not slap Talmadge's back. He couldn't flatter Byrd."[20]

And yet Carter was tolerant of the shortcomings of people in his own executive family. He stood by Bert Lance, who was under fire for his financial dealings as a banker, and thereby tarnished his own reputation for rectitude. He never withdrew confidence from Hamilton Jordan, Frank Moore and other assistants who were constantly under fire for serving him poorly. He was worried about the loyalty of Joe Califano but never called him on the carpet. One may see here a hope of familial unity that is not extended to outsiders—an attitude conceivably imbedded in Carter's religious background. He hoped for a community of believers, a good Baptist concept, yet he remained the Baptist preacher you didn't tell jokes in front of.[21] Politicians found it difficult to relax with him. But of course, in keeping with his understanding of leadership, he was afraid of being co-opted into political games.

A companion criticism is that Carter did not take sufficient care to guard his professional reputation in Washington or with the public. His withdrawal of the fifty dollar tax rebate may have sent a message to congressional Democrats that if one risked going out on a limb for Carter he might chop it off.[22] Neustadt's analysis of the response of the Carter White House to the disclosures of Bert Lance's financial difficulties charges a failure to appreciate the field day the press would have in pointing out the credibility gap between the moralistic Carter, promising honesty in government, and the stubborn, prolonged defense of Lance. Neustadt believes that Carter's staff should have protected him on the Lance affair, though it is not clear that the president understood his need for protection. As a result, he spent the Summer of 1977 in damage limitation on that issue just when he needed to repair his relations with Congress over the rebate and water projects disputes and to recover from the initial failures of the energy program and the SALT overture.[23] But as one of his closest aides remembered, as governor and as president, Carter, once elected, did not pay enough attention to the public presentation of what he was doing. As president he focused on making decisions and in his mind separated campaigning and governing.[24] Government was not, for him, a continuous campaign, even though political scientists were then contending that the presidential selection process had turned presidential governance into just that. His aides thought him to be very good at campaigning. But once elected he addressed a different job.

It is difficult to imagine how Carter could have incorporated the insights of his critics about his deficiencies in the political arts into his style of leadership without giving up his very great strengths as a leader. Whether these strengths were sufficient for presidential leadership is an issue to be considered later.

Another major criticism was that Carter lacked a sense of history. "Anything he didn't believe or had not chosen to master was not worth knowing," observed a close adviser, for he "had the pride an uneducated man takes in his intelligence. History and experience were not important to him. He had the vain belief that he could move into an area and master it." Another assistant believed that since Carter's policy ideas developed from things he had done in Georgia, if it had worked there he expected it to work in Washington. Thus, his own experience told him that the protection of civil rights in the South could be a model for the protection of human rights around the world. Another illustrated Carter's lack of a sense of history by citing his promise of tax reform in his speech accepting the Democratic nomination. He had no historical knowledge of how difficult it had been to achieve such reform.[25]

Neustadt and May believe that Carter entered the presidency in the grip of the mistaken historical analogy that, much like Roosevelt in 1932, he could use the honeymoon period with Congress to win support for an avalanche of proposals.[26] Thus he proposed the economic stimulus package and election law reforms which included public financing of congressional elections, he tried to kill pork barrel water projects, asked for extensive authority to reorganize the executive branch and announced his goal of putting a lid on hospital costs. In foreign affairs he unfurled the banner of human rights, called for a ban on nuclear weapons tests, suggested a new diplomatic relationship with Cuba, attacked nuclear proliferation among nations, spoke in favor of a Palestinian homeland and sent Secretary Vance to Moscow with a proposal for deep cuts in nuclear weapons stocks beyond the terms of any past negotiation. He also sent Congress a comprehensive energy program, though this issue had received little attention in the presidential campaign. These ambitious proposals produced a "monstrous jam up," and most of them went nowhere. Carter repudiated the rebate. Many of the water projects were restored. Hospital cost containment was rejected. Tax reform and welfare reform were never given a chance. His public language on the Palestinians complicated diplomacy and relations with Congress. The Russians rejected the SALT overture. The energy program was delayed for almost two years.

Neustadt and May argue that Carter bought trouble by asking for so much so soon. A more modest program might have been more successful, both in terms of achievement and his professional reputation. Times were quiet, the economy was recovering, no foreign policy crises or military traps faced the United States. A more careful identification of priorities and marshaling of political resources might have produced greater success. This is the same criticism Heineman and Hessler make, but Neustadt and May blame Carter's deficient sense of history. He was laboring under the false analogies of FDR's hundred days and Lyndon Johnson's burst of legislative creativity in 1965. Historical and political conditions, however, were different. Roosevelt and Johnson achieved their programs on the high tide of decisive election victories which also swept extraordinary numbers of Democrats into Congress. The agenda of acute, unresolved problems was long and many vocal constituencies were demanding action. Those presidents could ride the tide of reform and guide the energies of many policy entrepreneurs in Congress and elsewhere. In contrast Carter came into office at a time of disillusionment with government, with no election mandate and without the partnership of a partisan coalition in Congress and the country.

Neustadt and May accept the argument that effective presidential leadership often must reach beyond what is thought to be attainable. But because Carter did not understand, and thus could not invoke, his historical context, he missed out on a valuable political resource for presidential persuasiveness. The central task of leadership is to articulate the dilemmas and unresolved issues of a particular time and to propose remedies in terms that strike home to large numbers of people.[27] Overkill can injure plausibility just as much as can a failure to lead in time of crisis. The more difficult assignments, of course, are those ambiguous periods when the tolerance of politics for change is unclear. In such cases the president's understanding of relevant historical experience is crucial to success. For Neustadt and May a president may compensate for limited personal experience by widespread consultation among academia, the media, president watchers and politicians. Carter and his lieutenants, they feel, failed to do this.[28]

Carter's insights into the emerging policy problems of his time created the task of winning support for fresh definitions of problems. The new positions must first be articulated and then political support cultivated until the time for action is ripe. John F. Kennedy acted in terms of this historical logic, introducing innovations in his first term with the intention of enacting most of them after he was reelected for a second term.[29] Carter's fresh, original insights about the issues facing the nation placed him far ahead of the Democratic coalition in his understanding of the inappropriateness of answers from the past. A more careful selection of objectives, couched in terms of the emerging historical context, might have made him a more plausible leader.

Another often-repeated criticism was that Carter stood alone in failure. Some of his lieutenants charge that by personally taking on hard issues that might have been better delegated to others, Carter had to assume sole responsibility when things went wrong. "Carter didn't seem to realize that by forcing conflicts to be decided in his office he would take the blame," said one. "Cabinet officers liked it. The President took the heat."[30] Thus when the secretary of interior could have taken the blame for cuts in water projects Carter muscled his way in instead.[31] He dramatized the intractable problem of winning release of the hostages in Iran by refusing to campaign against Senator Edward Kennedy in presidential primaries in order to stay home and work for their release. Several of his aides believed this to be a great error which eventually left him alone in the Rose Garden without anything to show for it. He had inadvertently called attention to his failure.[32] Carter recognized this, writing in his memoir, "It was very likely that I had been defeated . . . because I had kept these hostages and their fate at the forefront of the world's attention and had clung to a cautious and prudent policy in order to protect their lives."[33]

In the same context, his comment, "It is impossible for me to put into words how much the hostages had come to mean to me," demonstrated the degree to which he engaged himself with the substance of an issue rather than with the task of managing the images of decision making. If he saw an issue as his responsibility he seized it. The important thing was to resolve the issue, and credit would then come from the achievement rather than from clever management of appearances. The strength and weakness of this approach go hand in hand. When it succeeded Carter received attention and credit; when it failed he was blamed and isolated. In some conceptions of politics an effective politician must find ways to get the credit but avoid the blame. Carter did not reason that way. He was acting out the central theme of his career, which was to test himself against obstacles, and much of the time he was confident that he would win.

Carter's lieutenants did not regard him as a man who was testing himself in order to overcome a sense of insecurity. Quite the reverse. One assistant spoke for others in his comment that Carter reacted to hard problems "with extraordinary serenity. . . . I can't recall an incident in which he was really crushed, upset or demoralized."[34] This particular person believed Carter's religious faith to be the basis of his serenity. He was relaxed in his conviction that he was doing the right thing. Such a relaxed conviction of having made the right effort may explain a leader's willingness to accept the blame that comes with failure.

Carter was criticized for being a poor manager of relationships among his lieutenants. He did not have clear ideas about the division of labor between line and staff functions and gave uncertain signals about the degree to which he wished to delegate policy development to cabinet officers in relation to the need for coordination and arbitration by White House staffs. And he was thought to be ineffective in managing conflict among his lieutenants, simply shouldering the additional burden of incorporating differences himself.

Carter's aides found him indifferent to the organization of executive decision processes, and indeed he says very little in his memoir about such questions. According to one aide this silence reflected a belief that intelligent people could solve problems without elaborate machinery, a stance that underestimated the complexity of the task of governing since the White House staff was required by necessity to coordinate the work of complex departments. Heineman and Hessler regard Carter as having little appreciation for the skill of balancing the competing needs of centralization and decentralization in decision making. The widespread confusion about how White House staffs, Executive Office of the President staffs and department staffs were to relate to one another caused much wasted time and effort. A domestic policy assistant comments, "I don't think that Carter ever resolved in his own mind the balance point he wanted between the White House staff and Cabinet secretaries."[35]

As discussed earlier, Carter's strategy for the organization of decision making was catch-as-catch-can with the implicit principle of integrating diversity through collegiality and homework. Lieutenants would supply collegiality in response to the president's desire for unity, and the president would supply the homework. The difficulty was that it didn't always work that way. Too often Carter found himself saddled with more options than he wanted because he had not used his staff to refine and limit those options. This was partly because, as one administration economist put it,

"Carter liked to delve into the details himself. He didn't like to have potential sub options that he hadn't thought about." Eizenstat and the DPS reduced this problem in domestic policy making by laying the DPS memo on the top of the stack of recommendations from the departments; more often than not Carter would follow the advice of his own staff. The problem was more acute in economic policy making because he would not delegate the custodian role to anyone. As a result, instead of getting three options he sometimes got six. Too many minor issues reached him because subordinates disagreed on how they should be handled. Carter asked Eizenstat to be an informal coordinator of economic policy development, complaining that he was getting too many memos on economic policy. But he gave Eizenstat no additional staff with which to do this work. In Eizenstat's view Carter needed someone to play the role that William Seidman had played for President Ford as the custodian of economic policy options. Internal observers believed that the disjointed character of the economic policy-making process made for disjointed policy in which issues were decided without continuity. A long-term economic policy was less possible in this sort of arrangement.[36]

Critics of foreign policy making identified the same flaw in process and policy. Carter's preference for using Brzezinski as a policy thinker and not a custodian sometimes led to poor coordination of the development of policy options. Foreign policy thus never developed a clear, coherent pattern. Vance and Brzezinski seemed alternately up or down, and their pushing and pulling in opposite directions necessarily detracted from the management task of establishing agreement on long-term policy goals and searching for ways to implement them.[37] Critics credited this failure to more than Brzezinski's actions as an advocate, since Carter seemed not to understand his need for a custodian and failed to see that an incoherent decision process, riven with conflict, could not produce a coherent policy.[38] When three people—the president, the secretary of state and the assistant for national security—are all three expected to address the same policy problems, without any division of labor at the onset, cordiality may not be sufficient to produce agreement. But Carter evidently counted on cordiality, rather than a more explicit division of labor, to make the collegial approach work.[39] Consequently neither Vance nor Brzezinski could count on the president's support with sufficient consistency to maintain a broad policy direction for the administration. A specific decision might undercut either one at any moment.[40]

Presidential executive style usually varies in response to the president's perception of the stakes of a given issue, and any characterization of a uniform style is misleading. Carter was no exception. He was quite comfortable with delegation of the policy development role to associates and he necessarily delegated much diplomatic negotiation. Robert Strauss managed the multilateral trade negotiations. James Schlesinger developed the first energy plan. Alan Campbell, head of the Office of Personnel Management, and Alfred Kahn, chairman of the Civil Aeronautics Board, were given full rein to develop and manage the legislative fights on civil service reform and airline deregulation respectively. Carter delegated to others the responsibility for developing most domestic and economic policy initiatives, which permitted Eizenstat and, to a lesser extent, Schultze to act as custodians of presidential options though without authority to reconcile disputes before they went to the president. Carter assumed direct responsibility for those issues on which he believed only the president could provide a lead and on which he could rely on his strength for problem solving. This was most clearly seen in diplomacy, where Carter was his own custodian. Brzezinski deferred to Carter and acted as coordinator of details in such cases, but when Carter was uncertain of the right policy and Vance and Brzezinski were at odds, Brzezinski moved to an advocate role. The Carter executive style therefore varied across policy areas and issues. However, the search for collegiality, the underrating of the custodian role and the president's commitment to achievement are present in all areas.

Jack Watson, who was secretary to the Carter cabinet, assistant to the president for intergovernmental relations and, in 1980, White House chief of staff, believes that Carter's failure to establish a chief of staff in the White House at the outset was a big mistake. At the beginning of the administration he wrote the president a memorandum warning that Carter's very voraciousness as a student of policy problems might involve him in too many issues too deeply. He needed a buffer. In Watson's view the president's attempt to be his own chief of staff, with eight or ten White House lieutenants reporting directly to him, pulled him in too many competing directions.

It results in a lack of cohesion, a lack of organization and cutting in on decision making before it reaches the Oval Office, the presidential level. That was in my judgement, a mistake that President Carter made in the first two years of his administration. He didn't actually appoint a chief of staff until late in the summer of 1979. I think that many of our problems on the Hill, many of our congressional relationships, difficulties, who's speaking for the President, would have been solved had we started from the very beginning with a strong chief of staff.[41]

Watson's most interesting insight is the claim that lack of explicit coordinating functions makes for disjointed policy as well as a disjointed decision process. He and the critics of Carter's style of managing policy formation clearly believe that policy would have been more coherent, consistent and geared to the long term if the president had used custodians to help him formulate his choices. Such lieutenants would have been buffers to keep the president one step removed from details and the exploration of sub-options. They might have also been guardians of the continuity of perspective that might have come with greater presidential detachment.

The difficulty with this argument is that Carter didn't want it that way. He was clear at the outset that it was not his nature to have aides report to assistants who then reported to him. He wanted the information directly.[42] He saw homework as his strength and knowledge as a resource for political persuasion. In another context Roger Porter has argued that presidents are inclined to engage in "fine tuning" in economic policy making, making continuous adjustment of decisions in the light of new knowledge and events because of the great uncertainties inherent in economic policy. Control may reduce the sense of uncertainty.[43] This very desire to control events through knowledge, which was so strong in Carter, may help account for the zigzag fine tuning of both economic and foreign policy, areas in which serial decisions were the very stuff of policy. In contrast a president like Ronald Reagan, who has no interest in mastery of subjects or problems, finds it easy to adhere to a consistent policy line. Jimmy Carter did not like the disarray among advisers that his own system guaranteed. But his insistence on being his own custodian ensured it.

How legitimate is the argument that Carter policies would have had greater consistency and coherence if the policy-making process had been less disjointed? The policy problems that Carter and his lieutenants faced were filled with contradictions. The Democratic coalition was torn between those who would continue reform and those who would consolidate in domestic matters. The path between inflation and unemployment was perilous and detente was fragile as new tensions between the United States and the Soviet Union emerged. A less disjointed policy-making process would not, by itself, have made policy more coherent, for the contradictions within policy problems had to be addressed. We therefore turn to the management of contradictions.

Carter's conception of politics did not accept the inherent reality of policy contradictions or the need to manage such contradictions through policy that would account for and resolve them for that time. The Thomas Hughes discussed Carter's seeming rejection of the idea of contradiction in foreign policy in a 1978 essay which forecast many of the difficulties that finally beset the president. American political culture, in its universalism, rejects the existence of contradiction, and Carter's beliefs were consistent with that rejection. His language promised that all good things were simultaneously possible. Hughes regards this view as simply mistaken; not all goals can be achieved at any one time. He gives Carter high marks for liberal idealism in foreign policy in regard to human rights and for rooting this idealism for the world in the American national experience. He also praises the effort to anticipate and prevent potential conflicts in Panama, the Middle East and Africa. To Hughes this adds up to a cultural revolution in foreign policy.[44] But the president had not reconciled this revolution with competing views of the world and international politics.

The contradictions Hughes regards as potentially treacherous for the Carter presidency include the fight between absolutists and relativists. Absolutists would press any principle to the nth degree whereas relativists recognize that reality is recalcitrant and are prepared to trim. Human rights might be treated as an absolute regardless of national security needs, or resistance to aggression could become an absolute regardless of limits on United States power. Polarization and conciliation are in conflict insofar as politicians may seek to polarize or to reduce conflict in the Middle East or Africa. American globalism is confronted by critics who see no need to stake out United States interests everywhere. And substantive contradictions arise between a Cold War emphasis on security and attention to greater equality among the developed and developing nations.[45]

Rather than being adept at handling such contradictions Hughes saw Carter as intent on mastering subjects. But presidents are paid to manage contradictions more than to resolve concrete issues. He feared that if Carter could not take the curse off contradictions he would be accused in the public mind of allowing the contradictions to happen and they would thereby overwhelm him. In this way Carter would learn that foreign policy can damage a president politically. The remedy was to make conscious choices among the contradictions and persuade others to agree. The president had to make his imprint. And "to the degree that his posture remains one of surprise and impressionability he will appear the more manageable and he will become an object of management by others." Hughes concludes that Carter's capacity to internalize contradiction was his greatest personal strength and his chief political weakness.[46]

These insights into Carter's approach to foreign policy are applicable to domestic and economic policy as well. He faced extremely difficult contradictions in domestic policy among competing forces in the Democratic camp and his choices in economic policy were seriously constrained by the realities of economic life. However, Hughes argues that a president can overcome such inherent policy contradictions if he will only choose and then win acceptance for his choices. If so it is not enough to plead that the conflicts besetting a president were beyond his control. He must somehow rise above them. But one can argue that contradictions may in fact be overwhelming and beyond the capacity of a president to overcome.

Did Carter see contradictions? We cannot be sure. The working hypothesis of this study has been that he saw them and hoped to integrate them in new policy syntheses. The key was synthesis rather than choice. Thus the intensity of conflict among parties sometimes eluded him because he was so intent on reconciliation. And he often rejected the necessity to choose between competing principles because he hoped to bring them together. He wished for new balance between equity and efficiency in domestic programs, for a fiscally responsible economic expansion and for subordination of conflict among nations through cooperation. He deliberately incorporated these contradictions into his political appeals and in so doing embodied in his presidency the contradictions of public policy of the 1970s. This incorporation was accompanied by the confidence that hard issues could be resolved by goodwill and homework. This worked for a number of specific thorny issues but not for contradictions that ran like a fault across broad policy areas. In this sense Carter's belief that contradictions could be overcome was found wanting. Eventually the conflicts overwhelmed his presidency, which became increasingly reactive. Was Carter's wish to incorporate and resolve policy contradictions beyond his grasp because the problems were intractable or because he did not provide plausible solutions? No problem has a final solution. The Carter period was characterized by a politics of incompatible solutions to problems with a striking lack of consensus about the right course. Carter refused to side with any camp. He would not, for example, be either a conventional Democratic reformer or a conservative who might appeal to Republicans. It is not clear that his many audiences would have accepted his choice of any policy contradiction. His strategy of attempting integration among opposites was plausible and rational.

But insofar as Carter incorporated unresolved issues on the national policy agenda into his presidency and failed to persuade others of his integrated solutions or found those visions broken apart by events his presidency was sure to appear beleaguered. As Hughes predicted, he would seem to be managed by others, and by events. Carter may have been mistaken in thinking that he could achieve such grand syntheses. He clearly set himself up for a fall, since his presidency was sure to disappoint the public. The final irony was that he became the scapegoat for all unresolved national and international problems. Everybody—politicians, the public, interest groups and media—piled on him.[47] This may explain his great unpopularity in the years after his presidency. His memory left a bad taste.

SKILL IN HISTORICAL CONTEXT

With a clear sense of a political leader's skills in relation to his deficiencies one can then examine the historical context in which those skills were used. In effective leadership skill is well matched to the task undertaken.[48] Skillful leaders realize this and seek problems that maximize their strengths. However, a role such as the presidency and the many demands and problems it attracts cannot possibly be played superbly in all its aspects by any individual. Every president will be found wanting in some respects. The question then in evaluating individual presidents is whether their skills were matched not only for the tasks they undertook but for the challenges presented to the presidency in their time as understood by the observer. The criteria of observers for effective performance will, of course, vary. Clashing beliefs about policy purposes and prevailing norms about the skills required to be an effective president both influence judgment. Political scientists are inclined to leave aside purpose as a basis for judgment and ask about skill. But skill norms are likely to be incompletely drawn from the work of particular presidents. Certainly Franklin Roosevelt is the basis for Neustadt's model of skill in the presidency. Commentators sometimes forget that skillful presidents often failed to live up to the norms established in their names. One would not base a model for presidential leadership on Roosevelt's disappointing second term, for example. Skill must therefore be assessed within historical context.

The relevant questions about Carter's skill are: Was he effective in performing the principal tasks that he set for himself as president? Did he make the most of the opportunities for presidential leadership in the context of the political resources and constraints available to him at his time in history? In assessing how well matched Carter's skills were to the tasks of policy leadership that he undertook, we will focus on the three general areas of action he addressed.

1. Carter's skills were well matched to the tackling of specific problems in situations where his capacity for mastery of the details and his ability to negotiate could make an important difference in the outcome. These were most often situations of closed politics in which Carter could control the list of participants. The Camp David accords and his subsequent trip to the Middle East provide the best illustration. The same skills were seen in other diplomatic negotiations in regard to Panama, China and SALT II, although clearly many individuals contributed to success, perhaps more than Carter did.

2. Carter had the ability to place new issues on the policy agenda and capture attention for them. The commitment of United States foreign policy to human rights around the world is one of his legacies. Carter's conception of presidential leadership may have made him an agenda setter more than a power maximizer. For example, he did not believe that it was his sole responsibility to solve the problems of inflation or energy conservation.[49] He would lead but the Congress and public must do their part. This was one of the central arguments of his dramatic speech to the nation on the crisis of national will, with energy as an example, on July 15, 1979.

Carter's skills in this respect may not have been sufficiently appreciated. What appeared to critics as a failure to take political soundings and provide "strategic" leadership may have been simply an effort to place new items on the policy agenda. Prevailing expectations of leadership call upon the leader to develop a vision for the group and then skillfully manage others to get it accepted. In this conception followers are passive pawns and other leaders become objects for skillful manipulation. A more realistic understanding of leadership would call upon the leader to get something started and then manage the process by which the group itself resolves the problem. A leader would help a community deal with its problems rather than provide answers.

Carter was good at foreseeing problems for the near future and placing them on the policy agenda. But his belief that others should take over at that point, that his primary task as president was to develop good ideas, clashed with expectations that the president should develop the muscle and power to get his ideas accepted. His forbearance may have been a virtue rather than a failing in terms of this conception of democratic leadership. However it must be admitted that he was not particularly good at managing processes of discussion and conflict.[50]

3. Carter did not manage the seamless web of purpose, politics and process smoothly. His strategic leadership had a disjointed character in which discrete decisions jarred and jostled each other. He fastened too much on particular decisions without relating them to decisions that had come before and those that would follow. Although he was guided by clear general principles and policy objectives his capacity for homework caused him to treat decisions in isolation from each other and to separate policy and politics. By the same token he did not often impose his own policy priorities on the management of decision processes and his lieutenants and their subordinates consequently were often uncertain about his purposes. Thus welfare reform without budget increases made political sense but Carter never conveyed that idea convincingly to Califano. Inflation fighting required budgetary discipline but Carter handed interest groups benefits and took them away in the same breath. He reversed his course often in response to immediate situations. The B1 bomber was canceled because of inefficiency without considering its potential use in SALT bargaining; the MX missile was added to United States armories in order to get the Senate to support SALT II. Constant reversals in economic policy confused everyone. Carter did not know how to extract a strong strategic sense of direction from a welter of discrete decisions. The decisions rather than the direction were his focus.

Theoretically skill and historical conditions are separate factors. But since the purpose of our analysis is to examine combinations of the two, we can pose four possible relationships between leadership skill and the historical forces that reinforce or impede the exercise of that skill.

1. Skill under favorable conditions
2. Ineptness under favorable conditions
3. Skill under unfavorable conditions
4. Ineptness under unfavorable conditions

In situation 1, skill and favorable political conditions reinforce each other. Success cannot be reduced to either factor since each contributes to the outcome. One can, of course, imagine successes in which the historical conditions were so favorable that leadership skill was beside the point. But the study of political leadership suggests that highly skillful leaders usually add something to the favorable conditions that buoy them up. It is the combination that makes the difference.[51]

Situation 2, ineptness under favorable conditions, contains two opposite possibilities. The inept leader may fail to take advantage of favorable conditions and thus miss an opportunity to succeed. The very strategies the leader chooses may thwart success. Or despite leadership weakness favorable conditions may carry the leader along to some degree of success.

The third situation—skill operating under adverse conditions—is the most problematical and holds most of the dilemmas of political leadership. The skillful leader may overcome unfavorable conditions by sheer virtuosity. Or, if conditions are intractable, the leader may fail despite a highly skillful attempt.

In the fourth case ineptness and intractability reinforce each other. Each may contribute to the outcome, the reverse of the happy combination of situation 1. Or ineptness may be incidental to an impossible historical situation.

Jimmy Carter had very few, if any, cases in which his skills were reinforced by favorable historical forces or by strong political resources at his disposal. The best example would be his capturing the nomination for the presidency, a feat of skill in which Carter sold himself to a plurality of Democratic voters. The match of his moral appeal with the post-Watergate climate was perfect. He hoped to use such idealism as a political resource for his presidency, particularly in foreign policy, but it went against the grain of growing public unhappiness with detente. Carter's initiatives meshed with a rising tide of politics in only a few minor instances, such as economic deregulation.

Situation 2 contributes little to an understanding of the Carter presidency. One can find plenty of examples of Carter ineptness but they seldom occurred under conditions favorable enough to assume that greater skill might have brought success. In such cases ineptness almost has to strangle the possibility for success. Carter made big mistakes in his early relations with Congress and in the organization and management of policy making in the first years, but the politics of the policy issues involved seldom contributed favorably to his position. Nor can one find instances of success in which favorable forces simply swept ineptness aside.

Much of the Carter presidency can be found in situation 3. Using considerable skill the president struggled in unfavorable conditions with weak political resources and achieved some notable successes and some failures. The foreign policy successes belong here, particularly the canal treaties and the Camp David accords, as do the few domestic policy successes, such as the energy program. But skill was often not enough. Carter failed to get the SALT II treaty ratified for reasons beyond his control. He managed the negotiations of the hostage crisis with great acumen and eventually succeeded, but not in time to save his presidency.

The fourth situation produces a number of puzzles. Carter's somewhat clumsy style of policy leadership may have contributed to the early problems of his energy package, the failure of welfare reform and a number of other domestic policy measures as well as to the failure to take a steady course in economic policy. But the political conditions surrounding these issues were very unfavorable and the economic policy dilemmas were downright intractable. A good many of the most disastrous occurrences of his presidency were beyond his control, such as the Iranian revolution, the 1979 OPEC oil shock and the Soviet invasion of Afghanistan. Carter may not have always made his own good luck but he was certainly a victim of bad luck.

This analysis tells us what we already know—that Jimmy Carter was president at a time of transition, after a Democratic period of reform and achievement and before a Republican resurgence. The Ford and Carter presidencies belong together in this respect, both providing few possibilities for heroic leadership. Many conditions were highly unfavorable to the exercise of leadership at all and, indeed, a number of events were simply bad luck for the president. Most of the achievements were personal, and it is not clear that anyone else could have done as well. Carter's ineptness was most evident in those areas of leadership, especially with Congress, in which any brand of leadership would have had trouble succeeding. The Democrats provided a limited audience for decisive leadership that dared to challenge the prevailing pattern of Democratic policy demands.

Jimmy Carter anticipated many of the themes of the presidency that was to follow his. He was trying to lead the Democratic coalition toward a new combination of liberal centrism, but both politics and problems overwhelmed him. The balance tipped in favor of a Republican president who promised to act boldly to overcome the contradictions of the Carter presidency. Carter's message for the future was therefore reserved for the Democratic search for a new agenda after the Reagan presidency. Ronald Reagan took the political initiative away from the Democrats and defined a new policy agenda to which Democrats had to respond. The Mondale candidacy of 1984 was an attempt to restore the traditional Democratic coalition which Carter had wished to move beyond. Carter's search for liberal centrism was thus ahead of its time and a guide to the search for a fresh Democratic response to the Reagan presidency.

With more political skill, particularly at protecting his professional reputation, and a good bit more luck, Jimmy Carter might have been a second-term president. But it seems unlikely that the achievements of either his first or second term would have changed much. He was a president of transition, and in this sense he made the most of his opportunities.

The puzzle about the Carter presidency which may never be fully answered is why Jimmy Carter became so unpopular, with media, politicians and the public, and stayed unpopular during the presidency of his successor. There were political reasons. Many Democrats found him too conservative and many Republicans thought him too liberal. He had few constituents of his own. And though his style of leadership coincided with the reaction against the "imperial" presidency that carried him to the White House, the presidency must promise the effective use of power rather than merely presenting a set of norms against the abuse of power. The reaction against the imperial presidency was therefore sure to be temporary. Carter, with his democratic style of leadership, benefited from that reaction in winning the presidency but suffered when popular expectations inevitably shifted back to demand effectiveness. Finally, Carter incorporated but failed to transcend the policy contradictions of his time. His virtues and shortcomings were an almost perfect match for the period in American history in which he was president of the United States.

NOTES

PREFACE

1. Ben W. Heineman, Jr., and Curtis A. Hessler, *Memorandum for the President: A Strategic Approach to Domestic Affairs in the 1980s* (New York, 1980), Chap. 1.
2. Bert A. Rockman, *The Leadership Question: The President and the American System* (New York, 1984).

CHAPTER 1

1. Personal communication to the author.
2. White Burkett Miller Center of Public Affairs, University of Virginia, Project on the Carter Presidency, Transcripts (hereinafter cited as PCP), Vol. XVII, p. 37
3. Erwin C. Hargrove, *Presidential Leadership, Personality and Political Style* (New York, 1966), 3–4.
4. William McKinley Runyon, *Life Histories and Psychobiography: Explanations in Theory and Method* (New York, 1984), 93.
5. James David Barber, *Presidential Character: Predicting Performance in the White House* (Englewood Cliffs, N.J., 1977), 8.
6. Betty Glad, *Jimmy Carter: In Search of the Great White House* (New York, 1980), 46, 57.
7. Jimmy Carter, *Why Not the Best?* (New York, 1976), 9, 11, 12, 60–61.
8. *Ibid.*, 13.
9. Daniel J. Levinson *et al.*, *The Seasons of a Man's Life* (New York, 1978), Chap. 5.
10. Carter, *Why Not the Best?*, 96.
11. *Ibid.*, 99.
12 *Ibid.*, 101.
13. *Ibid.*, 105–106.
14. *Ibid.*, 110.
15. Washington *Post*, May 11, 1976, Sec. A, p. 19. Taken from Bill Moyers' interview with Carter on the PBS program, "Campaigning 1976," May 6, 1976.
16. Glad, *Jimmy Carter*, Chap. 6.
17. Levinson *et al.*, *The Seasons of a Man's Life*, Chap. 13.
18. Glad, *Jimmy Carter*, 111.
19. Allen Otten of the *Wall Street Journal* to the author, October, 1976.
20. Carter, *Why Not the Best?*, 62.
21. PCP, Vol. XIX, p. 7.
22. PCP, Vol. XX, p. 7.
23. William C. Havard, Jr., "Southern Politics: Old and New Style," in Louis D. Rubin, Jr. (ed.), *The American South: Portrait of a Culture* (Baton Rouge, 1979), 56–59.
24. Dewey W. Grantham, *Southern Progressivism: The Reconciliation of Progress and Tradition* (Knoxville, Tenn., 1983), xv, xviii, xxii, 413–21.
25. Washington *Post*, May 11, 1976, Sec. A, p. 19.
26. Carter, *Why Not the Best?*, 114.
27. Glad, *Jimmy Carter*, 139–40.
28. Gary Fink, *Prelude to the Presidency: The Political Character and Legislative Leadership of Governor Jimmy Carter* (Westport, Conn., 1980), 3–4.

PAGES 9–23

29. Glad, *Jimmy Carter*, 158, 127–37; Fink, *Prelude to the Presidency*, 17–18.
30. Fink, *Prelude to the Presidency*, 91, 165.
31. PCP, Vol. VII, p. 16; Fink, *Prelude to the Presidency*, 171, 180.
32. PCP, Vol. VII, pp. 2–3, 16–17.
33. Jules Witcover, *Marathon: The Pursuit of the Presidency, 1972–1976* (New York, 1977), 109–10.
34. Carter, *Why Not the Best?*, 3; PCP, Vol. XVI, p. 11.
35. Carter, *Why Not the Best?*, 173–74.
36. William Lee Miller's interpretation of Carter's political personality is close to my own in many respects. I did not read Miller until my interpretation was fully developed. Rather than attempt to combine the two interpretations I have presented my own picture of Carter from the evidence before me, just as Miller did. I have made no effort to see where we may differ, but I think we agree in understanding religious faith to be an important key to Carter's leadership style. See William Lee Miller, *Yankee from Georgia* (New York, 1978).

CHAPTER 2

1. White Burkett Miller Center of Public Affairs, University of Virginia, Project on Carter Presidency, Transcripts (hereinafter cited as PCP), Vol. XIX, pp. 6, 69.
2. PCP, Vol. XVI, p. 85.
3. PCP, Vol. XIV, pp. 84–85.
4. Interview with Carter White House assistant, Washington, D.C., August 25, 1983; James Fallows (Transcript of "Rhetoric and Presidential Leadership," workshop at the Miller Center of Public Affairs, University of Virginia, March 1, 1979), 5.
5. PCP, Vol. X, p. 85.
6. Charles O. Jones, *The Trusteeship Presidency: Jimmy Carter and the United States Congress* (Baton Rouge, 1988), 7–8.
7. Jimmy Carter, *Keeping Faith: Memoirs of a President* (New York, 1982), 65; PCP, Vol. XIX, p. 70.
8. PCP, Vol. XVII, p. 11.
9. PCP, Vol. XIII, p. 60.
10. PCP, Vol. XIV, p. 30, Vol. III, p. 99, Vol. XII, p. 31.
11. PCP, Vol. VII, p. 14, Vol. XVII, p. 41, Vol. X, pp. 111–12.
12. Carter, *Keeping Faith*, 35, 47.
13. PCP, Vol. XI, pp. 65–66.
14. PCP, Vol. XIII, pp. 7–8, 51–55, 63.
15. PCP, Vol. VI, p. 36
16. PCP, Vol. IX, p. 66; Interview with Carter White House assistant, Washington, D.C., April 4, 1983.
17. Robert Shogan, *Promises to Keep* (New York, 1979), 193; PCP, Vol. XVII, p. 47.
18. Stuart Eizenstat to the author, August, 1986.
19. PCP, Vol XIV, p. 29.
20. Interview with Carter White House assistant, Washington, D.C., August 24, 1983.
21. PCP, Vol. XIX, pp. 70, 72.
22. Carter, *Keeping Faith*, 89. Carter's memoir provides some confirmation in his discussion of how difficult it is for a president to prevail with Congress on domestic policy.
23. Ben W. Heineman, Jr., and Curtis A. Hessler, *Memorandum for the President: A Strategic Approach to Domestic Affairs in the 1980s* (New York, 1980), Chap. 1.
24. Zbigniew Brzezinski, *Power and Principle: Memoirs of the National Security Adviser, 1977–1981* (New York, 1983), 30–31, 432.
25. PCP, Vol XIX, p. 47.
26. Interview with OMB official in the Carter administration, Washington, D.C., April 4, 1983; PCP, Vol VIII, p. 118; Fallows, Miller Center Workshop, 5, 25; PCP, Vol. XIII, p. 22.
27. PCP, Vol. XIII, p. 34; Brzezinski, *Power and Principle*, 56–57.

28. Carter, *Keeping Faith,* 35.

29. PCP, Vol. XIX, p. 8

30. Author conversation with Stephen Hess, Washington, D.C., 1977; Stephen Hess, *Organizing the Presidency* (Washington, D.C., 1976).

31. PCP, Vol. XIII, p. 21.

32. PCP, Vol XIX, p. 16.

33. *Ibid.,* 16–17.

34. James Fallows, "The Passionless Presidency," *Atlantic Monthly,* CCXXXXIII (May, 1979), 35.

35. PCP, Vol. XX, pp. 8–9.

36. PCP, Vol. XV, pp. 37–38.

37. PCP, Vol. XIX, pp. 32–33.

38. Cyrus Vance, *Hard Choices: Critical Years in America's Foreign Policy* (New York, 1983), 35.

39. Carter, *Keeping Faith,* 56–57.

40. PCP, Vol. XIII, pp. 38, 58.

41. Alexander L. George, *Presidential Decisionmaking in Foreign Policy: The Effective Use of Information and Advice* (Boulder, Colo., 1980), 148–49.

42. Heineman and Hessler, *Memorandum for the President,* Chap. 1.

43. Interview with former Carter White House aide, Washington, D.C., August 25, 1983.

44. PCP, Vol. III, pp. 51–53.

CHAPTER 3

1. Jules Witcover, *Marathon: The Pursuit of the Presidency 1972–1976* (New York, 1977), 8, 225, 306.

2. Theodore J. Lowi, *The End of Liberalism: The Second Republic of the United States* (New York, 1979), 50.

3. White Burkett Miller Center for Public Affairs, University of Virginia, Project on Carter Presidency, Transcripts (hereinafter cited as PCP), Vol. XIII, pp. 10–11.

4. Robert Shogan, *Promises to Keep* (New York, 1977), 51.

5. *Public Papers of the Presidents of the United States: Jimmy Carter* (2 Vols.; Washington, D.C., 1977), I, 1–4, 656–62.

6. PCP, Vol. XIII, pp. 101–102.

7. Interview with Carter White House assistant, Washington, D.C., August 24, 1983.

8. PCP, Vol. X, p. 91, Vol. XIII, p. 63.

9. Erwin C. Hargrove and Michael Nelson, *Presidents, Politics and Policy* (Baltimore, 1984), 178–82.

10. PCP, Vol. XI, p. 65.

11. PCP, Vol. XIII, pp. 7–8, 54, 55.

12. PCP, Vol. XIV, p. 15.

13. "An Inside Look at How the White House Operates," *Nation's Business,* LXV (August, 1977), 37.

14. Hargrove and Nelson, *Presidents, Politics and Policy,* 176–84.

15. *Ibid.,* Chap. 6.

16. *Ibid.,* 181, 237–38.

17. Interview with Carter White House assistant, Washington, D.C., August 24, 1983.

18. Interview with Carter White House assistant, Washington, D.C., April 4, 1983.

19. PCP, Vol. XIII, p. 63.

20. *Ibid.,* 63–64.

21. *Ibid.,* 62.

22. PCP, Vol. VI, p. 57.

23. Interview with Carter White House assistant, Washington, D.C., April 4, 1983.

24. PCP, Vol. XIX, pp. 18–19.

25. Dom Bonafede, "The Emergence of Eizenstat," *National Journal,* June 1, 1977, p. 865.

26. PCP, Vol. XIV, p. 20; Interview with Carter White House assistant, Washington, D.C., August 24, 1983.

27. PCP, Vol. XIII, p. 33.

28. *Ibid.,* 42–43.

29. *Ibid.,* 45, 47; PCP, Vol. XIV, p. 17.

30. PCP, Vol. XIII, p. 48.

31. *Ibid.,* 50.

32. Charles O. Jones, *The Trusteeship Presidency: Jimmy Carter and the United States Congress* (Baton Rouge, 1988), 135–36.

33. Jimmy Carter, *Keeping Faith: Memoirs of a President* (New York, 1982), 93.

34. Interview with Carter White House assistant, Washington, D.C., August 25, 1983.

35. Carter, *Keeping Faith,* 92–93.

36. PCP, Vol. XIII, pp. 37–38.

37. Stuart Eizenstat Diary, December 9, 1976, to August 11, 1977 (Copy in possession of author), 1–2; Shogan, *Promises to Keep,* 234; Interview with Carter White House assistant, Washington, D.C., August 25, 1983; PCP, Vol. XIII, p. 38.

38. PCP, Vol. XIII, p. 28; Eizenstat Diary, 7.

39. PCP, Vol. XVII, p. 54.

40. PCP, Vol. I, p. 3.

41. Eizenstat Diary, 8.

42. *Ibid.,* 9; Shogan, *Promises to Keep,* 235.

43. Eizenstat Diary, 13–14, 21.

44. *Ibid.,* 8.

45. Bob Rankin, "Carter's Energy Plan: A Plan of Leadership," *Congressional Quarterly Weekly Report,* April 23, 1977, pp. 727–32.

46. Jones, *The Trusteeship Presidency,* 138–39.

47. *Ibid.,* 140, 155–56.

48. Bob Rankin, "Many Factors Lead to Energy Stalemate," *Congressional Quarterly Weekly Report,* December 24, 1977, pp. 2631–35; Richard Carigan, "Chalk One Up for President's Energy Lobbyists," *National Journal,* September 30, 1978. p. 1556; Barbara Kellerman, *The Political Presidency: Practice of Leadership* (New York, 1984), 212; James R. Schlesinger, "Adjusting Public Policy to the Energy Watershed" (Paper prepared for ASEA Symposium, Stockholm, Sweden, May 5–6, 1983, copy in possession of author), 11; Carter, *Keeping Faith,* 102.

49. Schlesinger, "Adjusting Public Policy," 11.

50. PCP, Vol. XIII, pp. 30–31.

51. *Ibid.,* 77–78.

52. Stuart Eizenstat, "The Presidency in Trouble" (Paper, 1983, copy in possession of author), 94–95.

53. PCP, Vol. XIX, p. 48.

54. Lawrence E. Lynn, Jr., and David def Whitman, *The President as Policymaker: Jimmy Carter and Welfare Reform* (Philadelphia, 1981), 44.

55. PCP, Vol. XIII, pp. 10–11.

56. Lynn and Whitman, *The President as Policymaker,* 44; PCP, Vol. XIV, p. 19; Interview with Carter White House assistant, Washington, D.C., August 24, 1983; Ben W. Heineman, Jr., and Curtis A. Hessler, *Memorandum for the President: A Strategic Approach to Domestic Affairs in the 1980s* (New York, 1980), 282.

57. Joseph A. Califano, Jr., *Governing America: An Insider's Report from the White House and the Cabinet* (New York, 1981), 283.

58. *Ibid.,* 325–26.

59. Lynn and Whitman, *The President as Policymaker,* 51–52.

60. *Ibid.,* Chap. 4.

61. Califano, *Governing America,* 325.

62. Lynn and Whitman, *The President as Policymaker,* 86–87.

63. *Ibid.,* 88–89; Califano, *Governing America,* 329–34.

64. Lynn and Whitman, *The President as Policymaker,* 91; PCP, Vol. XIII, p. 100.

65. Califano, *Governing America,* 100–104; PCP, Vol. XI, p. 71.

66. Califano, *Governing America,* 338–39; Lynn and Whitman, *The President as Policymaker,* 122–25.

67. PCP, Vol. XI, p. 70.

68. Lynn and Whitman, *The President as Policymaker,* 126–28, 131.

69. *Ibid.,* 134, 136; Califano, *Governing America,* 341.

70. Califano, *Governing America,* 343; Lynn and Whitman, *The President as Policymaker,* 149–52.

71. Califano, *Governing America,* 344.

72. *Ibid.,* 354; Heineman and Hessler, *Memorandum for the President,* 286–87, 110.

73. Lynn and Whitman, *The President as Policymaker,* Chap. 2; Califano, *Governing America,* 361–64; PCP, Vol. XIX, p. 23.

74. Lynn and Whitman, *The President as Policymaker,* 250.

75. PCP, Vol. XIII, p. 29; Vol. XIV, p. 124; Interview with Carter White House assistant, Washington, D.C., August 24, 1983.

76. Joseph Califano, *Governing America,* 274.

77. Stuart Eizenstat, "The Presidency in Trouble," 18–19.

78. Califano, *Governing America,* 276–77.

79. Willis D. Hawley and Beryl A. Radin, "The Presidency and Domestic Policy: Organizing the Department of Education," in Michael Nelson (ed.), *The Presidency and the Political System* (Washington, D.C., 1984), 456–57.

80. Interview with Willis Hawley, Nashville, Tenn., June 22, 1983.

81. Hawley and Radin, "The Presidency and Domestic Policy," in Nelson (ed.), *The Presidency and the Political System,* 459.

82. Interview with Willis Hawley; Nashville, Tenn., June 22, 1983.

83. Interview with PRP official, Washington, D.C., August 25, 1983; Interview with Willis Hawley; Nashville, Tenn., June 22, 1983.

84. Interview with PRP official, Washington, D.C., August 25, 1983.

85. *Ibid.*

86. Hawley and Radin, "The Presidency and Domestic Policy," in Nelson (ed.), *The Presidency and the Political System,* 464; Interview with Carter White House assistant, Washington, D.C., August 24, 1983.

87. Carter, *Keeping Faith,* 88–89.

88. *Ibid.,* 89.

CHAPTER 4

1. Erwin C. Hargrove and Samuel A. Morley (eds.), *The President and the Council of Economic Advisers: Interview with CEA Chairmen* (Boulder, Colo., 1984), 6–10.

2. Roger Porter, "The President and Economic Policy," in Hugh Heclo and Lester M. Salamon (eds.), *The Illusion of Presidential Government* (Boulder, Colo., 1981), 216, 225–26.

3. Hargrove and Morley (eds.), *The President and the CEA,* 428.

4. I. M. Destler, *Making Foreign Economic Policy* (Washington, D.C., 1980), 223.

5. White Burkett Miller Center of Public Affairs, University of Virginia, Project on the Carter Presidency, Transcripts (hereinafter cited as PCP), Vol. XI, pp. 6–7.

6. Hargrove and Morley (eds.), *The President and the CEA,* 193–94, 424–25.

7. PCP, Vol. XI, p. 12.

8. *Ibid.,* 12–13.

9. *Ibid.*

10. *Ibid.,* 14; Destler, *Making Foreign Economic Policy,* 233.

11. PCP, Vol. XI, pp. 14–16, Vol. I, pp. 121–22; Destler, *Making Foreign Economic Policy,* 222–24.

12. PCP, Vol. XI, p. 13.

13. Options paper on Economic Policy Group, April 30, 1977, and Presidential Reorganization Project draft paper on Economic Policy Group, May 19, 1977; in President Reorganization Project Files, Carter Presidential Library, Atlanta.

14. Destler, *Making Foreign Economic Policy,* 222–25.

15. PCP, Vol. XI, pp. 13–16, 20, 24.

16. PCP, Vol. XIII, pp. 74–75.

17. PCP, Vol. XI, p. 13; Interview with Carter White House assistant, Washington, D.C., April 4, 1983.

18. PCP, Vol. XI, pp. 13, 22, Vol. I, pp. 96–97, Vol. VI, pp. 40–41, Vol. XII, p. 87, Vol. IX, p. 27.

19. PCP, Vol. XI, p. 24.

20. PCP, Vol. IX, pp. 101, 108–109.

21. PCP, Vol. XVII, p. 23; Dom Bonafede, "Stuart Eizenstat, Carter's Right-Hand Man," *National Journal,* June 9, 1979, p. 496; "Stuart Eizenstat: The Power Behind Domestic Policy," *Business Week,* March 20, 1978, pp. 1, 126.

22. Colin Campbell, *Governments Under Stress: Political Executives and Key Bureaucrats in Washington, London and Ottawa* (Toronto, 1983), 122–24; PCP, Vol. XIX, p. 20.

23. PCP, Vol. XI.

24. Interview with Ray Marshall, Nashville, Tenn., March 22, 1985.

25. Robert Samuelson, "Whatever Happened to the Promise of an Ever-Expanding Economy?" *National Journal,* January 9, 1980, pp. 86–92.

26. PCP, Vol. XIII, pp. 34–35, 62, 113.

27. PCP, Vol. XIV, p. 19.

28. Interview with Carter White House assistant, Washington, D.C., April 4, 1983; Interview with Carter White House assistant, Washington, D.C., August 14, 1983.

29. PCP, Vol. XI, pp. 3–4, 46–47, 79.

30. Hargrove and Morley (eds.), *The President and the CEA,* 39, 474.

31. PCP, Vol VI, pp. 27, 18, 49, 52–54.

32. *Ibid.,* 57.

33. White House Domestic Policy Assistant, "Memorandum on the Development of the Economic Stimulus Package," 1983, p. 18, in Carter Presidential Library, Atlanta.

34. "Decision Analysis, Administration Minimum Wage Position," (Paper written for the President's Reorganization Project study of the Executive Office of the President, 1977, in Carter Presidential Library, Atlanta), 1–4.

35. *Ibid.,* 4–6; "Memorandum on Econmic Stimulus Package," 23–24.

36. "Memorandum on Economic Stimulus Package, 27–28, 30, 34–35.

37. PCP, Vol. XI, pp. 31–32.

38. *Ibid.,* 32–33.

39. James E. Anderson, "Economic Policy Formation in the Carter and Johnson Administrations: The Case of the Wage-Price Guidelines" (Paper, Southern Political Science Association, Birmingham, Ala., 1983, copy in possession of author), 26–28. Anderson's analysis is based on interviews with participants in the decisions described.

40. Hargrove and Morley (eds.), *The President and the CEA,* 489–90.

41. Anderson, "Economy Policy Formation," 31, 35–37; W. Kip Viscussi, "The Political Economy of Wage and Price Regulation: The Case of the Carter Pay-Price Standards," in Richard J. Zeckhauser and Derek Leebaert (eds.), *What Role for Government? Lessons from Policy Research* (Durham, N.C., 1983), 159.

42. PCP, Vol. XI, pp. 40–41.

43. Anderson, "Economic Policy Formation," 337–39; Viscussi, "The Political Economy," in Zeckhauser and Leebaert (eds.), *What Role for Government?,* 161.

44. PCP, Vol XI, p. 98; Vol. IX, pp. 44, 54, 123–24.

45. PCP, Vol. IX, pp. 121–22, 132, 145–46.

46. Ben W. Heineman, Jr., and Curtis A. Hessler, *Memorandum for the President: A Strategic Approach to Domestic Affairs in the 1980s* (New York, 1980), 252.

47. Herbert Stein, *Presidential Economics: The Making of Economic Policy from Roosevelt to Reagan and Beyond* (New York, 1984), 215–16.

48. PCP, Vol. XI, p. 7.

49. "Memorandum on Economic Stimulus Package," 1–2.

50. PCP, Vol. XI, p. 27; "Memorandum on Econmic Stimulus Package," 11.

51. Hargrove and Morley (eds.), *The President and the CEA*, 476–77.

52. "Memorandum on Economic Stimulus Package," 8–11.

53. *Ibid.*, 11.

54. *Ibid.*, 4–5, 12–13, 15.

55. *Ibid.*, 14.

56. PCP, Vol. XVI, pp. 18–19.

57. *Ibid.*, 20.

58. Hargrove and Morley (eds.), *The President and the CEA*, 463, 478.

59. PCP, Vol. XVII, p. 39; "Memorandum on Econmic Stimulus Package," 32; PCP, Vol. XI, p. 28

60. "Memorandum on Economic Stimulus Package," 22–23.

61. PCP, Vol. XIX, p. 12.

62. Jimmy Carter, *Keeping Faith: Memoirs of a President* (New York, 1982), 77–78.

63. *Ibid;* PCP, Vol. XIX, p. 69.

64. Hargrove and Morley (eds.) *The President and the CEA*, 200–202.

65. PCP, Vol. XI, pp. 2–4.

66. Heineman and Hessler, *Memorandum for the President*, 254.

67. Council of Economic Advisers, *The Economic Report of the President* (Washington, D.C., 1981), 235, 269, 293.

68. Stein, *Presidential Economics*, 218; Heineman and Hessler, *Memorandum for the President*, 253–56; Hargrove and Morley (eds.), *The President and the CEA*, 461.

69. Robert Shogan, *Promises to Keep* (New York, 1977), 231–32.

70. "Memorandum on Economic Stimulus Package," 22, 24, 25, 28.

71. PCP, Vol. XVII, pp. 59–60.

72. PCP, Vol VI, p. 48.

73. Heineman and Hessler, *Memorandum for the President*, 254.

74. PCP, Vol. XI, pp. 4, 36

75. Heineman and Hessler, *Memorandum for the President*, 258.

76. "Memorandum on Economic Stimulus Package," 69.

77. Heineman and Hessler, *Memorandum for the President*, 257.

78. Hargrove and Morley (eds.), *The President and the CEA*, 483.

79. Hargrove and Morley (eds.), *The President and the CEA*, 488–89; PCP, Vol. VI, pp. 6–7, 115.

80. Bowman Cutter, "The Presidency and Economic Policy: A Tale of Two Budgets," in Michael Nelson (ed.), *The Presidency and the Political System* (Washington, D.C., 1984), 476–80.

81. Hargrove and Morley(eds.), *The President and the CEA*, 486; Heineman and Hessler, *Memorandum for the President*, 258–59.

82. PCP, Vol. VI, p. 36; Hargrove and Morley (eds.), *The President and the CEA*, 495; Stuart Eizenstat, "The Presidency in Trouble" (Paper, 1983, copy in possession of author), 74; Heineman and Hessler, *Memorandum for the President*, 259.

83. Heineman and Hessler, *Memorandum for the President*, 264.

84. PCP, Vol. VI, pp. 37–38.

85. Hargrove and Morley (eds.) *The President and the CEA*, 482, 487.

86. Cutter, "The Presidency and Economic Policy," in Nelson (ed.), *The Presidency and the Political System*, 482.

87. *Ibid.*

88. Hargrove and Morley (eds.), *The President and the CEA*, 487–89.

89. *Ibid.,* 490.

90. *Ibid.,* 484–85.

91. PCP, Vol. XIII, p. 89; Interview with Carter White House assistant, Washington, D.C., April 4, 1983.

92. Heineman and Hessler, *Memorandum for the President,* 259–60.

93. Cutter, "The Presidency and Economic Policy," in Nelson (ed.), *The Presidency and the Political System,* 479.

94. Interview with Carter White House assistant, Washington, D.C., April 4, 1983.

95. Hargrove and Morley (eds.), *The President and the CEA,* 486.

96. "Carter's Election Year Budget: Something for Practically Everyone," *National Journal,* February 2, 1980, pp. 176–87.

97. Cutter, "The Presidency and Economic Policy," in Nelson (ed.), *The Presidency and the Political System,* 482.

98. David P. Calleo, *The Imperious Economy* (Cambridge, Mass., 1982), 148; Stein, *Presidential Economics,* 231.

99. PCP, Vol. XI, p. 96.

100. Eizenstat, "The Presidency in Trouble," 67–68; PCP, Vol. XI, pp. 43–44; Cutter, "The Presidency and Economy Policy," in Nelson (ed.), *The Presidency and the Political System,* 483.

101. PCP, Vol. XI, 44, 98.

102. PCP, Vol XIX, p. 61.

103. Carter, *Keeping Faith,* 526–30.

104. Hargrove and Morley (eds.), *The President and the CEA,* 493–94; PCP, Vol. VI, pp. 114–15.

105. Calleo, *The Imperious Economy,* 149.

106. Hargrove and Morley (eds.), *The President and the CEA,* 474, 494–95.

107. PCP, Vol. XI, p. 103; Heineman and Hessler, *Memorandum, for the President,* 259.

108. Cutter, "The Presidency and Economic Policy," in Nelson (ed.), *The Presidency and the Political System,* 403.

109. Heineman and Hessler, *Memorandum for the President,* 264–65.

110. Interview with Carter White House assistant, Washington, D.C., April 4, 1983.

111. Robert J. Samuelson, "The Missing Policy," *National Journal,* April 1, 1978. p. 524; "The Inflation paradox," *National Journal,* October 20, 1979, p. 1777.

112. PCP, Vol. XI, p. 99; Interview with Carter White House assistant, Washington, D.C., April 4, 1983.

113. Heineman and Hessler, *Memorandum for the President,* 260.

114. PCP, Vol. XIX, pp. 67–68.

115. PCP, Vol. XVII, p. 62, Vol. IX, p. 142, Vol. XII, p. 80; Interview with two Carter White House assistants, Washington, D.C., April 4, 1983.

CHAPTER 5

1. Cyrus Vance, *Hard Choices: Critical Years in America's Foreign Policy* (New York, 1983), 157, 257.

2. Jimmy Carter, *Why Not the Best?* (New York, 1976), 177–78.

3. Jimmy Carter, *Keeping Faith: Memoirs of a President* (New York, 1982), 144.

4. Zbigniew Brzezinski, *Power and Principle: Memoirs of the National Security Adviser, 1977–1981* (New York, 1983), 48, 49, 520–21.

5. White Burkett Miller Center of Public Affairs, University of Virginia, Project on the Carter Presidency, Transcripts (hereinafter cited as PCP), Vol. XVIII, p. 20.

6. Interview with Carter White House assistant, Washington, D.C., August 25, 1983.

7. Raymond A. Moore, "The Carter Presidency and Foreign Policy," in M. Glenn Abernathy *et al.* (eds.), *The Carter Years: The President and Policymaking* (New York, 1984), 55–56, 77. Moore discussed these topics with the president after he left office.

8. David K. Hall, "Implementing Multiple Advocacy in the National Security Council, 1947–1980" (Ph.D. dissertation, 2 vols., Stanford University, 1982), II, 656; PCP, Vol. XIX, pp. 16–17; Brzezinski, *Power and Principle*, 63.
9. Brzezinski, *Power and Principle*, 57–63.
10. *Ibid.*, 57, 63–64.
11. Alexander L. George, *Presidential Decisionmaking in Foreign Policy: The Effective Use of Information and Advice* (Boulder, Colo., 1980), 195–96.
12. Vance, *Hard Choices*, 459–60.
13. *Ibid.*, 34.
14. Brzezinski, *Power and Principle*, 74.
15. Vance, *Hard Choices*, 35; Brzezinski, *Power and Principle*, 522.
16. Hall, "National Security Council," 662–63.
17. Carter, *Keeping Faith*, 53–55.
18. *Ibid.*, 51–53.
19. William B. Quandt, *Camp David: Peacemaking and Policies* (Washington, D.C., 1986), 35.
20. Hamilton Jordan, *Crisis: The Last Year of the Carter Presidency* (New York, 1982). 46–47, Vol. XVIII, p. 58, PCP, Vol. XX, p. 42, Brzezinski, *Power and Principle*, 523.
21. Vance, *Hard Choices*, 40.
22. George, *Presidential Decisionmaking*, 195–96.
23. Brzezinski, *Power and Principle*, 44–47.
24. Hall, "National Security Council," 657.
25. Brzezinski, *Power and Principle*, 515.
26. *Ibid.*, Chaps. 3–6, 10–11, p. 70.
27. PCP, Vol. XV, pp. 72–73. Revisions in the Miller Center text were suggested to the author by Zbigniew Brzezinski.
28. Brzezinski, *Power and Principle*, 31; PCP, Vol. XIX, p. 39.
29. Carter, *Keeping Faith*, 54.
30. Vance, *Hard Choices*, 441–42.
31. PCP, Vol. XV, pp. 66–67.
32. Brzezinski, *Power and Principle*, 52–53.
33. Vance, *Hard Choices*, 31–34, 442–62.
34. *Ibid.*, 31.
35. PCP, Vol. XIX, p. 5.
36. William McKinley Runyon, *Life Histories and Psychobiography: Explanations in Theory & Method* (New York, 1984), 93. Runyon describes how individuals go through life creating situations that will evoke actions they wish to take.
37. Carter, *Keeping Faith*, 155, 279.
38. PCP, Vol. XIX, p. 70.
39. *Ibid.*, 60.
40. Rosalyn Carter, "Late Night America," The Public Broadcasting Systems, August 27, 1984.
41. Carter, *Keeping Faith*, 155.
42. Brzezinski, *Power and Principle*, 145.
43. Carter, *Keeping Faith*, 155–56.
44. Brzezinski, *Power and Principle*, 137.
45. Carter, *Keeping Faith*, 173; PCP, Vol. VII, pp. 50–51, 54.
46. Carter, *Keeping Faith*, 168, 178, 184.
47. Carter, *Keeping Faith*, 279.
48. Brzezinski, *Power and Principle*, 85–86, 88–89.
49. Vance, *Hard Choices*, 167–68.
50. Carter, *Keeping Faith*, 279.
51. Quandt, *Camp David*, 48–49, 60–62, 130–32, 137, 163.
52. Vance, *Hard Choices*, 174; Brzezinski, *Power and Principle*, 24, 93, 236.

53. Carter, *Keeping Faith*, 290–92, 294–96; Brzezinski, *Power and Principle*, 110–11.
54. Vance, *Hard Choices*, Chap. 10.
55. Carter, *Keeping Faith*, 305, 306.
56. Brzezinski, *Power and Principle*, 243.
57. Quandt, *Camp David*, 120.
58. Brzezinski, *Power and Principle*, 246, 251; Carter, *Keeping Faith*, 312; Vance, *Hard Choices*, 216, 217.
59. Carter, *Keeping Faith*, 315–26.
60. Quandt, *Camp David*, 197, 201.
61. Carter, *Keeping Faith*, 319–403; Vance, *Hard Choices*, Chap. 10; Brzezinski, *Power and Principle*, Chap. 7.
62. Brzezinski, *Power and Principle*, 88, 238.
63. Stanley Hoffman, "In Search of a Foreign Policy," *New York Review of Books*, September 29, 1983, p. 48.
64. Vance, *Hard Choices*, 226.
65. Quandt, *Camp David*, 179, 207, 218.
66. *Ibid.*, 219, 235–39, 247.
67. Vance, *Hard Choices*, 249–50.
68. Brzezinski, *Power and Principle*, 279–81.
69. PCP, Vol. XIX, p. 72; Quandt, *Camp David*, 290–91.
70. Vance, *Hard Choices*, 78.
71. Brzezinski, *Power and Principle*, 201.
72. Vance, *Hard Choices*, 114; Brzezinski, *Power and Principle*, 189, 201–203, 206–207; Carter, *Keeping Faith*, 194, 196.
73. Carter, *Keeping Faith*, 194, 197–98.
74. *Ibid*, 194.
75. Brzezinski, *Power and Principle*, 198, 233.
76. Carter, *Keeping Faith*, 199.
77. Vance, *Hard Choices*, 109–110, 116, 118–19.
78. *Ibid.*, 110–12; Brzezinski, *Power and Principle*, 330; Strobe Talbott, *Endgame: The Inside Story of SALT II* (New York, 1979), 247.
79. Carter, *Keeping Faith*, 192, 194.
80. Talbott, *Endgame*, 32–35.
81. Vance, *Hard Choices*, 445–46.
82. Talbott, *Endgame*, 39.
83. Carter, *Keeping Faith*, 216.
84. Brzezinski, *Power and Principle*, 151–55.
85. Talbott, *Endgame*, 46–48, 54–55, 58–59.
86. Brzezinski, *Power and Principle*, 159–60.
87. Vance, *Hard Choices*, 46–49, 52.
88. *Ibid.*, 53, 55; Brzezinski, *Power and Principle*, 162–64; Talbott, *Endgame*, 65–67.
89. Vance, *Hard Choices*, 49, 55; Talbott, *Endgame*, 72–73, 75–76.
90. PCP, Vol. XIX, p. 58; Carter, *Keeping Faith*, 149, 219.
91. Carter, *Keeping Faith*, 220–21, 231–32, 233–34, 240, 261; Brzezinski, *Power and Principle*, 168–70, 325, 340–41; Talbott, *Endgame*, 127–28; Vance, *Hard Choices*, 63.
92. Brzezinski, *Power and Principle*, 358; Vance, *Hard Choices*, 326; Gary Sick, *All Fall Down: America's Tragic Encounter with Iran* (New York, 1985), 67.
93. Sick, *All Fall Down*, 91–92, 165–70.
94. *Ibid.*, 68.
95. Gaddis Smith, *Morality, Reasons and Power: American Diplomacy in the Carter Years* (New York, 1986), Chap. 8.
96. Sick, *All Fall Down*, 173; Michael Ledeen and William Lewis, *Debacle: The American Failure in Iran* (New York, 1981), 158.
97. Sick, *All Fall Down*, 103, 109, 114, 155–56, Ledeen and Lewis, *Debacle*, 114; Brzezinski, *Power and Principle*, 358, 370, 382, 397, 398.

98. Vance, *Hard Choices*, 328.

99. Sick, *All Fall Down*, 145–52.

100. Hall, "National Security Council," 672–73; Ledeen and Lewis, *Debacle*, 236.

101. Sick, *All Fall Down*, 142–45.

102. *Ibid.*, 210–11.

103. PCP, Vol. XIX, p. 53.

104. Sick, *All Fall Down*, 222–24.

105. Quandt, *Camp David*, 317.

106. George, *Presidential Decisionmaking*, 141.

107. Graham Allison and Peter Szanton, *Remaking Foreign Policy: The Organization Connection* (New York, 1976).

108. Philip Odeen, "National Security Policy Integration" (President's Reorganization Project report, September, 1979, in "The National Security Adviser: Role and Accountability") *Hearings Before the Committee on Foreign Relations*, U.S. Senate, 96th Cong. 2nd Sess., April 17, 1980.

109. Dick Kirschten, "Beyond the Vance-Brzezinski Clash Lurks an NSC Under Fire," *National Journal*, May 17, 1980, pp. 814–15.

110. *Ibid.*

111. Odeen, "National Security Policy Integration," 107, 109–10.

112. *Ibid.*, 110–11.

113. *Ibid.*

114. PCP, Vol. XV, pp. 46–47.

115. *Ibid.*, 55, 57.

116. Seyom Brown, "Power and Prudence in Dealing with the USSR, " in Richard A. Melanson (ed.), *Neither Cold War Nor Detente? Soviet American Relations in the 1980s* (Charlottesville, Va., 1982), 216–17.

117. Brzezinski, *Power and Principle*, 174.

118. Vance, *Hard Choices*, 88–89.

119. Kenneth W. Thompson, "Human Rights and Soviet American Relations," in Richard A. Melanson (ed.), *Neither Cold War Nor Detente? Soviet American Relations in the 1980s* (Charlottesville, Va. 1982), 146–47.

120. Leslie Gelb, "Muskie and Brzezinski: The Struggle over Foreign Policy," *New York Times Magazine*, July 20, 1980, p. 39.

121. Brzezinski, *Power and Principle*, 37, 146, 177–78.

122. PCP, Vol. XV, pp. 30–33.

123. Phil Williams, "Carter's Defense Policy," in M. Glenn Abernathy *et al.* (eds.), *The Carter Years: The President and Policymaking* (New York, 1984), 91–92.

124. PCP, Vol. XV, pp. 33–34.

125. *Ibid.*, 72.

126. Vance, *Hard Choices*, 87–88, 185.

127. Gelb, "Muskie and Brzezinski," 39–40; Carter, *Keeping Faith*, 54; PCP, Vol. XIX, p. 40.

128. Brzezinski, *Power and Principle*, 38, 316.

129. *Ibid.*, 188, 317–18; Vance, *Hard Choices*, 99, 100.

130. Vance, *Hard Choices*, 101–102.

131. *Public Papers of the Presidents of the United States: Jimmy Carter* (Washington, D.C., 1977–78); 1052–1057; Vance, *Hard Choices*, 102; Brzezinski, *Power and Principle*, 320–21; Carter, *Keeping Faith*, 229–30.

132. Brzezinski, *Power and Principle*, 322–24.

133. PCP, Vol. XV, p. 56.

134. Brzezinski, *Power and Principle*, 520.

135. Jewel A. Rosati, "The Impact of Belief on Behavior: The Foreign Policy of the Carter Administration," in Donald A. Sylvan and Steve Chan (eds.), *Foreign Policy Decision Making* (New York, 1984), 176.

136. PCP, Vol. XV, pp. 52–55.

137. Brzezinski, *Power and Principle*, 29.
138. PCP, Vol. XV, pp. 31, 34, 39–41.
139. Brzezinski, *Power and Principle*, 44–47; Carter, *Keeping Faith*, 241; PCP, Vol. XVIII, pp. 13–14.
140. Carter, *Keeping Faith*, 262–64; Brzezinski, *Power and Principle*, 344–53; Vance, *Hard Choices*, 358–64.
141. Stuart Eizenstat, "The Presidency in Trouble" (Paper, 1983, copy in possession of author), 95–96.
142. Vance, *Hard Choices*, 394; Brzezinski, *Power and Principle*, 429, 432.
143. Vance, *Hard Choices*, 394–95; "The National Security Adviser," in *Hearings Before the Senate Committee on Foreign Relations*, April, 1980; Hall, "National Security Council," 675–76.
144. Hall, "National Security Council," 676, 678; Brzezinski, *Power and Principle*, 469, 502; PCP, Vol. XV, p. 70.
145. Stanley Hoffman, "Detente," in Joseph S. Nye, Jr. (ed.), *The Making of America's Soviet Policy* (New Haven, Conn., 1984), 253–59.

CHAPTER 6

1. Alexander L. George, *Presidential Decisionmaking in Foreign Policy: The Effective Use of Information and Advice* (Boulder, Colo., 1980), 56, 148–49.
2. Charles O. Jones, *The Trusteeship Presidency: Jimmy Carter and the United States Congress* (Baton Rouge, 1988). James S. Young and Robert Strong are writing another volume on the Carter presidency in the Miller Center series.
3. Jameson W. Doig and Erwin C. Hargrove, "Leadership and Political Analysis," in Jameson W. Doig and Erwin C. Hargrove (eds.), *Leadership and Innovation: A Biographical Perspective on Entrepreneurs in Government* (Baltimore, 1987), Chap. 1.
4. Richard E. Neustadt, *Presidential Power: The Politics of Leadership from FDR to Carter* (New York, 1980); Samuel Kernell, *Going Public: New Strategies of Presidential Leadership* (Washington, D.C., 1986); Jeffrey K. Tulis, *The Rhetorical Presidency* (Princeton, 1987); Fred I. Greenstein, *The Hidden Hand Presidency: Eisenhower as Leader* (New York, 1982).
5. Theodore J. Lowi, *The End of Liberalism: The Second Republic of the United States* (New York, 1979), 51.
6. Ben W. Heineman, Jr., and Curtis A. Hessler, *Memorandum for the President: A Strategic Approach to Domestic Affairs in the 1980s* (New York, 1980), 290–300.
7. White Burkett Miller Center of Public Affairs, University of Virginia, Project on the Carter Presidency, Transcripts (hereinafter cited as PCP), Vol. XIX, p. 48.
8. Richard E. Neustadt and Ernest R. May, *Thinking in Time: The Uses of History for Decision Makers* (New York, 1986), 111–33.
9. PCP, Vol. XIII, p. 58.
10. PCP, Vol. III, p. 52.
11. PCP, Vol. XIV, p. 18.
12. Interview with Carter White House assistant, Washington, D.C., August 24, 1983; Jimmy Carter, *Keeping Faith: Memoirs of a President* (New York, 1982), 409; Stanley Hoffman, "Jimmy's World," Review of Gaddis Smith's *Morality, Reason and Power: American Diplomacy in the Carter Years*, in *New Republic*, October 20, 1986, p. 40.
13. Paul C. Light, *The President's Agenda: Domestic Choice from Kennedy to Carter* (Baltimore, 1982), Chap. 9.
14. Heineman and Hessler, *Memorandum for the President*, xix, 13, 51.
15. *Ibid.*, xvii–xviii, xix, 13, 36, 50.
16. Interview with former Carter cabinet officer, Washington, D.C., August 25, 1983.
17. PCP, Vol. XV, pp. 88, 90–91.
18. PCP, Vol. XIX, p. 23.
19. PCP, Vol. XVII, p. 52.

20. Interview with former Carter White House assistant, Washington, D.C., August 25, 1983.

21. Author conversation with James Wall, editor of the *Christian Century*, former Carter political associate and expert on southern religion, Chicago, September 2, 1983; Author conversation with writer John Egerton, Nashville, Tenn., June, 1986.

22. White House Domestic Policy Assistant, "Memorandum on the Development of the Economic Stimulus Package," 1983, p. 30, in Carter Presidential Library, Atlanta.

23. Neustadt, *Presidential Power*, pp. 228–30.

24. PCP, Vol. III, p. 101.

25. Interview with former Carter White House assistant, Washington, D.C., August 25, 1983; PCP, Vol. VIII, p. 19; James Fallows, "The Passionless Presidency," *Atlantic Monthly*, CCXXXXIII (May, 1979), 41.

26. Neustadt and May, *Thinking in Time*, 66–74.

27. For a full development of this idea see Erwin C. Hargrove and Michael Nelson, *Presidents, Politics and Policy* (Baltimore, 1984), Chap. 4.

28. Neustadt and May, *Thinking in Time*, 72.

29. Hargrove and Nelson, *Presidents, Politics and Policy*, 67–68, 100–105.

30. Interview with former Carter White House assistant, Washington, D.C., August 25, 1983.

31. PCP, Vol. V, p. 62.

32. Stuart Eizenstat, "The Presidency in Trouble" (Paper, 1983, copy in possession of author), 9.

33. Carter, *Keeping Faith*, 14, 594.

34. PCP, Vol. XV, p. 89.

35. Interview with former Carter White House assistant, Washington, D.C., August 15, 1983; Heineman and Hessler, *Memorandum for the President*, 51; Eugene Eidenberg (Transcript of panel on the presidency and the White House staffing operations, Annual Meeting of the American Political Science Association, New York, September 4, 1981, in Miller Center of Public Affairs, University of Virginia), 12.

36. PCP, Vol. XI, pp. 15–16, 77, Vol. XIII, pp. 75–76, Vol. I, pp. 121–22.

37. I. M. Destler, "National Security II: The Rise of the Assistant," in Hugh Heclo and Lester M. Salamon (eds.), *The Illusion of Presidential Government* (Boulder, Colo., 1981), 273–74.

38. David K. Hall, "Implementing Multiple Advocacy in the National Security Council, 1947–1980" (Ph.D. dissertation, 2 vols., Stanford University, 1982), II, 680.

39. George, *Presidential Decisionmaking*, 160.

40. Destler, "National Security II," in Heclo and Salamon (eds.), *The Illusion of Presidential Government*, 272.

41. Jack Watson, "Up on the Bridge and Down in the Engine Room" in Samuel Kernell and Samuel L. Popkin (eds.), *Chief of Staff: Twenty-Five Years of Managing the Presidency* (Berkeley, Calif. 1986), 71–72.

42. PCP, Vol. XIX, pp. 7–8.

43. Roger Porter (Remarks prepared for panel on advising the president, Annual Meeting of the American Political Science Association, Washington, D.C., September, 1986).

44. Thomas L. Hughes, "Carter and the Management of Contradictions," *Foreign Policy*, XXXI (Summer, 1978), 35–36.

45. *Ibid.*, 39–43.

46. *Ibid.*, 52–53, 54

47. Gary W. Reichard, "Early Returns: Assessing the Presidency of Jimmy Carter" (Paper, 1986, copy in possession of author).

48. Doig and Hargrove, "Leadership and Policy Analysis," in Doig and Hargrove (eds.), *Leadership and Innovation*, Chap. 1.

49. White House Domestic Policy Assistant, "Memorandum on Economic Stimulus Package," 29.

50. Conversation with Ronald Heifetz, John F. Kennedy School of Government, Harvard University, April, 1987.

51. Doig and Hargrove, "Leadership and Political Analysis," in Doig and Hargrove (eds.), *Leadership and Innovation,* Chap. 1.

INDEX